READING THE *MAHĀVAMSA*

SOUTH ASIA ACROSS THE DISCIPLINES

SOUTH ASIA ACROSS THE DISCIPLINES

Funded by a grant from the Andrew W. Mellon Foundation and jointly published by the University of California Press, the University of Chicago Press, and Columbia University Press

South Asia Across the Disciplines is a series devoted to publishing first books across a wide range of South Asian studies, including art, history, philology or textual studies, philosophy, religion, and the interpretive social sciences. Series authors share the goal of opening up new archives and suggesting new methods and approaches, while demonstrating that South Asian scholarship can be at once deep in expertise and broad in appeal.

For a list of books in the series, see page 225.

READING THE *MAHĀVAṂSA*

THE LITERARY AIMS OF A THERAVĀDA BUDDHIST HISTORY

Kristin Scheible

COLUMBIA UNIVERSITY PRESS
NEW YORK

Columbia University Press
Publishers Since 1893
New York Chichester, West Sussex
cup.columbia.edu

Library of Congress Cataloging-in-Publication Data
Names: Scheible, Kristin, author.
Title: Reading the Mahāvaṃśa : the literary aims of a Theravāda Buddhist history / Kristin Scheible.
Description: New York : Columbia University Press, 2016. | Series: South Asia across the disciplines | Includes bibliographical references and index.
Identifiers: LCCN 2016002531 (print) | LCCN 2016038697 (ebook) | ISBN 9780231171380 (cloth : alk. paper) | ISBN 9780231542609 (electronic)
Subjects: LCSH: Mahānāma, active 5th century. Mahāvaṃśa. | Buddhist literature, Pali—History and criticism.
Classification: LCC BQ2607 .S35 2016 (print) | LCC BQ2607 (ebook) | DDC 294.3/824—dc23
LC record available at https://lccn.loc.gov/2016002531

Columbia University Press books are printed on permanent and durable acid-free paper.

Printed in the United States of America

c 10 9 8 7 6 5 4 3 2 1

Cover design: Kat Lynch/Black Kat Design
Cover image: Bhikkhuni Sanghamitta delivering Bodhi scion, honored by nāgas en route to Laṅkā. Mural by Solias Mendis, Kelaniya Raja Maha Vihara. Pictures from History / Bridgeman Images

CONTENTS

Acknowledgments *vii*
A Note on Transliteration and Translation *ix*

INTRODUCTION 1

1. INSTRUCTIONS, ADMONITIONS, AND ASPIRATIONS IN *VAṂSA* PROEMS 13

2. RELOCATING THE LIGHT 38

3. *NĀGAS*, TRANSFIGURED FIGURES INSIDE THE TEXT, RUMINATIVE TRIGGERS OUTSIDE 67

4. *NĀGAS* AND RELICS 94

5. HISTORICIZING (IN) THE PĀLI *DĪPAVAṂSA* AND *MAHĀVAṂSA* 117

CONCLUSION 155

Notes *161*
Bibliography *201*
Index *215*

ACKNOWLEDGMENTS

THIS BOOK began during my studies at Harvard. I was enchanted by many detours through semantic fields in Charlie Hallisey's Pāli classes and charged (as well as somewhat awed) by the bricolage of his social history seminar. I benefited from an array of Sanskrit courses taught by Stephanie Jamison. Kimberley Patton's classes (on images and animals) enabled me to write obsessively about *nāgas* and take seriously the power of things to make people feel, cultivate, and sustain devotion. I taught for Diana Eck and thought comparatively and productively about myth, image, and pilgrimage. John Strong's seminar "Relics of the Buddha" made its lively debut at the Divinity School, which led me to my dissertation and to my adviser, Anne Monius. I am so thankful for the time I shared with these teachers.

This book simmered as I began my teaching career at Bard College, where I had many supportive colleagues. I am profoundly grateful for the enduring friendship of historian and classicist Carolyn Dewald and professor of religion and Asian studies Richard H. Davis. As a mentor, Richard helped me search through my personal oscillating universe for the elusive balance among teaching and student-centered activities, research, professional obligations, college committees and commitments, and family life.

The organizers of the Five College Buddhist Studies Faculty Seminar didn't have to include me in their cohort of regulars, but they did, luring me month after month from the Hudson to the Pioneer Valley. I have benefited from these enriching conversations and look forward to future collaborations. I received extraordinarily helpful feedback when I presented some of my work to the group. I especially value Andy Rotman and Maria Heim as friends and interlocutors; their questions and insights have been invaluable as I have given shape to this project. A workshop at Amherst College in 2014, "The Exegesis of Emotions and the Body in Text," permitted me to further develop my material before I relocated to Reed College. Engaging conversations with supportive colleagues in the Reed Religion Department (Ken Brashier, Mike Foat, Kambiz GhaneaBassiri, and Steve Wasserstrom) and teaching and lecturing in the humanities curriculum have helped to hone my arguments. I am fortunate to have found an intellectual and pedagogical home at Reed, where I am doing my part to help the humanities thrive.

Several people have read and commented on the manuscript and deserve great thanks. As the book took shape, it benefited from the expert editorial eyes of Janna White and the enthusiastic readings by adventurous undergraduates at both Bard and Reed. Comments from an anonymous initial reader for the South Asia Across the Disciplines series encouraged me, and I feel such gratitude for the time and effort as well as the heartening commendations and constructive feedback from the two anonymous manuscript reviewers. The entire editorial team at Columbia University Press, especially Associate Editor Christine Dunbar and Publisher for Philosophy and Religion Wendy Lochner, as well as freelance copyeditor Annie Barva have been attentive, supportive, and patient through what has been an unusual time. As this book took shape, my youngest son was diagnosed with alveolar rhabdomyosarcoma and has suffered years of doctors, hospitals in three states, chemotherapy, radiation, surgeries, and more. This book is dedicated to my family, the most supportive and loving crew: Pat, for reading everything as well as for holding down the fort and my anxiety level, and my kids, Aidan, Elias, and Jasper—may the *saṃvega* turn to *pasāda*.

A NOTE ON TRANSLITERATION AND TRANSLATION

SANSKRIT AND Pāli terms herein follow conventions of transliteration, and I have sought to align terms with religious contexts (so, Sanskrit *dharma* when talking about Sanskrit texts and Pāli *dhamma* when immersed in the world of Pāli texts; the same pattern goes for *bodhisattva/bodhisatta*, *sūtra/sutta*, and so on).

The transliterations of the *Dīpavaṃsa* and *Mahāvaṃsa* provided in the text and notes are from *Dīpavaṃsa: An Ancient Buddhist Historical Record*, ed. and trans. Hermann Oldenberg (1879; reprint, New Delhi: Asian Educational Services, 1982), and Mahānāma, *The Mahāvaṃsa*, ed. Wilhelm Geiger (London: Frowde for Pāli Text Society, 1908).

All translations from the Pāli are mine unless otherwise indicated.

READING THE *MAHĀVAṂSA*

INTRODUCTION

In the study of religions, we find that certain key texts come to define their interpretive communities, for both the communities themselves and the scholars who study them.[1] Texts are an appealing source for the cultivation of understanding; they seem stable and fixed in a way that a religious community, comprising people who change through time and contexts, simply is not. But a text is not a source unless it is brought to life through reading and interpretation, irrespective of the vicissitudes of time and context. Reading and interpretation necessarily negate, to some extent, the stability or fixedness of a given text, and the imagination at work in reading and interpretation opens up possibilities for transformation.

The *Mahāvaṃsa* is one such key text, a work central to the real and imagined community of Sinhalese Theravādin Buddhists of Sri Lanka. This text explicitly announces its objective: to present a narrative that will engender certain reading strategies and emotional consequences. It provides reading instructions to prime its audience and introduces powerful metaphors and colorful, evocative characters to guide a productive reading. Yet the way the *Mahāvaṃsa* has been read by scholars, monks, and laypeople alike as a political "charter" for the moral authority of its particular textual community has allowed for accreted interpretations to ossify. Can the *Mahāvaṃsa* be exhumed from the weighty expectations and work of generations of readers? What happens when we examine it not as a political charter but as a work of literature illustrative of its textual community's religious imagination?

The composition of the Pāli *Mahāvaṃsa* is generally dated to the reign of the Laṇkan king Dhātusena in the mid-fifth century. Since then the

Mahāvaṃsa has been read and used as a historical source for early Sri Lanka by scholars, Theravādin monks, and laypeople, especially those interested in the constructions of legitimacy that a historical record provides. It preserves a running narrative of some of the historical highlights of mainland Indian Buddhism, such as the events of the Third Buddhist Council convened by King Aśoka (Asoka)[2] and the establishment of the *sāsana* (the Buddhist teachings and traditions), relics, and great kings in the island of Laṇkā.[3] It opens with the coming of the Buddha to the island of Laṅkā and moves through the subsequent coming of the hero-founder Vijaya, an account of the three Buddhist councils, consecrations of various kings, the coming of the great *thera* (monk) Mahinda to convert the island, and the arrival of relics. What is known as the "Duṭṭhagāmaṇī epic" makes up roughly one-third of the *Mahāvaṃsa*'s narrative before it returns to recount the reigns of various kings. The narrative itself is hardly original; there likely existed a composite collection of stories within the *aṭṭhakathā*, the commentarial literature on canonical sources, that included the general narrative first redacted in the Pāli *Dipāvaṃsa* and then refined in the *Mahāvaṃsa*.[4] For the compiler of the *Mahāvaṃsa*, originality was not the aim. The text was instead meant to retell stories in a way that would have a very specific impact on its readers and interpreters.

The *Mahāvaṃsa* has been read and interpreted for centuries. Its commentary, the *Vaṃsatthappakāsinī*, is typically dated to around the eleventh century; that it warranted a critical commentary six centuries after its composition indicates its prominence in the Sri Lankan tradition.[5] In more recent years, it has been read and interpreted as a charter for the Sinhalese Buddhist nationalist claims for hegemony over the entirety of Sri Lanka. This argument is predicated largely upon the basic narrative of the *Mahāvaṃsa*'s first chapter, where the Buddha visits the island three times and prognosticates its primary position in the Buddhist world of the future. Scholarship on the *Mahāvaṃsa* to date, with an eye toward the text's continued relevance and usage, has tended to buttress this politicized reading of what is undoubtedly a far more complex and nuanced text.

To consider the purpose, relevance, and intention of this text on its own terms, we must peel away the layers of interpretation and use that have been piled onto it and question the characteristics and qualities it has been assumed to have. We should begin at the most fundamental level by questioning the validity of the common definition of this text as a "history." What is meant by the attribution *history*, and what might the contours of historical consciousness have been for the fifth-century compiler? And in terms of content, whose history is it? Although the text does contain an account of the various kings of the land, the narrative's main focus is the establishment of the *sāsana*, especially the relics, on the island. In each "establishment" account, much attention is paid to the mythical circumstances and supernatural forces surrounding the events. Why are these narratives peppered with events and characters that challenge what can conceivably be called "historical"? Insofar as the *Mahāvaṃsa* is a history, it is a history of the way a past Sri Lankan textual community sought to engender particular emotions and behaviors through the act of reading and interpreting the text.

Scholars of the past century poured much ink considering the *Mahāvaṃsa* as a reliable textual account of history dating back to the Buddha himself. Authoritative attempts to determine a timeline for Buddhism and a history of the Buddha are predicated on the dates in this text. Jonathan Walters has more recently put a spin on this standard iteration by understanding the *Mahāvaṃsa* as a history of dispensations or successions of the Buddha's presence.[6] But even Walters's nuanced reading focuses largely on what vestiges of history are redeemable within the text and what they in turn may reveal about the Mahāvihāran monastic complex claimed to be the locus of the text's compilation.

There are explicit and implicit cues in the *Mahāvaṃsa* that its agenda is not solely historical. The presence of *nāga*s (snakelike beings) in the *vaṃsa* (history, chronicle, or lineage) literature has largely been ignored or glossed over as mythical or whimsical accretion to otherwise trustworthy historical documents. The *Mahāvaṃsa*, however, begs for a critical reading as aesthetically and emotionally pleasing, transformative poetry, a partial corrective for the study of early Theravāda Buddhism.[7] A focused examination of the *nāga*s present in these ethically inspiring, religiously motivating stories can help facilitate such a reading. My perspective differs from other scholars in that I pay attention to the explicit literary aims and the more subtle cues within the *Mahāvaṃsa* to explore a different, religious reading.

In chapter 1, I consider subtle and blatant cues in the text that lead me to suggest a new, literarily sensitive reading of the *Mahāvaṃsa* as a partial corrective to the predominant historicizing focus. The *Mahāvaṃsa* exclaims its literary prowess outright within its proem (opening poem) and declares its purpose to "avoid the faults of that one [the earlier narratives]" and to be "easy to grasp and bear in mind, producing anxious thrill [*saṃvega*] and serene satisfaction [*pasāda*], and handed down through tradition."[8] Moreover, the proem reiterates this claim in the imperative: "Listen to this one causing *saṃvega* and *pasāda*, in this way the grounds for making [more] *saṃvega* and producing [more] *pasāda*."[9] Just in case the reader-hearer has missed this explicit declaration, or perhaps as a literary device for a compounded sense of urgency and purpose, every chapter of the text concludes with the same buttressing phrase: "Made for the anxious thrill and serene satisfaction of good people."[10]

I thus examine the proems of the *Dīpavaṃsa* and *Mahāvaṃsa* as reading instructions. The proems directly articulate the ethically transformative potential of the texts, a potential realized through proper reading by an appropriate audience (of "good people," *sujana*). The proems explicitly place the two *vaṃsa*s in a literary realm where narrative has power, through the manipulation of human emotions, to transform the hearer and by extension the community that sustains the text's continued relevance. How do these proems prepare a particular kind of reader and circumscribe a particular kind of textual community not only to engender individual ethical transformation but also to envision the Buddhist landscape with Sri Lanka at its center? Can these proems help us read the *Mahāvaṃsa* in a new light? I argue that the text goes beyond the work of a chronicle and presents itself as an aesthetically riveting, poetic work that trains a reader how it should be read as the reading unfolds. I outline a method for reading informed by the work of scholars such as Martha Nussbaum, Hayden White, Paul Ricoeur, and Umberto Eco to prepare for the applied reading performed in subsequent chapters.[11] The world conjured by the text, replete with *nāga*s, requires a certain emotionally charged reading. Finally, I argue that structurally significant patterns manifest in the proem itself are what determine the text's narrative arc.[12]

The *Mahāvaṃsa* proclaims its own literary greatness, but how is its literary power manifested in the text? Chapter 2 delves into the use of literary tools such as metaphor and double entendre by training our attention on the opening chapter of the *Mahāvaṃsa*. Both the *Dīpavaṃsa* and the *Mahāvaṃsa* open with the narrative of the Buddha's three visits to the island of Laṅkā, where he has significant relations with the *nāga*s of the island. I explore how the metaphor of light is used in the narrative and examine how this metaphor will resonate with and affect the reader who has been primed for it in a particular way by the proem. We will see how a certain pattern of transformation is developed: the physical space of Laṅkā is transformed to a lamp of the *dhamma* (Buddhist teaching), a *cetiya* (object or place to trigger memory of the Buddha) for the future remembrance and representation of the Buddha through relic veneration,[13] while individual hearers are transformed ethically, resulting in a moral community prepared for the responsibility of the *dhamma*. Just as a lamp is primed with oil to effectively receive the flame, so the reader of the *Mahāvaṃsa* is primed for the full, transformative force of the text by the text's proem and narrative strategies.

To bring about the affective response the text claims it will produce, it employs rhetorical strategies that demand work on the part of the reader-hearer. Pāli is not typically considered a language that allows for much literary flourish; *literary* is a designation reserved for Sanskrit.[14] But literary moves are made in Pāli nonetheless, anticipating the later explication of literary concerns in the vernacular, such as the ninth-century work *Siyabaslakara*. The *Mahāvaṃsa* prefigures literary concerns such as the use of metaphor and particularly riveting characters such as the *nāgas*, a class of being and valuable type of literary device.

In chapter 3, I consider the character of the *nāga*, who drives the opening narrative of the *Mahāvaṃsa*. A fighting family of *nāgas* provokes the Buddha's first visit to the island, and the invitation proffered by a converted *nāga* prompts his subsequent return. I briefly define and situate the *nāga* in Pāli Buddhist literature, providing a survey of sorts to amplify its meaning, utility, and semantic field. Crucial here are the various (and useful) indications of this character's slippery ontological nature and the soteriological repercussions of that nature.[15] *Nāgas* are liminal—neither human nor fully animal, these semidivine agents are nonetheless capable of converting to Buddhism and are fairly far along in the process of cultivating the conditions for buddhahood. And they are key agents in the transmission of the *dhamma*, particularly to border regions. *Nāgas* are thus critical characters to effect the transfer of the *sāsana* to Sri Lanka, just as they are critical characters to provoke the imaginative capacity required for the ethical transformations in readers that the text calls for. In this context, I consider the role of the *nāgas* in Buddhist literature in general as didactic and morally provocative tropes and use one of three salient, *nāga*-centered *Jātaka* tales, the *Bhūridatta Jātaka*, to help flesh out the character of the *nāga*.

Chapter 4 surveys the world illuminated by the particular reading of the *Mahāvaṃsa* I advocate and the especially salient character of the *nāgas* in that world. Here I argue that the *nāgas* in fact drive the entire narrative arc of the text from conversion by the Buddha's initiatory, physical visit at the outset through the acquisition, enshrinement, and right veneration of his relics. In this chapter, we question how the textual community envisions the world without the Buddha's enduring, living presence. Relics are a viable technology developed by a community seeking continuous proximity to the Buddha, and the *nāgas* are utilized as particularly salient characters to facilitate the ongoing connection with the Buddha via his relics. After exploring the tripartite classification of relics operative in the early medieval textual community responsible for the *Mahāvaṃsa*, I investigate the *nāgas*' relationships to relics of use (*pāribhogika*), of the body (*sarīrika*), and of the imagination through representation or image (*uddesika*).

Chapter 5 considers the conundrum in which we find ourselves as we read the *Mahāvaṃsa* and uncovers the various threads of the historical context and the historicizing interpretive culture that surrounds it. The majority of scholarship to date has treated this "chronicle" as a "history," provoking all the concomitant responsibilities, expectations, and methods of interpretation assumed to be at work when one encounters "history."[16] I suggest that one of the primary concerns for the Mahāvihāran monks responsible for compiling the *Mahāvaṃsa* and its predecessor, the *Dīpavaṃsa*, was to provide a vehicle for the continued presence and proximity of the Buddha through evocative, transformative literature. The *vaṃsa* thus works on the reader-interpreter in ways not entirely unlike the way history works on the modern scholar, but there is a significant difference—the *Mahāvaṃsa* explicitly states its objectives in religious terms. The text not only is didactic but also intends to create or support an ethically inspired community in its religious program. This chapter reflects on my central argument—namely, that a new, literarily sensitive reading of the *Mahāvaṃsa* is warranted and explicitly called for in the text's proem and through its consistent use of metaphor and imagination-exercising characters such as the *nāgas*. In an eager search for sources of historical data, scholars have tended to overlook or ignore the more literary aspects of the *Mahāvaṃsa*, experiencing a sort of mythic myopia.[17] Because we will have read and examined the text's proem, especially in light of the proem of the earlier, related text, the *Dīpavaṃsa*, we will recognize that the traditional scholarly way of reading and using the *Mahāvaṃsa* misses the point. The true intention of the *Mahāvaṃsa* is to effect a transformation in the reader-hearer through the cultivation of the highly prized Buddhist emotions of *saṃvega* (anxious thrill) and *pasāda* (serene satisfaction).[18]

Several recent works in Buddhist studies have initiated a change in the interpretive tide and have influenced the way I have approached the

Mahāvaṃsa. Each offers a partial corrective to the overbearing historicist approach taken by earlier generations of Buddhologists. In terms of the *Mahāvaṃsa* proper, Jonathan Walters has been sensitively and productively reading the *vaṃsas* with a concern for the history of religions, suggesting that the social historical context they indicate is more of an argument made by the compilers than an accurate description of how things were.[19] Stephen Berkwitz's recent work is especially useful for his interpretation of *vaṃsa* literature, especially later medieval *vaṃsas* composed in the vernacular Sinhala language, as "Buddhist histories."[20] Also relevant here is his argument that narrative Buddhist histories about the past lead readers in their contemporaneous present to a sense of dependency on and gratitude for the acts of past agents, an urgent gratitude that compels ethical behaviors. However, Berkwitz's work gives the impression that the poetic methods and ethically resonant effects of literary production are original to later medieval, vernacular texts such as the thirteenth-century *Sinhala Thūpavaṃsa*. I extend his general argument and method of interpretation back to the translocal, Pāli *Mahāvaṃsa*, compiled eight centuries earlier.

Kevin Trainor has written productively on *saṃvega* and *pasāda*, the profusion of their references throughout the *vaṃsas*, and the relationship these emotions have with relic veneration, although he, too, focuses on the later, more dramatic *vaṃsas*.[21] Andy Rotman has explored the often overlooked yet commanding function of *saṃvega* and *pasāda* in Buddhist sources.[22] Maria Heim delves into the mutual constitution of the affective and cognitive in the production of meaning in Buddhist texts.[23] Charles Hallisey rethinks what is "literary" in vernacular Sinhalese sources as well as the work of narrative in Pāli sources, prompting important questions about the *Mahāvaṃsa*.[24] And Yigal Bronner considers the work of rhetorical devices, namely *śleṣa* (double meaning), in Sanskrit.[25]

John Strong has solidly affirmed the centrality of relic veneration in the Theravāda tradition even in an early text such as the *Mahāvaṃsa* and the special relationship between the relics and the *nāgas*.[26] Robert DeCaroli pays attention to the importance of the Buddha's nonhuman attendants, though he does not consider the *nāgas* on their own terms but rather within the larger class of deities (*devatā*) and as literary "hooks."[27] Steven Collins provides an original interpretation of such familiar concepts as *nirvāṇa* and karma mapped by issues of time that necessitates a rethinking of what is happening in the *Mahāvaṃsa* narrative, in terms of both the structures it sets up and the processes it describes and encourages.[28]

Anne Blackburn thinks critically about the role of the textual community in the type, production, and perpetuation of texts, which helps us think through the processes at work in the production and continued relevance of the *Mahāvaṃsa*.[29] Finally, Anne Monius likewise considers the aims of the textual community around two disparate (in terms of historical period and genre) Tamil Buddhist texts that argue for a recentering of the Buddhist world, much like the narratively enacted recentering project (both of the *sāsana* and of the practices, as in the emphasis on relic veneration) to Sri Lanka ostensibly at the heart of the *Mahāvaṃsa*.[30]

There has been no reading of the *Mahāvaṃsa* such as the one I advocate and lay out here.[31] I know of little scholarship on the work of proems generally and none regarding the genre of Buddhist histories.[32] And although a few texts focus on the metaphor of light or narratives featuring *nāgas*,[33] most scholars consider these topics ancillary to their own foci simply because they are pervasive in Indic texts and cultures.

Light, metaphorically or physically employed in ritual practice, suffuses all religious traditions.[34] The metaphor of knowledge as light is ubiquitous in all Indic traditions; words that embody light—such as *prakāśa, prabhā, āloka*—abound in literature,[35] in the epithets for significant personae (such as in the epithets for the Vedic fire god Agni[36] and the Mahāyāna Buddha Amitābha, such as Limitless Light),[37] and in artful representations of these personae haloed by a nimbus representing *tejas* (power, light). In his exploration of vision and metaphor in the Mahāyāna and citing numerous primary sources, David McMahon sketches the domain:

> Just a few of the many possible examples will suffice to give a basic idea of how the light metaphor is used in Buddhist literature: perfect wisdom is seen to be both a light and source of light; bodhisattvas are "lights and leaders of the world"; the six perfections are a bodhisattva's light, torch, and illumination; the bodhisattva's compassionate work is an abundant light that purifies the eyes of all beings, freeing them from *samsāra* and a light to the blind. The essential nature of mind or wisdom in many texts, both Mahāyāna and non-Mahāyāna, is said to be transparently luminous (*prabhāsvara*, Pāli: *pabhassara*) by nature and only adventitiously obscured by mental afflictions. All dharmas are often declared to be by nature transparently luminous as well.[38]

Light, whether of the sun, moon, or lamps, provides Indic texts a salient metaphor for enlightenment, clarity, and truth. Light also is a means for worship in South Asia; the central act of *pūja* is to offer light to a deity or Buddha, whether candles or butter lamps, at a home altar, roadside shrine, or more formal place of worship, daily or during Diwali. Light represents theophany, as made very clear in the image of the *jyotirliṅgaṃ*, Śiva's shaft of light.[39]

Snakes, too, have universal metaphorical resonance in religious imagination.[40] Shedding skin is a visceral representation of rebirth and renewal, and snakes' unusual (phallic) shape, unique means of locomotion, and generally secretive nature have inspired their use as provocative characters in religious literature.[41] *Nāgas* in particular—the semidivine, sometimes polycephalous serpents who are at times represented as rather human in physical stature—are a category of being that pervades all Indic religious traditions. Ophiolatry has had a mark on the Indian landscape, as demonstrated in roadside shrines to *nāgas* and in the popularity of the Nāg Panchamī festival, where milk offerings are brought to shrines and to the *nāgas*' homes (typically in anthills or at the base of trees).[42]

We see *nāgas* slithering through Jain, Vaiṣṇava, and Śaiva texts as well as Buddhist ones. Frequently in the stories, they rather transparently represent autochthonous disorder, something that needs restraint or subjugation by the god or enlightened protagonist.[43] Once subdued, *nāgas* become model worshippers and stick close to their "saviors"; in parallel stories and iconography, *nāgas* curl around the *tīrthaṅkara* (Jaina, enlightened teacher of dharma) Pārśvanātha and the Buddha Gotama, serving as an umbrella to protect their honored one from the elements; and sometimes *nāgas* even become accoutrements, as in the depictions of Śiva adorned with *nāga* garlands and Gaṇeśa wearing the *nāga* Vāsuki as his sacred cord.

Even a most cursory survey of the classic tales reveals the special salience of the *nāgas* in South Asian imagination. They are critical agents in foundational Hindu myths. For example, the *devas* (gods) and *asuras* (power-hungry antigods) use the *nāga* Vāsuki as a rope, winding him around Mount Mandara to churn the Milk Ocean to procure *amṛta*, the elixir of immortality.[44] The competitive Kadru (mother to one thousand *nāgas*) and Vinatā (mother to *garuḍa*, an eaglelike being), co-wives of the sage Kaśyapa, trigger the mutual distrust and hatred between the *nāgas* and *garuḍa*. As in many Hindu myths, a bet is made, and *garuḍa* becomes the miserable servant of the *nāgas*. To obtain release, he steals the *amṛta* that was churned. Stories have it that *nāgas* lick drops of *amṛta* that fall on the sharp-edged grass, resulting in the split tongues we see on snakes. An angry Kadru curses her own *nāga* offspring to die in King Janamejaya's snake sacrifice, though many are saved.

Nāgas are closely associated with periods of creation in Vaiṣṇava traditions. The colossal *nāga* Śeṣa's name means "remainder" because he is the only thing that remains after the cycle of dissolution that occurs at the end of each *kalpa* (world period)—the *nāga* is the only thing that perseveres, unrestricted by time (Śeṣa is also known as Ananta, "Endless"). Floating on the cosmic sea between world periods, resting on Śeṣa like a raft, Viṣṇu contemplates creation anew. Images of this manifestation of Viṣṇu as Nārāyana abound. When Viṣṇu incarnates as the *avatāra* (incarnate god) Kṛṣṇa, Śeṣa also incarnates as Kṛṣṇa's older half-brother, Balarāma. As a youth, Kṛṣṇa subdues the vitriolic *nāga* Kāliya, who has been poisoning the river Yamunā. Playing with friends, Kṛṣṇa falls into the river, and when Kāliya grabs him, Kṛṣṇa begins to expand his body to the point where the *nāga* can no longer hold him. Kṛṣṇa then dances on Kāliya's head, not for fun but to pound him into submission. Kāliya's *nāginī* (female *nāga*) wives beg for his life, and when Kṛṣṇa relents, the *nāgas* then become his ardent worshippers.[45]

The Kashmiri *Rājataraṅgiṇī* is a twelfth-century Sanskrit chronicle parallel to the *Mahāvaṃsa*, another case of a South Asian literary chronicle frequently read as a historical source alone. In it, *nāgas* factor in controlling water, rain, and fertility. *Nāgas* were clearly good characters to think with; the *Rājataraṅgiṇī* composer's father was employed in the court of King Harṣa, who is credited with his own composition of a rare Sanskrit tragedy about *nāgas*.[46]

And *nāgas* are a pervasive presence in Buddhist texts beyond the Pāli sources that are my focus. For example, in the early and central Mahāyāna text *Saddharmapuṇḍarīkasūtra* (Lotus Sūtra), a famous episode reveals a *nāginī*, strikingly an eight-year-old, female *nāga* (as liminal a character as could be imagined in terms of her age, gender, and birth status).[47] After hearing the bodhisattva (enlightened, salvific being) Mañjuśri preach the *sūtra* (sermon), the *nāginī* transcends her female birth, takes a brief turn as male, and then achieves enlightenment. Her transformation underscores the transformative capacity of the hearing of a text, in this case the Lotus Sūtra, but in our case the *Mahāvaṃsa*. This is only one of countless examples of the work, conveyed in narrative form, that the literary character of the *nāga* performs in the religious imagination.

My project here mirrors to some degree the compelling work by theologian Paul D. L. Avis, who takes the work of the imagination in Christian faith seriously:

> I will contest the assumption made by both the Enlightenment and postmodernism that metaphors, symbols and myths belong to the realm of the trivial, the arbitrary and the false. I will show that symbols are not arbitrary or at our disposal, but powerful, cognitive and to be handled with care. I will claim that metaphors are the vehicles of fresh insight and thus constitutive of our apprehension of truth; that symbols mediate the transcendent because they participate in what they symbolise, and that myths, which are archetypal stories studded with numerous symbols, embody a sacred narrative of human identity in the face of the divine reality.[48]

As described by George Lakoff and Mark Johnson, metaphor is not a "transfer of meaning but a restructuring of the world."[49] Metaphors make you work; they require your active participation in what is tantamount to world creation.

I have referred to the "work" the text expects from its audience, and this concept requires clarification. Dominic LaCapra offers a helpful distinction between the "documentary" and "worklike" aspects of texts that frame the way I approach the proem of the *Mahāvaṃsa* in chapter 2. Simply stated, "The documentary situates the text in terms of factual or literal dimensions involving reference to empirical reality and conveying information about it. The 'worklike' supplements empirical reality by adding to and subtracting from it. It thereby involves dimensions of the text not reducible to the documentary, prominently including the roles of commitment, interpretation, and imagination."[50]

As we will see, the documentary and worklike aspects of the *Mahāvaṃsa* are not easily separable and instead represent two perceptible strains within the narrative itself; when these aspects are activated by the reader, there are two modes of reading and interpreting the text. I argue that the more documentary aspects are those that promote the typical historicist reading, and although the latter is one of many valid readings, it is far from an exclusive one. Rather, the *Mahāvaṃsa* is a multivalent text, and it is by paying attention to the worklike dimensions that a new reading becomes warranted, especially in terms of the study of religion.

The terms *religion* and *religious* also beg for clarification. It is beyond my project to define what is religion or religious here, but I do employ these terms heuristically to help define a circumscribed set of expectations, practices, values, and anticipated audiences that are exemplified in the *Mahāvaṃsa*. The *Mahāvaṃsa* was written by a monk or monks for a monastic audience, with the explicit intention of deepening religious attitudes, including those that would encourage the activity of relic veneration. The term *religion* generally refers in this book to what has become known as Theravāda Buddhism, although, as we will see in chapter 5, the exact constitution of the textual community is itself unattested—it is only assumed, not definitively known, to be the domineering Mahāvihāran monastic complex, and this claim was made explicit only once the commentary on the *Mahāvaṃsa*, the *Vaṃsatthappakāsinī*, was written.

By the term *textual community*, I refer to the useful idea that Brian Stock introduces in his work on eleventh-century literary culture and that Blackburn and Monius fruitfully apply to the Buddhist context.[51] Stock defines "textual communities" as "types of microsocieties organized around the common understanding of a text."[52] I have already demanded a literary reading of the text, but what I mean by "literary" is not an exclusive category. I do not want to set up an artificial dialectic of literary and historical, nor do I want to limit the work of the *Mahāvaṃsa* to a singular method. An awareness of these very rhetorical maneuvers may in fact underscore the predominant historical argument, and we will find that a textual community is one that writes, reads, hears, and interprets as a creative and legitimating act.

The questions I bring to this text illustrate a wider set of implications and concerns in the discipline of religious studies: How do interpreters (scholars, laypeople, and virtuosi) read religious texts? What cues (internal to the text and external) shape the reading process? And to what end? How we read a text such as the *Mahāvaṃsa* has implications for the larger field of religious studies; the *Mahāvaṃsa* is not the only religious text that features talking snakes who provoke agents within the narrative and readers outside it into ethical consideration, enrichment of faith, and practical action.

Religious texts enshrine the worldview and the imaginative hopes of the communities that shaped their production. In such a way, texts themselves act as *cetiya*, sites to spark remembrance and veneration of sanctified beings (the Buddha in this case). The *Mahāvaṃsa* is more than a Buddhist history; it conveys a presence of the Buddha to an ever-evolving textual community, making accessible pathways for ethical transformation. Insofar as the text provokes affective response, it acts as a relic.

{1} INSTRUCTIONS, ADMONITIONS, AND ASPIRATIONS IN *VAṂSA* PROEMS

THE PROEMS (introductory verses) of both the *Dīpavaṃsa* and the *Mahāvaṃsa* call for their audience's active participation through the act of reading or hearing the stories. The *Dīpavaṃsa* clearly aims for what I am calling "religious satisfaction" (*pasāda*)—namely, the feeling of confidence and inclusion in the Buddha's *sāsana* that results from the performed reading by "good people" (*sujana*).[1] The text suggests that the act of reading or hearing will be transformative for the right reader-hearer; the *Dīpavaṃsa*'s proem constructs and anticipates a certain expected community of reception and transformation. The *Mahāvaṃsa*'s proem recapitulates this construction of a "textual community" (following Brian Stock[2]) and reiterates the *Dīpavaṃsa*'s claim about the efficacy of its content. However, the *Mahāvaṃsa*'s proem also makes a structural, functional claim—a claim that begs further examination—about its relationship to the source material "told by the ancients,"[3] perhaps including the *Dīpavaṃsa* itself. Why does the *Mahāvaṃsa* begin its narrative with a boastful proem, urging the reader-hearer to disregard the interpretations of the narratives of old in favor of this new compilation? How do these claims play out in the text's narrative? Does the text live up to its own expectations?

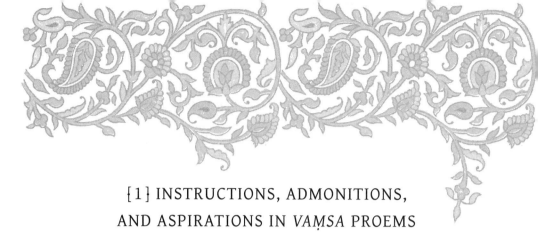

We know that originality is not the primary objective of Pāli texts from the premodern Buddhist world. In fact, overt originality challenges truthfulness, authority, and convention as well as confounds the traditional modes by which good poetry is assessed. Pāli texts frequently assert the importance of continuity over originality. Imitation is thus a valid and even desirable textual practice for our fourth- and fifth-century compilers. The literary technique of imitation also provides would-be innovators with an ideal medium to effect subtle but profound adjustments to a traditional discourse. In other words, if continuity is key, any deviation (barring scribal errors), however slight, becomes a conscientious choice and even an argument by the compiler. The attuned and primed reader would recognize the slightest nuances of the new argument, and thus a new layer of the textual community would develop. The *Mahāvaṃsa* builds on this discursive tradition and benefits from its legacy, authenticity, and authority. But it does not simply imitate the *Dīpavaṃsa* and other source materials.[4] In its proem, the compiler makes a point to draw the reader-hearer's attention to his primary objective in producing the text and its most original content: the text's literary turn.

If both the *Dīpavaṃsa* and the *Mahāvaṃsa* arose out of the arguably nascent, orthodox, textual community of Anurādhapura's monastic complex, the Mahāvihāra, why would the *Mahāvaṃsa* make outright claims of superiority over the *Dīpavaṃsa*? Within the tense, even turbulent times of these texts' composition, the *Mahāvaṃsa*'s claim as a singular, authoritative voice over the claims of other "ancient" texts is at stake. These two early *vaṃsa*s reflect the fraught circumstances in which they were produced vis-à-vis other outside lineages vying for royal patronage, and they also reflect a particularly tumultuous time within the Mahāvihāra itself as it grappled with internal divisions about what made for a poetic, effective history of its establishment and continued authority in Laṅkā. The extended *Mahāvaṃsa* and the later commentary on it, the *Vaṃsatthappakāsinī*, claim that, in addition to competitive rival sects, internal rabble-rousers also threatened the stability of the Mahāvihāra enough to warrant expulsion. Does the *Mahāvaṃsa* represent an attempt by the "winners" of this internal feud to shore up more widespread support? Or does it represent a minority voice making assertive claims of authority? Whatever the political context or motivations that surrounded the *Mahāvaṃsa*'s production, its internal aims are clear—to break new and fertile literary ground.

PROEMS AS INSTRUCTIONS

How are we to approach a sensitive reading of the ethically provocative, aesthetically pleasing dimensions of a text so far removed from our own cultural location? Drawing heavily on pioneering interpretive work in the context of European Christendom, Anne Blackburn has suggested that scholars of Theravādin textual communities must train themselves to read Buddhist texts the way that the medieval participants in the textual community might have read them.[5] Framed in this way, the *vaṃsa*s speak to us as living texts that are part of an ongoing, dynamic process of reinterpretation and application by Theravādin Buddhists. But it is impossible to be sure that the reading we perform in the twenty-first century approximates that of a member of the intended textual community. There is no single proper way to read a text, even an authoritative text such as the *Mahāvaṃsa*, but there are better readings and less-compelling ones. My method, therefore, will be to read the proems to reveal the range of expectations they conveyed to their original textual communities. As Umberto Eco says, "A theory of interpretation—even when it assumes that texts are open to multiple readings—must also assume that it is possible to reach an agreement, if not about the meanings that a text encourages, at least about those that a text discourages."[6] To understand the vision of the world constructed by the textual community responsible for the *Mahāvaṃsa*, it is helpful to use Blackburn's modification of Stanley Fish's reader-response theory: "[Fish] argued that a shared institutional location makes possible common interpretive responses to a text. I suggest that, in addition, common exposure to textual representations makes possible shared interpretive responses to social institutions."[7]

The *Mahāvaṃsa* constructs as much as reflects its textual community. I believe the best way to sensitively engage with both the *Dīpavaṃsa* and the *Mahāvaṃsa* is to pay particular and deliberate attention to the reading instructions contained within each text's respective proem. We may not have access to the actual parameters and demographics of the textual community anticipated or constructed by each text. Nevertheless, we may read the proems to begin to understand something of each text's aspirations or the ethical and communally constitutive transformations the compilers hoped these texts would enact.

When we ignore the reading instructions contained in the proems and instead dive right into the narrative (as scholars and politicians alike almost universally do), fueled by our own ideas of what we might find, we would be, in Eco's terms, an "empirical reader": "The empirical reader is you, me, anyone when we read a text. Empirical readers can read in many ways, and there is no law that tells them how to read, because they often use the text as a container for their own passions, which may come from outside the text or which the text may arouse by chance."[8]

By disregarding "the law that tells them how to read" (in our case the proem is the law), a reader can use the text for various ends: to sate or inflame various political passions or to substantiate behaviors and theories.[9] The proems are very specific about their literary aims and the type of community they intend to create. Even for readers as far removed as we are from the immediate context of the Mahāvihāran textual community of the fourth and fifth centuries, I believe certain readings are better than others—and are perhaps even sanctioned or hoped for by the text.

Umberto Eco discusses the "spectatorly" aspect of the model reader's role in reading: "This type of spectator (or reader of a book) I call the model reader—a sort of ideal type whom the text not only foresees as a collaborator but also tries to create. If a text begins 'Once upon a time,' it sends out a signal that immediately enables it to select its own model reader, who must be a child, or at least somebody willing to accept something that goes beyond the commonsensical and reasonable."[10] The key to recognizing the "model reader" of the *vaṃsas* is the language employed in them. First, we must remember that the language of these texts was Pāli. This fact automatically circumscribes a subset of the community capable of reading and interpreting a text composed in this language. I have already examined the types of translocal claims that selecting Pāli entails; here I simply note that Pāli alienates some reader-hearers and anticipates others. The Pāli of the *Mahāvaṃsa* is, as the proem itself proclaims, poetically powerful, capable of eliciting a particular set of emotions from the primed reader. This relationship is reflected in later medieval South Asian theories on literature. Even though it may be anachronistic to apply the theories of the ninth-century *Siyabaslakara* to the *vaṃsas*, we can see how important the "model reader" is for the successful dissemination of the text: "Language is like a wish-conferring cow that gives what is desirable to those who can use it in the proper manner, but for others it will only impart bovine qualities."[11] The community is thus urged to be responsible for making good use of the text.

In the broader Buddhist case, we might think, for example, of the type of community that is both called for and constructed by the formulaic opening of each *sutta* (sermon): *Evaṃ me sutaṃ*, "Thus have I heard." These words call the audience into a certain relationship with the material about to be conveyed.[12] There is an element of temptation and seduction in being privy to hearsay. More important, however, is the way that "Thus have I heard" thrusts the speaker into a relationship with the *sutta* and, through it, with the Buddha himself. For the hearer concerned with establishing a feeling of proximity to the Buddha, this phrase collapses spatial and temporal distance. The community uttering this statement participates in a long lineage of members, of participants in the oral/aural practices of a diachronically potent textual community. Although "Thus have I heard" calls forth a different type of community than the "Once upon a time" that Eco refers to, in both cases the words uttered at the outset of a text create that text's model reader and shape that reader's orientation to the subject. So who is the model reader of the *Dīpavaṃsa* and the *Mahāvaṃsa*, and how is that reader called forth in each text's proem?

In the proems of our texts, the "catchphrase" takes the vocative form *suṇātha me*, "Listen to me!" or "Listen up!"—a direct, urgent command to virtuous members of the textual community. These words connect the text's compiler with his audience; here, the compiler reveals his goals and conveys the urgency and import of hearing these words. Although the urgent opener "Listen to me!" appears to be unique to the *Dīpavaṃsa* and the *Mahāvaṃsa*, other texts from this period begin with a similar personal entreaty to the audience to behave in certain ways for certain effects. For example, Buddhadatta states in the *Madhuratthavilāsinī*, a fifth-century commentary on the *Buddhavaṃsa*, that the commentary was solicited by his student Buddhasīha and that he felt compelled to produce the commentary:

> For the perpetuation of the Conqueror's Dispensation which always destroys people's evil, also for the rise and growth of my own merit and for the serene joy of the multitude, there will be this Commentary on the Chronicle of Buddhas, devoid of the fault of corruption, based on the textual course (tradition) transmitted in the Mahāvihara, and containing the essential matter in brief. . . . Therefore, (you) who are duly concentrated, abandoning dispersion (perplexity), with minds undivided, listen, lending your ears respectfully to (me) who am explaining this Commentary which is sweet and well lettered (composed). Now, this narration, which is very rare, should always be respectfully listened to and related by an intelligent man, leaving aside all other activity (work).[13]

We see that Buddhadatta anticipates a certain primed, "duly concentrated," intelligent reader-hearer. But the mere composition of the text is also beneficial "for the serene joy of the multitude" as well as for the commentator's merit.

The opening lines of Pāli texts indicate much about the ways they should be read and interpreted. Ronald Inden points to this constitutive aspect of South Asian literature:

> We wish to emphasize that once texts are seen as participating in the making and remaking of a living, changing scale of texts, we become aware of their political and polemical dimension. Every text, no matter what claims its authors or users may make about its transcendence, is *articulative* with respect to specific actors and situations. It is not merely a "source" that passively records events, but an intervention on the part of an agent in the world. It calls on its readers as they read the text not only to engage in (or refrain from) textual activity, but to engage, to some degree, in other acts as well. The very composition (and reiteration) of a text, the placement of it in relation to other texts, is itself an assertion of relative power.[14]

Both internal and external markers condition and appeal to the reader. In the *vaṃsas*, the direct appeal to "listen up!" creates the very textual community it seeks to attract. In her examination of how texts were used and received in the early Siyam Nikāya of the eighteenth century, Blackburn notes that

> readers' experiences were influenced by both [the inside and outside of the text]: by aspects of the work's form and content that provoked readers to respond in particular ways, and by expectations about monastic reading that carried authority within the order and thus influenced the ways students read and internalized what they read. By looking at the first aspect—the textual characteristics that influenced reading experiences—we remain open to the possibility that students' encounter with, internalization of, and subsequent use of the text proceeded with a certain amount of individual variation. By looking at the second aspect—external expectations that affected reading experiences—we also take seriously the fact that these readers shared an institutional location, and that this location affected acts of interpretation.[15]

The textual community of the *Mahāvaṃsa* is both constructed by and appealed to in the proem.

WHAT IS "LITERARY" IN PĀLI?

My claim that the *Mahāvaṃsa* argues to be read for literary effects rather than for literal historiography is contingent on what would have been considered "literary" in the Pāli textual world of the fifth century. In his article "What Is Literature in Pāli?" Steven Collins wonders, "Why is it that Pāli texts from the last few centuries BCE contain some of the earliest examples of literature in the *kāvya* [poetic literature] sense in South Asia, yet there is nothing more in this genre in Pāli, with one partial exception (*Mahāvaṃsa*), until the start of the second millennium?" Collins remarks that with one or two debatable exceptions all Pāli texts that persist into the modern period are from the Mahāvihāra. And yet he also explains that "during the first millennium the Mahāvihāra was a minority tradition alongside the Abhayagiri and Jetavana monastic fraternities."[16] The Mahāvihāra, then, found a particularly productive niche in the production and dissemination of Pāli texts. Other monastic communities were also productive on the literary front, but it is the corpus of the Mahāvihāra that endures.

As for the *Dīpavaṃsa*, Collins repeats the generally accepted notion that it "is a clumsy verse composition with grammatical and other errors, made probably in the third or fourth century C.E." The *Mahāvaṃsa*, which he dates to "perhaps the sixth century," he characterizes as "not high *kāvya*, but . . . an elegant poem, in *ślokas* with penultimate verses in each chapter in more complex meters, which either summarize the narrative or offer reflections on it."[17] The verses Collins chooses to illustrate the literariness of the *Mahāvaṃsa*, however, are XLII.1–5, which are technically part of the later section of the *Mahāvaṃsa* commonly called the *Cūlavaṃsa*. This extended part of the *Mahāvaṃsa* picks up the chronicle in the reign of Dhammakitti and concludes its narrative arc in the year 1815.[18] The *Mahāvaṃsa* may not adhere to the precise rubric of *kāvya*, but it operates as such with its use of metaphor, puns, riveting narrative, superhuman characters, and dramatic imagery. In his history of Sri Lanka, S. G. Perera goes so far as to call the *Mahāvaṃsa* a *mahākāvya* (great work of poetry) and a Mahāvihāran *purāṇa* (legend).[19]

The *Dīpavaṃsa* is poetic in intention, if poorly organized and grammatically imprecise. It is a challenge to translate with the standard *Pāli-English Dictionary*, and its nonconformity with conventional narrative structure proves challenging for even a patient translator.[20] Yet even at the height of his criticism of the *Dīpavaṃsa*'s lack of literary qualities, translator Wilhelm Geiger confesses that it stands at the threshold of epic poetry. He considers the *Dīpavaṃsa* to be a collection of strung-together fragments—a peculiar construction that leads to the overall impression of "clumsiness and an incorrectness of language and metre, and a number of other peculiarities."[21] He suggests that the text's redundancy in recounting the same incidents several times over is an indication of its origins in orally preserved literature, where the source texts preserved certain anomalies in form and content:

> If, for example, two independent versions of the same story are found beside each other, we may regard it as the outcome of an originally verbal tradition. Such versions as the [*Dīpavaṃsa*] shows can only be understood if we suppose that certain expressions and verses were fixed for the relater of any particular story by the regular custom of predecessors, but that the representation of the other parts was left to their imagination. Thus it happens that as we approach the period of decline of oral tradition, the same stories show many variants, together with many examples of identity of language. . . . The possibility is that the [*Dīpavaṃsa*] arranged together different versions from different sources, or that this had already taken place. The suggestion, however, that perhaps the authors did not realise that only variants of the same story were being dealt with, is quite out of the question. The compilation must have been done with a purpose: it was intended to keep the various traditions as more or less authorized, and to hand them on further.[22]

If the goal of the *Dīpavaṃsa* was to preserve variant traditions, one must accept that "traditions" can be contained in brief and entertaining narratives. This assumption in itself exposes the text's constitutive properties and the power of literature to create or perpetuate a tradition.

Geiger relates the form of the *Dīpavaṃsa* to the Indian predecessor to epic poetry, Ākhyāna poetry. His conclusion, based on T. W. Rhys Davids's assertion that "different stages of development in the Ākhyāna poetry are to be found in the canonical books of the Buddhists,"[23] is that the *Dīpavaṃsa* is a window into a certain stage in Pāli literary development.[24] It is in this vein that we may engage in a more generous reading of the text rather than dismiss it entirely as poor poetry. The repetitive passages may have been intentionally composed in this way—the abundant use of memory verses (*Memorialverse*) locates the *Dīpavaṃsa* in a particular moment in the course of literary evolution from oral to written literature and from proto-epic poetry to Ākhyāna epic.[25] Geiger sets out the techniques a fourth-century reader would likely have been expected to employ in his reading of the text:

> [Memory verses] lead us to the stage of development of the Ākhyāna poetry. With their help the one reciting holds in readiness in his memory the material essential for any recounting of the story. In this way, for example, he was able, according to the statements in 1,29 (v.p.10), to relate, one after the other, the whole of events of the life of the Buddha which happened between the night of his enlightenment to the first sermon at Benares, without running the risk of forgetting. But I do not therefore mean to say that the [*Dīpavaṃsa*] was a kind of handbook for rhapsodists reciting the history of Ceylon. In this respect the [*Dīpavaṃsa*] is only a reflex of its source or sources, and in its form there are still traces of former rhapsodic delivery.[26]

If this is the case, the lack of poetic style in the *Dīpavaṃsa* reflects a stage in literary development, bridging "rhapsodic" oral sources and the fuller poetic form of the *Mahāvaṃsa*.[27] It is highly likely that certain reading strategies made an impact on how the text was collated. This understanding can help us to forgive the rather choppy and repetitive delivery of the narrative and supports the theory that the *Dīpavaṃsa* demands an ethically primed reader (one whose memory would, in fact, be jogged by the memory verses). In so doing, we can turn our focus to both texts' aims to grab their audiences and communicate to them clear expectations of transformation. In other words, we open up the possibility to understand the texts as literature.

WORKLIKE AND DOCUMENTARY: READING THE *VAṂSAS* THROUGH LACAPRA

How can we assume that the *Dīpavaṃsa* and *Mahāvaṃsa* were intended to be read in a literary way? Because they say so, right at the outset, in proems that may be easily overlooked by readers in an urgent haste to enter the narratives of the *vaṃsas* to decode or liberate the "facts" they contain. By overlooking the proem or by simply treating the claims of poetic efficacy (that the text will provoke awe and satisfaction, for example) as hyperbole, however, we miss the opportunity to consider the work that the text imagines itself performing on us, the readers, and we refuse to perform any work ourselves. The proems' vocative opening, *suṇātha me*, initiates what Dominick LaCapra calls a "worklike" function, in contrast to the "documentary" function of chronicling events. LaCapra defines these helpful terms: "The documentary situates the text in terms of factual or literal dimensions involving reference to empirical reality and conveying information about it. The 'worklike' supplements empirical reality by adding to and subtracting from it. It thereby involves dimensions of the text not reducible to the documentary, prominently including the roles of commitment, interpretation, and imagination."[28] In other words, the documentary mode of any text describes and sets forth the narrative sequence in the structural manner of reportage: the point is to clarify the story, to set down events, to tell something. That is not to say that the documentary mode does not teach; the moral of a story, for example, may be conveyed in this style. The worklike, in contrast, is the mode or aspect of the text that demands a higher degree of interaction or effort on the part of the interpreter, who is constructed or instructed through the cumulative act of reading the text. The worklike element of a text requires commitment and readiness from the reader as well. It engages the imagination and transforms the interpreter-reader; it expects him or her to work and to be changed in the process. LaCapra explains: "The worklike is critical and transformative, for it deconstructs and reconstructs the given, in a sense repeating it but also bringing into the world something that did not exist before in that significant variation, alteration, or transformation. With deceptive simplicity, one might say that while the documentary marks a difference, the worklike makes a difference—one that engages the reader in recreative dialogue with the text and the problems it raises."[29]

The terms *documentary* and *worklike* here apply to both the form and the function of these texts. In our reading of these two *vaṃsa*s, we might say that on the surface the documentary aspect of each text conveys the story or the chronology of events of the narrative about the coming of Buddhism to Sri Lanka, and the worklike aspect reaches out beyond the narrative to make demands of and ethically transform the interpreter. Yet even in the most documentary passages, "work" is still going on because of the literary nature of these texts. There is no easy separation of the texts' documentary and worklike modes. The transformation that the "recreative dialogue" provokes in the reader may be gradual, but it is initiated in the very process of reading or hearing the text, beginning with the ostensibly documentary introductions in the proems. In other words, for the *Dīpavaṃsa*'s and *Mahāvaṃsa*'s textual communities, as for myself, the two modes may not be necessarily mutually exclusive, even if it is heuristically useful to consider them so.

Our reading of the texts is enriched if we read the proems as a moment of clarity, highlighting the texts' intentionally worklike aspects, to see how these two aspects are intertwined in the process of transmitting and receiving texts. Information can be effectively conveyed through the story regardless of the reader's ability (recalling here Eco's "empirical reader"); however, for the reader primed for the worklike dimension, initiated into the textual community, even the documentary aspects are imbued with a worklike quality.

Collins profitably applies LaCapra's distinctions specifically to Pāli texts, asking "how to balance a documentary interest in texts—what they can tell us about their time and place—and what [LaCapra] calls a dialogical approach, which asks questions about the relationship between [the] present historian and the past history he or she reconstructs, about the uses of language in both source material and historiography, and about various things to which he refers under the category of 'worklike' aspects of a text, as opposed to the 'documentary.' "[30] If the proem provides blatant, documentary information on the history of the lineages of monks and kings, it also initiates a certain worklike capacity that is at first transparent (as in the instructions for the proem's reader-hearer) and later more subtle and nuanced (as in the beginning of the narrative). To understand the form that the latter elements take, it may be helpful to see an example of the type of literariness that appears in our texts under the guise of pragmatic description. Something as seemingly innocuous as an epithet for the Buddha is revealed to have added potency and transformative power when it is encountered after one reads the instructions provided in the proems. In the narrative following the proem, *Dīpavaṃsa* I:14 reads, "Having become Enlightened and having made an utterance of all things, the Light Maker spent seven days just so on the excellent throne."[31]

At face value, such a descriptive passage can be read as a documentary chronicle of events: the Buddha became Enlightened, preached, and then sat in meditation for a week. But if we pause to consider the implications of the epithet used, "Light Maker" (*pabhaṃkaro*), we realize that the text performs yet another function here. By calling the Buddha "Light Maker," the text introduces or reinforces an image in the interpreter's imagination, thereby initiating the text's worklike function. In other words, in the simple act of reading the epithet we (the readers-hearers) tacitly agree to its semantic field and all of the work the words may induce. When we refer to the Buddha as "Light Maker," we are, in fact, praising the Buddha, which is a meritorious act in and of itself, and we envision him as a producer and disseminator of the *dhamma*, which is here imagined as light.[32] This work ideally results in a feeling of gratitude from the hearer, of being thankful for the Buddha's enlightenment in times past that enables one to be Buddhist in the present. In this way, certain names generate particular emotional states that a less symbolically rich name may not. Even in this most documentary of moments, describing a series of events in the Buddha's biography, the worklike aspect of the text permeates, in LaCapra's words, to "make a difference."

By evoking the Buddha in such loaded terms, the reader-hearer assumes a relationship of dependence on or gratitude for the Buddha. The text thus uses the epithet to construct an ideal devotee. The proem is explicit about its desired effect; when inspiring epithets are employed, we can assume it is an intentional move to buttress the poetic effect of the passage. Using "Light Maker" in this context, only fourteen verses into the entire *vaṃsa*, prefigures the way the Buddha is characterized throughout the narrative of his three visits to Laṅkā. This usage helps to prime the reader for the text's full desired aesthetic and ethically transforming effect.

The proems themselves illustrate how the reading methods previously outlined are not only salient but also in line with the expectations of the estimated fourth- and fifth-century textual community responsible for the textual production itself. At the outset, each text, before diving into the densely woven thicket of metaphors and the *nāga*-rich Buddha biographical narrative, provides instructions to guide an able interpreter through it.

A RELIGIOUS IMPERATIVE: THE PROEM OF THE *DĪPAVAṂSA*

Even in its rough-hewn state, the *Dīpavaṃsa* is a literary articulation of a religious worldview. As Geiger notes, it "can hardly be called a production of artistic merit, in spite of its rather bombastic proem."[33] That "bombastic proem," however, gives us a clear indication of the ideal reader, motives, and anticipated reactions for which the text was compiled.

And what should we make of this category of religious? What is it about the opening of either the *Dīpavaṃsa* or the *Mahāvaṃsa* that allows for this categorization, apart from the fact that both texts purportedly were written by monks in the monastic milieu of the Mahāvihāra and that they circulated within this limited monastic environs? The opening of the *Dīpavaṃsa* is explicitly religious insofar as it begins with the requisite line of praise, or *stotra*, prior to the numbered verses: "Homage to Him, the Blessed, Worthy, and Fully Enlightened One."[34] This eulogy is far from original; its inclusion is simply part of the composer's implicit argument that this *vaṃsa* is worthy of attention, just as other texts with the same preface are. Both the form of this verse and the content can be considered worklike elements. We should here recall part of LaCapra's definition of *worklike* as that element that "involves dimensions of the text not reducible to the documentary, prominently including the roles of commitment, interpretation, and imagination."[35] To this day, in Buddhist communities of various types around the world, this memorized phrase in homage to the "Fully Enlightened One" is uttered alongside the Three Refuges and the Five Precepts in a ritualized fashion. Its usage alerts a reader to and circumscribes a textual community and a community of faith.

After pronouncing the homage to the Buddha, the opening proem of the *Dīpavaṃsa* explicitly articulates the text's purpose, demonstrating the worklike element of both the form and the content. The proem is structurally set off from the regularized *śloka*s of the text itself, which makes its internal structural cohesion and uniqueness even more pronounced. The form itself calls out to the reader to take notice and heed its instructions. The content is most obviously worklike; it opens with the emphatic "Listen to me!" (*suṇātha me*), seemingly addressed directly and personally to the reader-hearer. The proem is here quoted in its entirety for the full emphatic effect:

> [1] Listen to me! I will relate the *vaṃsa* of the journey to the island of the Buddha and the coming of the bodhi tree and the relics, the collected traditional teachings, and the coming of the *sāsana* to the island and the coming of the King [Vijaya].
>
> [2] Listen to me, honoring [this *vaṃsa*] abounding in countless qualities, delightful, calming, producing joy and gladness.
>
> [3] Applying great attention, listen up all to this *vaṃsa*; I will explain the coming of the lineage.

[4] This extolled praise [text][36] indeed is praised by many, tied together as if all kinds of flowers [in a garland].

[5] Listen! This praise [text] of the island is honored by the virtuous, extolled by the greatest, this very one in truth well explained through the noble ones, which is new, which dwells upon the most meritorious *vaṃsa* (lineage), which is incomparable.[37]

As we pause to consider the full impact of this proem, we note first of all the overall tenor, the urgency with which the composer confronts his or her audience. The vocative *suṇātha* ("Listen!") is used four times in five verses. The author is direct and demanding, even downright urgent in his tone. A "listen up!" modified by "applying great attention" also buttresses the overall effect of urgency, agency, and persuasiveness in verse 3. The verse not only tells one to listen but explains *how* to listen. The fact that this story, according to the text, is "honored by the virtuous, extolled by the greatest" also conveys a subtle sense of reassurance to the reader-hearer. It indicates that other, more virtuous (*sādhu*) people are convinced by the text that is about to be revealed, and so the reader-hearer should likewise listen up and prepare to be convinced. The overall effect is that the hearer feels called into action and uniquely persuaded by the author to pay attention in a particular way for a particular intended effect.[38]

Apart from the direct command to pay attention and listen, these first five verses perform another more subtle and persuasive worklike function. The last verse of the proem provokes the very human need to be part of a group. Who would want to be excluded from the work of such a persuasive text? The turn this proem takes in verse 5 appeals to a most basic urge not to be left out: "This praise [text] of the island is honored by the virtuous, extolled by the greatest, this very one in truth well explained through the noble ones, which is new, which dwells upon the most meritorious *vaṃsa* (lineage), which is incomparable."

By understanding the *vaṃsa* correctly, one is thus included in the designation *virtuous*; it is through the process of reading or hearing that one is included in the textual community, a virtuous one. Blackburn argues for the utility of a term used in discussions of medieval literacy in Europe, *textual communities*, although she adapts it for the Buddhist monastic context. About *textual community*, she writes: "I use the term to describe a group of individuals who think of themselves to at least some degree as a collective, who understand the world and their appropriate place within it in terms significantly influenced by their encounter with a shared set of written texts or oral teachings based on written texts, and who grant special social status to literate interpreters of authoritative written texts."[39] Her characterization works very well for the *gantha-dhura* (bookish)[40] monks of the Mahāvihāra in the period before, during, and after Buddhaghosa's (and others') translation of the Sinhalese commentaries into Pāli—in other words, the period of literary productivity in Pāli beginning with the inscription of the Tipiṭaka and ending with the *vaṃsas*. The hearer is thus roped within the designation "good people" if he understands and respects the verse. To recognize oneself as the intended audience of the text is to initiate the ethical transformation.

This proem initiates the hearer-receiver into a particular, chosen community, one comprising likeminded people primed for the aesthetic and ethical effects of the following narrative. By giving an overview of the major events to follow, the *vaṃsa*'s proem acts as a microcosmic blueprint for the rest of the text. By establishing the receiver's relationship to the text, the proem presages the text's ethically transformative content as well. This early articulation of the relationship foreshadows the relationship we see within the later narrative between worshiper and the relics of the Buddha and even corresponds with the opening narrative about the *nāgas*' conversion by the Buddha. In all of these cases, the effect of proximity to the text's transformative power claims to be, of course, profoundly transformative. That the transmission of the chronicle itself should be "honored by the virtuous, extolled by the greatest" (*Dīpavaṃsa* I.5) indicates its value to the entire textual community.

The text's poetic merits and intentions are made clear in the images it conjures. Part of verse 4 reads: "This extolled praise [text] indeed is praised by many, tied together as if all kinds of flowers [in a garland]." This verse suggests that the composer was aware of poetic conventions and here was playfully rendering nascent *alaṃkāra* (ornamentation) theory. An obvious adornment is a flower garland, made up of various flowers tied together into a perfect whole. To imagine a text as a knitted collection of various flowers (*nānākusumaṃ va ganthitaṃ*) conveys a sense of beauty and adornment and constructs an image of distinct stories (here represented by the flowers) pieced together to be unified as a whole. Gathered together and understood as a whole, the piece of literature would augment the wearer's innate beauty or value. That the text itself suggests the ethical ornamentation it renders points to the sophisticated literary world in which it was composed.

Although it would be a historical impossibility for Daṇḍin, the seventh-century Sanskrit grammarian and systematic theorist on poetics, to have been known at the time of the composition of either of the *vaṃsa*s discussed here, we must assume that by the time he composed the *Kāvyādarśa* in the early seventh century, an interest in poetics was already widespread.[41] Daṇḍin certainly did not invent poetics; he wrote a compendium assessing the merits of poetry as he knew it. The theory of *rasa* was developed in the *Nāṭyaśāstra* (attributed to Bharata) sometime around the first century of the Common Era; it may be that the monastic textual community at the Mahāvihāra would have had some familiarity with *rasa* theory. The problem with this hypothesis is that the specific emotional responses specified as the goals in the texts (*pītipāmojja* [joy and gladness] and *manoramaṃ* [pleasing to the mind] in the *Dīpavaṃsa*; *saṃvega* [anxious thrill] and *pasāda* [serene satisfaction] in the *Mahāvaṃsa*) do not correspond with those articulated by Bharata or Daṇḍin. Not only that, but premodern South Asian theories of literature emphasize the audience's agency in producing the desired effects, yet with the *Dīpavaṃsa* (and the *Mahāvaṃsa*) we see the text itself asserting aesthetic agency.

The application of later medieval theories of aesthetics to the Pāli *Dīpavaṃsa* and *Mahāvaṃsa* is entirely anachronistic. Nonetheless, some understanding of the aesthetic work of poetry, nascent or well established, was obviously in general circulation within the community responsible for the early Pāli *vaṃsa*s and could have informed the way the compilers of the *vaṃsa*s framed their texts for maximum effect. Ranjini Obeyesekere's formulation of *rasa* may help us think through this deliberate choice to use worklike language and imagery: "[*Rasa*] was essentially a concept relating to the nature of aesthetic pleasure, experienced by an audience viewing a dramatic spectacle, comic or tragic. *Rasa* could be thus at once objective and subjective in that it was inherent in the work of art which had to be skillful enough to evoke *rasa*, and at the same time it was something inherent in the audience who had to be capable of appreciating *rasa*." Obeyesekere notes a similar interest in poetics and the innate potential to be moved in Sinhala audiences, so much so that Daṇḍin's text was generously translated and extended in the *Siyabaslakara*, likely composed around the tenth century. About the *Siyabaslakara*, Obeyesekere says: "That it was not the first work on literary criticism is clear from the evidence in the text itself. Verse 3 of the *Siyabaslakara* states that it was written for the benefit of two categories of students: those not conversant with Sanskrit, and those not familiar with earlier works on the subject. We can thus assume that both the works of the Sanskrit rhetoricians, and the works of Sinhalese writers on poetics, were known to the writer at the time."[42] We can also thus assume that the *vaṃsas*' self-conscious attempt at rendering the lists of kings in a poetic, pleasing form was the result of an unprecedented interest in poetry at the time of their production.

Through other early interpreters of the efficacy of poetics, we see that there is a general understanding that there are high expectations for the audience's participation. In the *vaṃsa* texts that make up our focus, all this work contributes to the text's religious work. The anticipated (or model) reader-hearer of the *Dīpavaṃsa* is primed in a direct and authoritative way for the reception of a text that is in turn about another kind of reception: that of the *dhamma* itself. The theme that is most important here is the exhortation to the reader-hearer: listen and listen joyously. And the first object of the audience's focus is not so much the glorious island of Laṅkā as it is the process of the transmission of the story from generation to generation, eventually linking the contemporary audience with the legitimating presence of the Buddha himself.

Finally, we must give thought to the form this proem takes. In the *Dīpavaṃsa*, it is concise, only five verses long, and its formulaic composition recalls the function of the *phalaśruti* (typically the concluding verses in Sanskrit *śāstras* [treatises] that articulate the intended consequences of hearing the text, literally the "fruits of hearing"). In the *Mahāvaṃsa*, the formula is further reduced to the single-line *phalaśruti* repeated at the end of each chapter, reiterating the ethical effect that reading catalyzes in the right audience. Interestingly enough, the self-consciously overt, ethically transformative work promised by the proem is not unambiguously or equally carried through every chapter of the *Dīpavaṃsa*. Although the proem of the *Dīpavaṃsa* commands the receiver to cultivate certain reading or hearing practices ("applying great attention, listen up") toward a text that will result in "joy and gladness," this directive is not reiterated at the end of every chapter, as it is in the *Mahāvaṃsa*. The *Dīpavaṃsa* frontloads its expectations; the *Mahāvaṃsa* reminds the reader-hearer at regular intervals of the emotional and ethical reasons for its narration.

Geiger suggests that the proem may represent the earliest stratum of the *Dīpavaṃsa* and that it may in fact be simply lifted from the proem of the source *aṭṭhakathā*:

> It may be correct that the base of that chronicle was such an introduction to the Tipiṭaka. The proem of the [*Dīpavaṃsa*] speaks at all events in favor of that. This proem was, as can be seen from the [*Mahāvaṃsa* Ṭīkā] QS. *a*, simply the proem of the old [*Mahāvaṃsa*]. The subjects were mentioned in it which were to be represented. These are without exception those which belong to the period before Mahinda. There is no account of later times, not even of the great deeds of Duṭṭhagāmaṇī. The proem thus belongs to an epoch in which the extent of work was smaller than at the time when Mahānāma developed the material into a poem, or when the [*Dīpavaṃsa*] was written. The old framework had burst, and out of the "historical introduction" of the [*aṭṭhakathā*], the "*Mahāvaṃsa* of the ancients," the extensive monastery chronicle of the Mahāvihāra, developed.[43]

This is a compelling argument to support reading the first few chapters of the *Dīpavaṃsa* in a new light. What if, as Geiger here suggests, the proem in fact introduces a coherent whole work that forms only part of what we have received as the *Dīpavaṃsa* proper? Turning to the *Mahāvaṃsa* with his provocative suggestion in mind, we see how its proem has lost this function and instead serves as a medium for the compiler to express his distaste for the aesthetically and emotionally inferior *Dīpavaṃsa*.

REPEATING THE IMPERATIVE: THE PROEM OF THE *MAHĀVAṂSA*

Although the most likely relationship between the *Dīpavaṃsa* and the *Mahāvaṃsa* is one of shared sources and perhaps a shared textual community, the *Mahāvaṃsa*'s ambitious proem eviscerates the literary aspirations of the "*Mahāvaṃsa* made by the ancients." Whether this phrase refers to the *Dīpavaṃsa* itself or not, it is indicative of a view against older source materials that highlights the *Mahāvaṃsa*'s intentionally literary turn.

Although all five lines of the *Dīpavaṃsa*'s proem are saturated with its hopes for the interpreter of the narrative to follow, the primary aim of the *Mahāvaṃsa*'s proem is to expound the flaws of the earlier *vaṃsa*. Where the *Dīpavaṃsa*'s proem declares the text's intention to tell the story of the coming of the Buddha and his *sāsana* to the island of Laṅkā and proclaims the effect the text will have on the audience, in three of the four verses of the *Mahāvaṃsa*'s proem the text's stated intention is to tell a better version of the story than the "*Mahāvaṃsa* of the ancients." It is an explicit statement that this narrative is not at all original, but a superior retelling. This argument hinges upon the text's claim of literary superiority, which is constituted specifically by its ability to bring about the emotional states of *saṃvega* and *pasāda*.

Why is the rhetoric of competition the focus of three-quarters of the *Mahāvaṃsa*'s proem? Was this vitriolic proem inspired by evolved stylistic concerns, perhaps as Pāli became a more acceptable option for literary flourish around the time of Buddhaghosa and the composition of the *Mahāvaṃsa*? Whatever the author-compiler's artistic ambitions, the rewriting of the same material used in the *Dīpavaṃsa* into what we know as the *Mahāvaṃsa* shows us that the story was an important one, capable of withstanding (and even warranting or benefiting from) revision.

The initial intention (of including and then transforming its audience into ethical interpreters and agents) expressed in the *Dīpavaṃsa*'s proem develops in the *Mahāvaṃsa* into a stylized refrain that is first articulated in verse 4 of the proem and then appends itself to the conclusion of each chapter of the text—even the chapters where it is a challenge to discern any literary or ethically didactic intent. But the *Mahāvaṃsa*'s proem omits the synopsis of the narrative that is the focus of the *Dīpavaṃsa*'s proem. By the time the *Mahāvaṃsa* was composed, the *sāsana* was already well entrenched, so much so that the common assumption is that rival *vihāras* (monastic complexes) competing for royal (and perhaps lay) attention and patronage may have provoked its composition by the threatened Mahāvihāra monastic complex concerned with protecting (or inventing) its own claims of authority and legacy. As noted in the introduction, scholars tend to agree that the beleaguered Mahāvihāran monks composed the *Mahāvaṃsa* to rearticulate their supremacy and their authoritative place in the lineage on the island. The tenor has changed between the two *vaṃsas*: whereas the inclusive *Dīpavaṃsa* extols its narrative's powerful, transformative ability to engender feelings of joy and gladness (and to promote conversion), the *Mahāvaṃsa* introduces in its revised proem an agitated emotional state (*saṃvega*). (*Saṃvega* is not unknown in the narrative of the *Dīpavaṃsa*, however; it occurs in the story of the *nāgas*' fear and subsequent assuagement.) The focus shifts from relocating the center of the Buddhist universe in the *Dīpavaṃsa* to reinforcing that location in the face of internal threats in the *Mahāvaṃsa*.

The *Mahāvaṃsa* proem begins the same way the *Dīpavaṃsa* begins, with the stylized homage that precedes just about every Pāli text: "Homage to Him, the Blessed, Worthy, and Fully Enlightened One."[44] Again, it is easy to jump over this stock-phrase *stotra* in order to proceed to the meat of the narrative, especially as it is such a familiar trope at the outset of Buddhist texts. But it may be worth our time to linger on it a moment and consider its worklike contribution to the text's structure, if not its content. In this reading, the act of rewriting the story of the development of Buddhism on the island of Laṅkā is itself an act of praise. Indeed, the homage itself is referred to as a prerequisite for entry into the proem—the first verse begins, "Having paid honor to the pure Saṃbuddha"—which in turn leads into the narrative, suggesting that this line is not just a stock phrase and instead a worklike act integral to the functioning of the whole text. Evoking the Buddha at the outset brings him into proximity, re-presents him to be the subject of praise.

Immediately after the *stotra* verse, the *Mahāvaṃsa*'s proem expresses its primary aim, which is to replace the *Dīpavaṃsa*, in three of its four verses. Even in the process of extolling the new text's virtues in the fourth verse, the critique of the older text is reinforced by the particular object of the vocative, "Listen to *this* one":

> [1] Having paid honor to the pure Saṃbuddha of the lineage of a pure race, I will explain the *Mahāvaṃsa* referring surely to its diversity of varied content.
>
> [2] That [*vaṃsa*], even though made by the ancients, was here told in too much detail, there exceedingly brief, and contained countless repetitions.
>
> [3] This [*vaṃsa*] avoids the faults of that one, [it is] easy to grasp and bear in mind, producing anxious thrill and serene satisfaction, and [it is] handed down through tradition.
>
> [4] Listen to this one, causing anxious thrill and serene satisfaction, in this way the grounds for producing anxious thrill and producing serene satisfaction.[45]

This proem critically dismisses the earlier competition (the *Dīpavaṃsa* or the *aṭṭhakathā*). Verses 2 and 3 explain the outdated and outmoded style of the earlier source and justify a new compilation. The grammar of the *Dīpavaṃsa* is indeed awkward at times,[46] and reading the text is anything but fluid,[47] so the *Mahāvaṃsa* proem could certainly be dismissing "that one."

In the final verse of the *Mahāvaṃsa*'s proem, attention is directed away from the superior quality of this text and toward its ethically transformative properties. The verse essentially means, "Listen to this text because it causes anxious thrill and serene satisfaction, so that it may continue to work on you to produce yet more anxious thrill and serene satisfaction." In other words, let this text provoke such a strong ethical and emotional response in the hearer that it establishes the foundation for further expressions of those same emotions. This verse establishes the refrain that is repeated at the conclusion of each chapter within the text, which reads, "Here ends [the number of the chapter, followed by its title], made for the anxious thrill and serene satisfaction of good people."[48]

This formulaic expression shows how the underlying agenda (the intended work) of the *Dīpavaṃsa* as stated in the proem has by the time of the *Mahāvaṃsa* become fixed and stylized. The *Dīpavaṃsa* does not conclude its chapters by repeating this verse or any other regular verse. In fact, in the *Dīpavaṃsa*'s proem the emotions singled out by the *Mahāvaṃsa*'s proem and its "tag lines" at the end of each chapter have yet to become fixed in a nominative way. The short declarative, vocative statements that close each chapter of the *Mahāvaṃsa* are a mechanism most likely developed to remind the readers-hearers of the text's transformative intention. This is where worklike content (content related to *saṃvega* and *pasāda*) evolves into worklike form (stylized, regularly repeated tag lines to close each chapter in a formal way). In the *Dīpavaṃsa*, it is crucial to present expected results at the outset to begin to prepare the reader. Insofar as the *Mahāvaṃsa* is a replacement or commentary on the *Dīpavaṃsa*, the initial invitation by which one is admitted to the community of interpreters morphs into a stylized, formulaic, and even iconic end phrase.

In the *Dīpavaṃsa*, the pairing of *pasāda* and *saṃvega* is not yet as explicit as it is in the later *Mahāvaṃsa* usage. Instead, we see *pasāda* embedded in a list of similar happy words in a causative, verbal form in verse 2: "Listen to me, honoring [this *vaṃsa*] abounding in countless qualities, delightful [*manoramaṃ*], calming [*pasādeyyaṃ*], producing joy and gladness [*pītipāmojjajananaṃ*]."[49] Here *pasāda* is seen as the causative form *pa + sad*, meaning to "render calm," "make peaceful," or "gladden." Compare this phrasing to the *Mahāvaṃsa* verse 4, where the pairing of *saṃvega* and *pasāda* takes a more stylized, stock-phrase approach: "Listen to this one, causing anxious thrill [*saṃvega*] and serene satisfaction [*pasāda*], in this way the grounds for making anxious thrill and producing satisfaction." Walpola Rahula has his own theory as to the derivation or necessity of this regularized stock phrase that peppers the *Mahāvaṃsa* text. He seems less concerned with the content of the verse than with the form as an indicator of the mode of writing, a sort of caveat for the orthodox readership, which exclaims something like "this text is kosher in spite of its quotidian subject." Rahula provocatively contends that the stock phrase provides a "cover" for the ambitious and creative *thera* (monk) responsible for composing the text:

> The *Mahāvaṃsa*, as we all know, abounds in stories of kings and ministers, rebels and wars, villages and cities and such "animal talk." It was improper for *bhikkhus* [ordained monks] to be engaged in such worldly talk. Mahānāma Thera, the author of the *Mahāvaṃsa*, knew it well. Yet he felt he should write the history of the Sinhalese race—a race that was destined to protect the religion of the Buddha. Nevertheless, to indulge in history as such was against the original teaching of the Master. So he discovered a new way out of the difficulty. The Commentaries maintain that at the end of a talk about kings and ministers and such others, if one reflects that even such powerful personages were subject to death and decay, the talk becomes a topic of meditation (*kammaṭṭhāna*) [Rahula's footnote 1 here refers to the *Dhammapādāṭṭhakathā*]. So, invariably at the end of every chapter of the *Mahāvaṃsa* the author includes a verse containing the idea of the impermanence of life or some spiritual admonition. There is spiritual advice interspersed in suitable places within the body of the chapters, too. And, further, each chapter ends with a formula which says that the *Mahāvaṃsa* was "written for the serene joy and emotion of the pious" (*sujanappasādasaṃvegatthāya kate Mahāvaṃse*). The author seems to have attempted to introduce his work not as a history dealing with the stories of kings and ministers and rebels and wars, but as a religious thesis, "a topic of meditation," intended to teach the impermanence of life and to infuse serene joy and emotion into readers' minds. This was how the learned Thera avoided "animal talk!"[50]

From Rahula's analysis, it seems that the desirable cultivation of *pasāda* and *saṃvega* represents some sort of aesthetic allowance to monks that is conducive to literary productivity. Perhaps then the *bhikkhus* would be able to delve into such distracting, banal matters as lists of kings and stories of their efforts for sheer didactic purposes. But this seems to me a maneuver one step ethically deeper than mere utilitarian instruction.

The composition of art (figurative and literary) could be justified as long as it incited certain religiously imbued emotions in the audience—namely, *saṃvega* and *pasāda*. *Bhikkhus* were not allowed to have figurative paintings, but there may have been some latitude with respect to the aesthetic reception of texts and the generation of desirable qualities such as *saṃvega* and *pasāda*. Rahula writes about the acceptability of aesthetically charged items for the express purpose of inciting the right response: "A *bhikkhu* should not request anyone to make even the figure of a gatekeeper (*dvārapāla*). But the Commentary [Samantapāsādikā] allows a certain measure of latitude by sanctioning the painting or moulding of such topics as *Jātaka* stories and such events as special alms-givings, which are apt to produce serene joy (*pasāda*) and emotion (*saṃvega*)."[51] I do not agree with Rahula that this technique was meant to covertly pass off inappropriate subject matter for literary composition. I read the stock phrase as a reminder to the reader-hearer of the express goals of heightened emotional states and the efficacy for the circumscribed audience of "good people" that reading the *Mahāvaṃsa* entails. I would not go so far as to imagine the *Mahāvaṃsa* as a "topic for meditation" on impermanence. I believe it is a "topic of meditation" of a different sort altogether—namely, the emotional states that it cultivates and the obligations thereof that firmly place one within the realm of "good people."

The cultivation of *pasāda* and *saṃvega* is considered to have implications not just for the reader-hearer's evolving emotional states but also for the actions and ethical choices he or she will make after being transformed by the experience of those emotions. Andy Rotman has considered the actively compelling side of the generation of *prasāda* (Pāli: *pasāda*) that has practical consequences for the laity. He suggests that Buddhist orthopraxy essentially "traps" individuals and forces the act of giving: "Individuals who come and see *prasāda*-generating objects are compelled to make offerings. Not doing so would be tantamount to admitting that *prasāda* has not arisen in one. And if *prasāda* has not arisen in one, then presumably one has not accrued the vast amounts of merit such objects are capable of generating. . . . [I]t is only the deviant who manages to get *prasāda* wrong."[52] As the *Mahāvaṃsa* illustrates, the story itself is what "traps" the hearer—a very worklike dimension of the text indeed. To be included among the virtuous listeners to whom the text is directed, a reader-hearer willingly submits to this form of entrapment and its concomitant acts of support of the religious community responsible for its production.

Finally, Collins reminds us of the actual oratorical utility of repeating such *phalaśruti* lines throughout the text. Concluding each chapter with a stylized nod to the intended aesthetic response creates an abiding sense of finality. Collins writes: "Public recitation of a text, like a sermon, resembles a dramaturgical performance as much as (perhaps more than) the static lines-of-text model of 'reading a book.' The dynamics of closure, in this perspective, are more than just a general point about texts providing 'the sense of an ending' which life (or death) cannot. They are quite literally moments in a (ritual) performance."[53] The worklike aspect of the form of this tag line functions much like the bell that ends a service. Structurally speaking, the closure of each chapter of the *Mahāvaṃsa* gives the *vaṃsa* enforced pauses, vantage points, throughout the running historical narrative. We can consider these pauses as temporal nodes that, like the bumpy joints of bamboo (*vaṃsa*), give this literary *vaṃsa* shape and connectivity.

◈ ◈ ◈

The proems of the *Dīpavaṃsa* and *Mahāvaṃsa* call for the reader-hearer to participate in the text in an active way and to invite him or her to belong to a particular type of community made up of "good people." By acquiescing to the proem's command to "listen up!" (in the *Dīpavaṃsa*, to listen to the stories of the coming of the Buddha and then his relics to the island of Laṅkā; in the *Mahāvaṃsa*, primarily to see how much better explained and more emotionally effective the story is in this version), and by acknowledging his or her situation as among the "good people" primed to have an aesthetically and ethically charged response to the text, the reader-hearer assertively participates in the work of the text at an ethically imbued level. Here is a distinct shift between the proem and the story in terms of the form and function: whereas the proems direct their attention assertively and personally at the audience, the rest of the narrative recedes into a narrated mode. The proem shows the narrator reaching out to impress the audience—using the vocative, imploring beyond the page for some interaction with the interpreter on the other side of the text. But then in verse 6 of the *Dīpavaṃsa* and verse 5 of the *Mahāvaṃsa*, the narrator's voice recedes into the story, and the vocative command to listen is replaced by the story itself, the focus for the audience's visual or aural attention. The first-person perspective disappears in favor of an unadulterated, omniscient presentation. As for the rest of the chronicle, except for the closing verses of each chapter of the *Mahāvaṃsa*, we see the events carrying the story rather than the narrator's stated ethically edifying objective. When the mode of narration switches from the vocative proemial statements to the narrative discourse of the rest of the text, as Émile Benveniste observes, "truly there is no longer a 'narrator.' The events are chronologically recorded as they appear on the horizon of the story. No one speaks. The events seem to tell themselves."[54]

[2] RELOCATING THE LIGHT

THE HEARER is primed by the explicit directions given in each proem, but the *Mahāvaṃsa* further elaborates on the transformative power of the text through its masterful use of metaphor to conjure the desired emotional states named in the proem. The *Mahāvaṃsa* does not just repeat the *Dīpavaṃsa*'s charge to the readers but extends it through the narrative of the text itself in its treatment of the metaphor of light in the story of the transformation of the *nāgas*. The *nāgas* are no longer read as simply the catalysts for the loving compassion and attention of the Buddha (as in the *Dīpavaṃsa*); the fact that they have been transformed into Buddhists seems more clearly established in the *Mahāvaṃsa*. In the *Dīpavaṃsa*, although there are several references to light, the metaphor is not fully developed the way it has been in the *Mahāvaṃsa*. It is in the rich, poetic use of the metaphor of light in the *Mahāvaṃsa* that we see the Mahāvihāran community reinterpreting for the reader its unique claim to the authentic lineage of the Buddha himself.

The proem of each text, then, seeks to train its audience's eyes to notice the more narratively rich aspects of the text. The blindness of ignorance is dispelled by the heightened sensitivity brought on through washing facts with the light of the *dhamma*. When one's vision has been thoroughly primed, one is able to encounter the *nāga* within the narrative and not dismiss it as "mythical accretion" but instead as an agent of the text's work. In this way, I draw inspiration from the intellectual project of Hayden White, who treats

> the annals and chronicle forms of historical representation, not as the imperfect histories they are conventionally conceived to be, but rather as

> particular products of possible conceptions of historical reality, conceptions that are alternatives to, rather than failed anticipations of, the fully realized historical discourse that the modern history form is supposed to embody. . . . What will be revealed, I think, is that the very distinction between real and imaginary events that is basic to modern discussions of both history and fiction presupposes a notion of reality in which "the true" is identified with "the real" only insofar as it can be shown to possess the character of narrativity.[1]

The narrative of the Buddha's three visits to the island of Laṅkā opens each of the two *vaṃsas*, revealing to the audience the overwhelming presence of the Buddha right at the outset. The overall narrative structure of the Buddha employing a terrifying darkness and then an enlightening light in the stories of the Buddha's three visits is somewhat mirrored in the presentation of the Buddha's story before the iteration of the various kings' works. The manifesting of darkness and the giving of light function both to bolster claims of authority for the textual community responsible for the vision the text presents and to provoke *saṃvega* (anxious thrill) and *pasāda* (serene satisfaction) both in humans and *nāgas* within the stories as well as in the audience outside the stories. The narrative structure itself supports the goal of transformation of the reader-hearer first articulated in each proem.

In the *Mahāvaṃsa*, dual goals are operative: first, to effect a transformation of the individual through the narrative and, second, to achieve better poetry through the conscientious manipulation of the tools of rhetoric, including metaphor, choice epithets of the Buddha, characters as fields of empathy, and a structure that culminates in a desired effect. In other words, the structure itself is a rhetorical strategy employed to prime the reader for the full impact of the narrative itself. As we will see, reading and remembering the instructions given in the proems are integral to comprehending the full effect of the narrative.

For the *Dīpavaṃsa*, the text's intended effect is both a personal, ethical transformation on the part of the hearer and perhaps a "plea for survival," a broader assertion of the potency and legacy of the Mahāvihāra among rival institutions vying for the king's attention and patronage.[2] The *Mahāvaṃsa* assumes these same goals and adds to them the full recentering of the Buddhist world to the island of Laṅkā. By keeping these goals and reading instructions in mind, we will be able to notice how the opening chapters' structure and content potentially catalyze ethical transformation within the well-primed interpreter and have an impact on the imagined world order. The metaphor of the revealing light of the *dhamma* working on the reader-hearer to effect the full transfer of *dhamma* to the new territory (whether the individual actor or the island of Laṅkā) manifests the text's worklike persuasion.

LITERARY DEVICES FOR ACHIEVING RELIGIOUS EFFECTS

In the *Mahāvaṃsa*, metaphors (along with similes) function as what Anne Blackburn, reflecting on the much later eighteenth-century text *Sārārthadīpanī*, has called "ruminative triggers," which are "stylistic characteristics of the text that draw the text and the reader more closely together and thus intensify the quality of the reader's reflective experience. The presence of these ruminative triggers . . . made it easier for monastic readers to read selectively and to interpolate elements of their personal experience (including their relationship to other texts and to people) into the work as they read."[3] The metaphor of light is a ruminative trigger particularly capable of effecting transformation, not just in these texts or even in Buddhism alone. Light "works" in all religious traditions; one need only consider the ubiquity of candles in worship. By first recognizing the range of meaning revealed by the focus on light, a reader is primed to appreciate, even be moved by, other ruminative triggers operating in the text.

To explore the literary devices and their effects, we should first take stock of the tools we are assumed to have garnered through our reading of the proems. From the *Dīpavaṃsa*'s proem, we understand that the first section of narrative about the Buddha himself coming to the island sets up a pattern of transference that is then replicated by the coming of the bodhi tree, the relics, the *sāsana*, and King Vijaya. According to that proem, by listening to and honoring this multivalent, delightful *vaṃsa*, joy and gladness will result. From the *Mahāvaṃsa*'s proem, we recognize that this text understands itself to be a replacement for the *Dīpavaṃsa*, relaying the same general narrative, but more efficiently and poetically. Easy to grasp and bear in mind, this text aims to produce emotional states in the reader-hearer, first *saṃvega*, which then transforms into *pasāda*, which in turn engender opportunities for these states' continued production. These emotions must be developed in this order (*saṃvega* first, then *pasāda*), as we will see in the narrative when the Buddha manipulates fear before resultant calm sets in. The more agitated or fearful the character (within the narrative) and reader (outside the text) become, the greater the sense of joy and satisfaction they feel upon resolution of the hardship.

According to Steven Collins, *saṃvega* is the more intense of the two emotions. He defines the two terms in his translation of the first chapter of the *Mahāvaṃsa* as follows: " 'Serene confidence' is *pasāda*, 'animation' *saṃvega*. One cannot convey all the nuances of these terms. The first is often said to occur at Buddhist Stūpas; it is a clarity of mind, calmness, and a conviction in the religious value of what, or who evokes that feeling. The second is a stronger emotion (from a root meaning to tremble or quiver), and is used when some shock inspires an increase in the intensity of religious feelings and intentions."[4] In other words, the text's desired effects are not simply emotional responses in the aesthetic realm. Instead, the expectation is that the hearer will be religiously moved.[5] These two emotional qualities are employed sequentially in the *Mahāvaṃsa* to heighten their religious effect. *Saṃvega* is not a banal shock and awe; it is explicitly the feeling of being awestruck. More importantly, it compels one to act on heightened "religious feelings and intentions." As Maria Heim notes, "*Saṃvega*, translated variously as agitation, urgency, thrill, fear, and anxiety, is often used in Pāli sources to indicate fear that is capable of instigating a sense of moral and religious urgency."[6] The resulting calm after the storm, *pasāda*, is integrally connected to the shock that precedes it. Concomitant with the satisfaction of *pasāda* is "a conviction in the religious value" of the catalyst of that emotion, typically the Buddha.

The semantic field of the term *pasāda*, which means "satisfaction" and "joy," also includes "clarity" and "light." This term is employed in both the *Dīpavaṃsa* and the *Mahāvaṃsa*, but in the *Mahāvaṃsa* it assumes the character of a countermeasure to the *saṃvega*, which is the initial response from the *yakkhas* (a class of nonhuman beings) and the *nāgas*. The darkness of ignorance, viscerally felt during the experience of *saṃvega*, is replaced with the clarity and light of the *dhamma*—namely, *pasāda*. This process occurs for the text's external readers-hearers also as their initial reaction in encountering the story, empathetic fear, is replaced by the serene confidence of clear understanding once the tension of the *saṃvega* is resolved.

The relationship between light, clarity, and understanding dominates Pāli texts of all eras. In her discussion of the Buddhist use of literary tropes, Blackburn quotes in its full, convoluted length a serial simile from the introduction of the *Saraṇāgamana* section of the overtly didactic eighteenth-century work *Sārārthadīpanī*.[7] The simile runs through some of the most common depictions of the Buddha, *dhamma*, and *saṅgha*, from the Buddha as a doctor dispensing the medicine of the *dhamma* to the Buddha as a prince decorated with the ornaments of virtue distributing the precious gift of the *dhamma* to other princes. The opening images in this extended simile caught my attention. Almost mirroring the structure of the *Mahāvaṃsa*, after a preliminary statement that declares the text to be about the Buddha, *dhamma*, and *saṅgha*, the *Sārārthadīpanī* launches into depictions of the Three Gems in paired terms of light and dark, heat and cooling rays:

> The three refuges are taught in this way: The Buddha is first [as] chief of all beings including men and māras and the dhamma following that because it appears as a teaching from that Buddha, and [then] the saṃgha, which is a receptacle for bearing that dhamma, like a golden bowl for lion's oil. Further, in this regard, the Buddha is like a full moon, the dhamma taught by the Buddha is like the moon's rays, and the saṃgha is like people made happy by the fact that that heat is calmed by the rays of the moon. Further, the Buddha is like the arc of daybreak on top of a high mountain, the dhamma is like the sun's rays which destroy darkness, and the saṃgha is like a population for whom darkness is destroyed [having] destroyed the darkness of the defilements by looking at good teaching. The Buddha is like a person who burns the forest, because [he] burns the forest which is the defilements. The dhamma taught by the Buddha is like the fire. The Buddha's listeners [in this case, monks] are like an area of land that has become a pure field after burning the forest of defilements.[8]

Rhetorical triggers for similes, such as the term *just as* and *like*, are markers that indicate that a reader-hearer is about to engage in the imaginative comparative leap. It is this encouraged imaginative leap that makes the *Mahāvaṃsa* such an effective literary text, provoking its readers-hearers through similes, metaphors, and encounters with imaginative characters. We can see the work of the imagination provoked by the text clearly in the case of similes. Blackburn writes: "These overt markers of a simile simultaneously indicate likeness and difference, emphasizing that the image presented is a verbal creation that gestures toward experience rather than directly describing it. This in turn provides what might be called an interpretive opening, or a point of entry for the reader to reflect upon the types of experience that the text describes. The reader is inspired to think about what he or she has read precisely because the simile's avowed failure to elaborate identity puts the attentive reader to work."[9] There is thus a palpable tension inherent in simile usage, where the term *similar* or *like* carries the simultaneous and competing weight of "also different." Although a simile inspires the reader primarily to picture what something (an emotion, event, or idea) is like, the reader's overall impression must be an awareness of the inherent difference between that imaginative depiction and "reality."

In the case of the "light of the *dhamma*" narrative in the *Mahāvaṃsa*, the tension between similar and different takes on a temporal hue. There is no overt reliance on serial similes to exaggerate the "interpretive opening" between text and reader. Instead, there is a sense that the events depicted occurred far in the past and were enacted on the reader's behalf. The metaphor is employed to corroborate the overall lesson of the *Mahāvaṃsa*, that to be a "good person" one engages in the transformative capacity enabled by the work of the text via the narrative's "interpretive opening." And this engagement is not solely the purview of virtuosi; as Charles Hallisey remarks, "analogies, similes, and metaphors are a common feature of Theravādin homiletics," and "analogy and simile were apparently considered very effective teaching tools, appropriate for even the dullest student."[10]

The connection between the text's explicitly stated ethical thrust and the image of light developed throughout this first narrative, I suggest, prepares the interpreter for his or her own encounter of the Buddha and his *sāsana* through the powerful medium of story. Once primed for what response to hope for or expect (joy, satisfaction), the reader encounters the narrative saturated in a particular light. Without the proem, and taken apart from the proem's location at the outset of the entire *vaṃsa*, the opening narrative of the Buddha's three visits to the island of Laṅkā in the *Dīpavaṃsa* and *Mahāvaṃsa* is still whimsical and interesting and a classic example of a story of the transference of *dhamma* to a new place. However, once the reader is aware of the expected result of his reading, he will be more susceptible to the emotional highs and lows, the agitation and relief, constructed in the narrative. The text may even inspire action in the form of supporting the textual community of the *Mahāvaṃsa*'s production.

An effective rhetorical strategy is employed in the very first chapter of the *Mahāvaṃsa*. Whereas the story of the Buddha's three visits to Laṅkā is told in the *Dīpavaṃsa*'s first and second chapters, the same narrative in the *Mahāvaṃsa* is reorganized into one single, self-contained unit that culminates in the successful transformation of the landscape of Laṅkā. There is no such climax in the *Dīpavaṃsa* account, even though the story seems the same. Could the use of the metaphor of light be the key to understanding this literary move made by the compiler of the *Mahāvaṃsa*? Susan Suleiman succinctly summarizes a series of questions that drive my own analysis of the *vaṃsas*:[11]

> Among the pertinent questions that the structural and semiotic variety of audience-oriented criticism allows one to formulate are the following: How (by what codes) is the audience inscribed within the system of a work? How does the inscribed audience contribute to the work's readability? What other aspects of the work, whether formal or thematic, determine readability or intelligibility? Finally, and in a slightly different perspective, what are the codes and conventions—whether aesthetic or cultural—to which actual readers refer in trying to make sense of texts and to which actual authors refer in facilitating or complicating, or perhaps even frustrating, the reader's sense-making activity?[12]

I believe these questions are best explored by reading the corresponding sections of the stories in the *Dīpavaṃsa* and *Mahāvaṃsa* against one another. In the proems, both texts reach out to an "inscribed audience," and the *Mahāvaṃsa* carries that prescriptive force into the verse that concludes each chapter.[13] It is in this juxtaposition that it becomes possible to ascertain what type of "semantic charter" is set forth in the two texts, what kind of textual community or audience they anticipate (and even desire), and what characteristics (such as the prevalence and prominence of the *nāgas* and of the metaphor of light) facilitate this audience's "sense-making" ability.

The use of narrative amplifies the dreamlike, otherworldly quality in both structure and content, inspiring the use of the imagination called for in the *Mahāvaṃsa*. As Hayden White notes,

> The relation becomes a problem for historical theory with the realization that narrative is not merely a neutral discursive form that may or may not be used to represent real events in their aspect as developmental processes but rather entails ontological and epistemic choices with distinct ideological and even specifically political implications. Many modern historians hold that narrative discourse, far from being a neutral medium for the representation of historical events and processes, is the very stuff of a mythical view

> of reality, a conceptual or pseudoconceptual "content" which, when used to represent real events, endows them with an illusory coherence and charges them with the kinds of meanings more characteristic of oneiric than of waking thought.[14]

In other words, any recounting of things past, especially those things far past, that are beyond the empirical knowledge of the agent responsible for their retelling, is a story. Even history recedes into something less than "real" by the nature of the passage of time; by reliving and representing a moment or an event, an agent is creating something anew, even if it is rooted in a "real" experience. By its very definition, history is story. White contends that a strain of modern historiography unnecessarily bifurcates history from narrative and extends a bias against storytelling as antiscientific. I agree with the view that these "histories" have much in common with oneiric thought, but I would not go so far as to cast aspersions on the result of such thought simply because it smacks of something less than refined, waking discourse. Rather, I would suggest that it is precisely this quality of the oneiric that helps the *vaṃsas* deliver their intended effect, the production of agitation and satisfaction. The oneiric atmosphere developed in the narrative and through the use of poetry reinforces my conclusion that what the Buddha does, where and how he conveys the *dhamma* as light to the *nāgas* of the island of Laṅkā within the world of the story, and how the reader interprets the Buddha's acts (ideally by experiencing abundant *saṃvega* and *pasāda*) are more important than the empirical historicity of his actions.

The development of *saṃvega* and *pasāda* and their direct correlation with the image of fear-inducing darkness and calming light, first prefigured for the reader within the proem's explicit reading instructions, become "verbal echoes"[15] throughout the rest of the text. Each reference recalls for the reader the first event in the narrative that evokes such emotions—namely, the Buddha's use of darkness and light in his conversion of Laṅkā. Even the particular formulation of the repeated end phrase at the conclusion of each chapter in the *Mahāvaṃsa* serves as a "verbal echo" to return the (primed) reader's attention to the text's ethically transformative potential.

The recentering imperative, the wish to have an impact on its own world and its audience, pervades the *vaṃsa* at many levels. These parallels reach the inscribed audience in such a way as to reinforce the archetypal story of the Buddha's visit, buttressing the effect of the recentered world because the familiar pattern reveals the eternal and effective nature of the process—it is "natural" that the Buddha and his relics would end up residing in Laṅkā. Just as the Buddha comes from India to subdue the indigenous, unworthy ones, so Vijaya later comes and reforms the *yakkhas*, and even later the monk Mahinda is sent by the Indian monarch Asoka to convert the indigenous population. The narrative in the first story of the coming of the Buddha organically sets up the structure that will sustain the rest of the text—it is a story about arrival, power, and transformation (through relocation and conversion). The Buddha must be the first, the model, and the catalyst for the pattern that will be followed. The Buddha initially brings the light of the *dhamma*, but it is only fully entrenched when the later Mahinda brings the Buddha's relics there.[16]

Returning to Suleiman's questions, we must ask, What are the codes, formal or thematic, to which the audience appeals in order to make sense of the *vaṃsas*? I explore here how the pervasive and saturating metaphor of *dhamma* as light appeals to the reader and helps to effect transformation, both geographic (of Laṅkā into the center of the Buddhist world) and individual (of a good person into an emotionally charged and satisfied person). Within the light-infused universe of the text, *nāgas* act as signifiers of a secondary code for meaning making, a code that deals with the individual's readiness to be transformed through contact with the *dhamma*. *Nāgas* are ontologically incapable of reaping the soteriological benefits of proximity to the Buddha, yet they are nevertheless effectively converted by the Buddha in Laṅkā. Laṅkā is thus a supercharged place where even one's destitute situation can be overcome so long as one is inclined to have faith in the Buddha. This inclination is provoked through heightened emotional states; just as the Buddha manipulates the *nāgas*' emotions in the text, so the text manipulates the reader's emotions. Even though the Buddha is far removed from the audience at the time of reading, the audience is brought into proximity to him, allowing transformation to occur through the power of narrative. From their situation internal to the narrative, the *nāgas* help to bring the Buddha to the island, and just as they have a crucial function in ferrying relics to Laṅkā (as shown in chapter 4), so they here serve as beings to empathize with, to share the status of liminality vis-à-vis the Buddha.

Our two texts, through their rhetorical force and vision at the outset of their narratives, effectively imagine and redraw the contours of the Buddhist landscape by positing, positioning, and articulating the island of Laṅkā as the new center of this landscape.[17] What exactly within the opening narrative of each text contributes to or effects this cosmically important transformation? Although the narrative building blocks in the *Dīpavaṃsa*'s account of the Buddha's three visits to Laṅkā are evident and compelling as well as effective in the construction of the Buddhist world, it is through the particularly illuminating metaphor of deeply penetrating light that the *Mahāvaṃsa* most forcefully effects the recentering of the Buddhist world. This metaphor does two things: it effects a transformation of the world (the recentering on Laṅkā), and it effects an emotional and ethical transformation in the primed audience. The rich, recentering, and atemporal metaphor of light even extends beyond the physical landscape of Laṅkā at the time of the Buddha into the very presence of the hearers of the *Dīpavaṃsa* and *Mahāvaṃsa* in the Mahāvihāra and beyond. The metaphor of light engages the text's worklike aspect; its efficacy depends on the salience of the image for the community at stake.

So who is on the receiving end of the metaphor of light, and how does the metaphor resonate for them? And what types of individual ethical transformations are engendered through the reading and interpreting of these texts? Although the proem of the *Dīpavaṃsa* gives clear instructions for how to achieve the desired, transformative, confidence-building effect, at first read the narrative seems more illustratively edifying than poetically, aesthetically powerful. How does the structure of the first story about the transformation of unethical agents (*nāgas*) into Buddhists serve as a model for the reader and interpretive community? I assert that the story is told to train readers-interpreters about useful methods to fulfill the expectations of the text itself. These expectations are contingent upon the heuristic suspension of disbelief, which allows the reader to enter a world that is other (temporally distant from the present) and yet shared, almost the same. The *Dīpavaṃsa* and *Mahāvaṃsa* aim to train the reader's vision; the reading process itself creates corrective lenses that enable the interpreter to come into direct contact with the powerful presence of the Buddha.[18]

With this view in mind, we can move away from the typical reading of the *Dīpavaṃsa* and *Mahāvaṃsa*, especially this first story comprising the Buddha's three visits, as a "charter of Sinhalese Buddhist nationalism"[19] and instead understand it as a different kind of charter. The structures and characters that make up this first story operate in a semantic realm rife with meaning. Pierre Maranda has explained what he calls "semantic charters" in several contexts, and it is through his work that I believe we can begin to make sense of the functions of the image of light:

> Semantic charters condition our thoughts and emotions. They are culture-specific networks that we internalize as we undergo the process of socialization. These mechanisms are at work both in category formation and in the establishment, consolidation, or rejection of relationships between categories: "Within a semantic universe, some combinations of, i.e., relations between, elements are common, others are permissible but rare, others are poetic or archaic, and others are excluded. . . . We could say, inspired by Rousseau, that human communication is a social contract which rests on a body of subliminal laws, and that a culture's myths contain its semantic jurisprudence."[20]

Reading the metaphor of light as a "semantic charter" clarifies its dual worklike function within the *vaṃsas*. Through the transformation of individual characters such as the *nāgas* (even if this occurs collectively) within the text, the light of the *dhamma* penetrates and saturates a new landscape, effecting the recentering of the Buddhist map. This occurs both within the text and outside of it by eliciting a transformative response from primed readers-hearers.

ANTICIPATING THE BUDDHA'S VISIT: *DĪPAVAṂSA*

After its proem, the *Dīpavaṃsa* proceeds to narrate the Buddha's enlightenment event, or the process by which he mastered states of meditation and insight, thoroughly penetrated the *dhamma*, and became emancipated from the rounds of rebirth in *saṃsāra* ("wandering on," the cycle of birth, life, and death). This connection back to the legitimating presence of the Buddha and specifically to his own moment of transformation lays a crucial foundation for the text.[21] At the point where he has become the perfectly enlightened one (*abhisaṃbuddha*) and has claimed the title of "Buddha" (*buddho buddho'ti*, I.13) , the new Buddha speaks out in his first postenlightenment act described in the *Dīpavaṃsa*. He is described here in terms of his light-giving capacity: "Having become Enlightened and having made an utterance about all things, / the Light Maker spent seven days just so on the excellent throne."[22]

Strictly speaking, when this epithet is first used in the *Dīpavaṃsa*, the Buddha has not brought any light anywhere yet. Thus, the text here either prefigures the narrative twist, preparing the interpreter to see the Buddha as the Light Maker, or it makes an assumption regarding the reader's familiarity with the story about the bringing of the light of the *dhamma* to Laṅkā. The name "Light Maker" in the latter case would serve as a mnemonic device, a loaded epithet that would recall for the right hearer ("good person") a familiar story.

Also embedded within the image of a Light Maker is the popular understanding of the physiological and ontological ramifications of becoming a Buddha: one actually glows, emanating the virtuous light of the *dhamma*.[23] An epithet such as "Light Maker" is thus as constructive as it is descriptive—it both anticipates and helps to create the image of the Buddha as the light-giving one and by extension creates the model reader, who is understood to be the light-receiving one. The use of this epithet engages the text's worklike aspect: it triggers an association with the vision, worldview, or, to employ Ronald Inden's concept, "world wish"[24] of the community who calls the Buddha by this name. The epithet thus functions as one of Blackburn's "ruminative triggers" by tapping into a metaphor that carries with it an aesthetic whose encoding is familiar to the primed interpreter.

The use of light, especially in epithets for the Buddha, may represent a very old rhetorical strategy. Richard Gombrich muses that the use of shining imagery for the Buddha may represent a co-optation of Vedic images of power and divinity, intentionally applied by an early Buddhist community seeking legitimacy: "In the Ṛg Veda, however, Aṅgīras is a class of supermen, standing between men and gods, and Agni, the personification of fire, is the first and foremost Aṅgīras (RV I, 31, 1). In other texts too the Buddha is called Aṅgīrasa when he is said to shine very brilliantly: at SN I, 196 he outshines the world; at AN III, 239 (=J I, 116) he shines and glows like the sun. So in this passage he is virtually impersonating Agni, the brahmins' fire god. This looks less like a debate than a takeover bid."[25] In other words, at a moment in a narrative where the Buddha is exerting his authority over another—namely, when he impresses the Brahmin Kassapa in the fire hut—the Buddha essentially takes on the characteristics of the utmost Brahmin, Agni, to sway Kassapa to the new *dhamma*. The Buddha uses salient tactics to convince and convert—light conversion (or takeover) works. Likewise, in the narrative told in the *Dīpavaṃsa* and *Mahāvaṃsa*, when the Buddha hovers over the island, the *yakkhas* interpret his superpowers as being within their own repertoire of *yakkha* powers—"Is he a *yakkha*?" they ask. Perhaps this most salient form of power exertion marks a special transformation tactic, a formula somewhat akin to "like begets like," where the *yakkhas* are most attentive to power in a familiar form. Immediately after his discussion of the fire hut event, Gombrich addresses a negotiation outside the world of the text that involves the situation of the earliest Buddhists (as Jonathan Walters calls it, the "text of its day mode," or reading the text for information about the textual community of its production[26]). Early Buddhists effectively co-opted salient and useful metaphors and images from Vedic sources as they developed their own world wishes. Outside the world of the text, the context might affect the production and interpretation of the world inside the text.

In the narrative, having been completely transformed by the process of enlightenment, the Buddha then makes use of his potent visionary acumen and surveys the whole world (*Dīpavaṃsa* I.16–22). His attention is drawn to the "most excellent Laṅkādīpa" (I.17, I.19, I.22),[27] a place where he knows the *dhamma* will take hold, replicating the pattern established by the visits of the former buddhas. This process is the voicing of *adhiṭṭhāna*, or determined resolution. Rhetorically and structurally, the authoritative, eternal, and repetitive nature of buddhas and their *dhammas* is initiated here. There is nothing inherently original about this buddha; in fact, the island's claims to legitimacy are underscored by attesting to the presence of a long lineage (*vaṃsa*) of buddhas there. But the positing of the island as a fitting place for the *dhamma*, a place that had fulfilled that same function in previous eras, also makes one problem obvious: the island is (in this story's present) currently inhabited by the nonvirtuous sorts of beings not inclined or even karmically able to inherit the *dhamma*.

Verses I.20–21 of the *Dīpavaṃsa* examine the Buddha's thought process: "At this time, *yakkhas*, *bhūtas*, and *rakkhasas* are in Laṅkādīpa, all are scorned by the Buddha; their strength I can take away. Having driven out the crowd of *yakkhas*, *pisācas*, and *avaruddhakas*, I will make this island a shelter and cause it to be inhabited by men."[28] What semantic charter is being appealed to here? We see a world with a hierarchy of beings where some beings are less than Buddha-worthy.[29] This world, which is also replete with various virtuous beings, is, to recall Maranda's definition of a semantic charter, a "culture-specific network." In this world, virtue is measured on a sliding scale. The counterexample of the unworthy beings tells us that one must be sufficiently primed for proper reception of the *dhamma*. The Buddha's thinking, as told through the narrative, makes a claim about the prerequisites required of the interpreter as well as of the various other beings referred to in the text. In a way, the text suggests that one ought not read on if one is insufficiently virtuous. What this says about those who continue to read, thus coming in contact (albeit of the literary sort) with the Buddha, is that they are not scorned by the Buddha but instead are sought out by him. And it is not simple exclusion from the list of unworthy ones that would lead one initiated into this semantic charter to have confidence in the Buddha's intentions. The Buddha here reveals his plan for the island, to "make this island a shelter."

Beyond the potential ethical agents' individual or collective readiness or worthiness, there is also a crucial temporal and even cosmic dimension to the equation. The *Dīpavaṃsa* informs its readers that there is a right and a wrong time (*kālaṃ akālaṃ*) to introduce the *dhamma* (I.19). This idea reinforces the argument introduced in the previous chapter about the necessity of priming the receptor, but this added temporal dimension shifts some of the agency away from the individual and onto a cosmic clock. The natural rhythm of the universe affects a "good person's" ability to be transformed. What good will it do to introduce the *dhamma* if it is the wrong time to do so? What does this qualification then say about the time at which this passage is being read, and what does it say about the present time? The text's diachronic presence and presumed efficacy indicates the endurance of the Buddha's *dhamma*; it is (still) the right time to initiate the transformative effect of the *dhamma*. The *dhamma*, like the Buddha, can still be accessed through the text—especially through the inclusive and worklike function of a passage like this—by an able, primed interpreter.

Within the narrative, the Buddha continues his prognostication of his connection with the island of Sri Lanka with his anticipation of his *parinibbāṇa* (final extinguishing upon corporeal death), which is again expressed with a metaphor of light ("like the setting sun").[30] He anticipates the rise of the virtuous ruler of Jambudīpa, Asoka, and, most important, the role of Asoka's son, Mahinda, in the establishment of the *sāsana* on the island of Laṅkā.[31] He puts a divine guard over the island because he needs to get on with the work of being a nascent buddha in the meantime. For the Buddha, his work in Laṅkā is still in the future; the text makes him stay true to his conventional biography and returns him to set up shop in Baranasi.

As we have seen, the Buddha is described by the text as being empowered by his sense of purpose to change the very nature of the island of Laṅkā. The play between the forward-thinking moral agency expressed by the Buddha's *adhiṭṭhāna* and the text's insertion of that act into the Buddha's conventional biography establishes a particular sense of time and nuances what is otherwise a rather black-and-white presentation of *kālaṃ akālaṃ*, a right and a wrong time, articulated in verse 19. In other words, the Buddha knows his own time (in the future he will set like the sun, the very measure of time itself), and he knows there is to be another time to finish the preparatory work. Here, we see light, time, and Buddha's omniscience coming together to weave the narrative and construct a particular vision of the world and of Laṅkā.

If we read the *Dīpavaṃsa* as an index or reflection of the time and textual community in which it was compiled, we may perhaps conclude that its main concern was to regain attention and support from the various rival sects around Anurādhapura in the fourth century. Walters identifies "four major moves" that ensured the *Dīpavaṃsa*'s goals would be met. First, the text was composed in Pāli, in *śloka* meter that related it directly to the *Khuddaka Nikāya*, "thus reviving that language as the medium for Buddhist textual production among the beleaguered Theravādins of the Lesser Vehicle." Second, it articulated a history that "claims that the disciplinary order of the Mahāvihāra in Sri Lanka is that of the original Theras." Third, it identifies the Sri Lankan kings with the Okkāka/Ikṣvāku lineage and as Sākyas, or "kinsmen of the Buddha himself." Finally, it connects Mahinda directly with the Mahāvihāra and "thus accorded that monastery the privilege of being the first to receive Buddhist teachings in Sri Lanka, a privilege that had no doubt also been claimed by their rivals at the Abhayagiri."[32] I would add that the composition of the *Dīpavaṃsa* in a specifically poetic form, in translocal Pāli, and replete with particularly resonant characters (*nāga*s) to represent in whimsical form the monks themselves was also a choice that ensured the *Dīpavaṃsa*'s long-reaching salience. In spite of its coarse poetry, it was a text that defied obsolescence even after the *Mahāvaṃsa* was composed, and it remained in circulation so that we still have it today. Perhaps its continued salience is a result of the compiler's translating the worldly concerns of his or her immediate community into narrative and then thrusting that narrative into the legitimating (and timeless) biography of the Buddha. As Umberto Eco has said, "To read fiction means to play a game by which we give sense to the immensity of things that happened, are happening, or will happen in the actual world. By reading narrative, we escape the anxiety that attacks us when we try to say something true about the world. . . . This is the consoling function of narrative—the reason people tell stories, and have told stories from the beginning of time."[33]

Even before the story of the Buddha's visit to expel the *yakkhas* is told, the *Dīpavaṃsa* contains a pregnant reference to a *nāga*. According to the timeline presented in the *vaṃsa* account of the biography of the Buddha, after his first rains-retreat in Isipatana (Sārnāth), he begins his peripatetic practice, initiating his model of ministry. Uruvelā, later known as Bodh Gayā, is geographically located at the very heart of this enlightenment narrative. The narrative sets up a pattern—namely, the movement of an auspicious, transformative character (the Buddha) from the very center region (Uruvelā) to an absolute peripheral region (Laṅkā). In Uruvelā, the Buddha happens upon Kassapa, an ascetic of the Jaṭila sect, which presents him with an opportunity to experiment with his powers of conversion. In this story, we encounter a *nāga*, but it is one with very little agency (he is not even given a name). The *nāga* serves as a means by which the Buddha can effect the transformation or conversion of his intended target, Kassapa. The story of the Buddha's conquering of the unnamed *nāga* is reduced to a single line of reference:

> [36] The Best-of-Men tamed a *nāga*-snake in the fire hut. Seeing this miracle, they all invited the Tathāgata:
> [37]"Gotama, we will look after you always with a continuous supply of food here in this *vihāra* through the four months of winter."[34]

The action provides the new Buddha with the opportunity to provoke several conversions within the central territory of Uruvela. This *nāga*-snake (*ahināga*) is not itself converted, but the image of it being overpowered is the tool the Buddha then uses to convert others. Although the episode with the *nāga* is reduced to a single line, its appearance alone is significant in that it foreshadows what will soon take place elsewhere—namely, the subduing of a multitude of *nāgas* in Laṅkā. It prefigures a structural equation, where to conquer *nāgas* equals to conquer people. The *nāga* in the private fire hut is conquered, and the result is that people outside the fire hut are converted. Later in the narrative, when the *nāgas* of Laṅkā are converted, it is the people outside the narrative, the interpreters, who are to be converted.

Why would the *Dīpavaṃsa* author-compiler dwell on the episode of the Jaṭila ascetic in Uruvelā but reduce the first sermon—the very establishment (the turning of the wheel, the setting in motion) of his *dhamma*—and the Buddha's first conversions to only two lines of text (I.31–32)? The *nāga* may have a reduced personality in the *Dīpavaṃsa* account of Kassapa's conversion, but it is here set up as a key figure in a paradigmatic, didactic encounter that will later be echoed in the establishment of the *dhamma* in another borderland, Laṅkādīpa itself.

I read this inclusion of the story of the conversion of Kassapa by subjugating the *nāga* as a dry run, a practice performance for the Buddha's prowess of conversion over other *nāgas* that prepares him for other encounters on the borderlands. Immediately following this conversion episode, the Buddha uses his *iddhi* (superpowers derived from meditation) to meditate by the Anotatta Lake in another borderland territory. Once primed through meditative practices, the Buddha has the ability to move from this border region to another: the island of Laṅkā in the middle of the ocean. Notice the obvious liminality issues: that the Buddha passes from one border region to another and that it is the light (in the form of fire) and the *nāgas* (our "codes") that are able to permeate these boundaries. It is in the midst of his meditation at Anotatta that the Buddha decides the time has come to rid Laṅkā of its demonic inhabitants, the *yakkhas*, and to turn over the island to human residents (I.48). In other words, the brief inclusion of the *nāga* story at this time highlights the Buddha's overwhelming power and shows that he can win converts such as Kassapa even in the borderlands through contact with and subjugation of the *nāgas*. Although the power exhibited by the Buddha to subdue the *nāga* may seem tame and understated here, in terms of the pattern established this episode is quite significant. The Buddha tames a serpent right in the heart of his *sāsana* as it emanates out from the bodhi tree, the site of enlightenment. This is a conversion event, but not of the serpent—the Buddha overcomes and tames the serpent (*ahināgaṃ damesi*); these acts enable him to convert the Jaṭila ascetic Kassapa.

As we will see, although the *yakkhas* are terrified and expelled after the Buddha's arrival in Laṅkā, it is the *nāgas* who provide the venue for the *dhamma* to take hold in the new land. *Nāgas* are locatively and ontologically liminal agents, betwixt and between water and land, always just outside the realm of worthiness. As such, they represent the willing but difficult potential converts (the audience) that the Buddha can infiltrate by means of his penetrating light (*dhamma*). Transformation occurs at the boundaries, effected by the rays that, like the sun, are constantly emanating outward from the dynamic center that is the Buddha himself. In this way, the *nāga* represents the edge, the frontier, the future, possibility, as well as the Buddha's amazing reach.

After meditating at Anotatta Lake, the Buddha senses that the time has come to give his attention to the island, so he transports himself to Laṅkā using his miraculous superpowers (*iddhi*). He stands in the sky above the *yakkhas*, where they mistake him for a *yakkha*, one of their own kind. After several awkward descriptive passages about his entry into meditative states, he performs magical miracles: "The man, standing like a *yakkha* of a measure of magical power and great psychic powers, instantly made dense clouds full of thousands of rain drops, rain, cold wind, and darkness."[35] The darkness terrifies the *yakkhas*; the empathetic reader, carried away by the narrative, should similarly feel a sense of awe, even terror, toward the Buddha at hearing of his exploits. The natural world is thus manipulated in the service of the Buddha's ethical mission as he restores the light. But this is not the gentle, penetrating light of the *dhamma*: "Just as the midday sun shining in the summer season, so terrifying heat was set in the body[36] of *yakkhas*. Just like the heat of the four suns at the conclusion of a *kappa* [aeon], even more so was the flame cast by the seat of the Teacher."[37] Here it is great heat, not explicitly light, that terrifies the *yakkhas*. The Buddha uses heat to help him purge the land of unwanted *yakkhas* and saves the light for his conversion of the *nāgas*.

The *yakkhas* are depicted as unable to embrace the *dhamma* as heat. The Buddha nonetheless is motivated through his compassion to provide the *yakkhas* with a new place: "The Buddha, the chief among sages, conducive to ease, having seen the suffering and terrified *yakkhas*, the merciful and compassionate great sage, thought about how to bring ease to the minds of the nonhumans."[38] He finds a mirror island to Laṅkā named Giridīpa that is endowed with all of the same attractive qualities as the *yakkhas*' current home. Transferring them to this other place, the Buddha explains that his reason for doing this is that Laṅkā is destined to continue to be ruled by men (not bodhi- or enlightenment-challenged *yakkhas*), just as it has been inhabited by men "since remote *kappas*": "Endowed with these and other good qualities, a residence for men, auspicious in various ways, the *sāsana* will shine [*dīpissati*] [there] among the islands [*dīpesu*], like the full moon in the sky at Uposatha."[39] The last line is especially interesting in terms of the developing metaphor of light. The double meaning of the word *dīpa* as both "lamp" and "island" works well as the phrase conjures a light-filled image: "[Laṅkā] will shine among the islands." Invoking the Uposatha, the bimonthly gatherings of the *saṅgha*, as a way of dating or timing the full moon is also interesting.[40]

After the Buddha rids Laṅkā of its *yakkha* inhabitants, at the end of chapter I of the *Dīpavaṃsa* the Tathāgata (Buddha) returns to the border region of Uruvelā, and his life story resumes in media res. At the outset of the second chapter, the setting shifts; now the Buddha is established in his most central and stable rains retreat, in Anāthapiṇḍika's Jetavana grove near Kosala: "In this Jetavana the Buddha, *dhamma* king, Light Maker, looking throughout the world, saw beautiful Tambapaṇṇi [Sri Lanka]."[41] The *nāgas* there are depicted as creatures that would challenge even the most naturally compassionate: they are ethically the lowest of the low and are very much depicted as snakes:

> All of the *nāgas* possessed great psychic powers, all were horrible and poisonous, all were steeped in malevolence, violence, and conceit.
> Moreover, those snakes were quick, powerful, corrupt, cruel, rough, harsh, irritable, angry, and bent on destruction.[42]

The Buddha is moved once again to relocate to the island, which is threatened by an impending family feud between two *nāga* families intent on each other's utter destruction. Can we read into this scenario an indication of the feud between the rival factions of monks at the time of the *Dīpavaṃsa*'s composition? In the case of the *nāgas*, there is no clear victor; the battle is avoided, and both parties defer entirely to the Buddha. Might the telling of this story be an attempt within the text to point toward the common, unifying authority of the Buddha himself? The Buddha is motivated by compassion and the desire to see happiness (welfare) in a future time (*Dīpavaṃsa* II.12–13). To stop the *nāgas*' fighting, the Buddha applies the same terrifying techniques he used with the *yakkhas* years earlier: he plunges the natural world into darkness so that "the terrified, trembling *nāgas* did not see one another, nor did they see the Subdued One, nor from where they should battle."[43] After thoroughly horrifying the *nāgas* into submission, the Buddha sends forth thoughts of loving kindness and emanates a warm light, adjusting his outward disposition to match his moral attitude. The Buddha is again described with the rich imagery of light: "It was a great sight, stupefying and hair-raising; they all saw the Buddha like the shining moon in the sky. Standing there, endowed with the six colors, shining in the middle of the sky, illuminating the ten directions, he addressed the *nāgas*."[44] Explaining the futility of anger and destruction, the Buddha delivers a fire-and-brimstone sermon about the sufferings in hell: "Then the Clear-sighted One agitated the *nāgas* with sufferings in hells, relating the nature of birth in the worlds of men and *devas* [gods], and [the nature of] *nibbāṇa* ['extinguishing,' the ultimate goal of Buddhist practice]."[45] The result of his compassionate sermon is that all the *nāgas* present (eighty *koṭis* [unthinkably high number][46] of *nāgas* [*Dīpavaṃsa* II.40–41]) take refuge in the Buddha, the first step in becoming Buddhist.

The next event in the story initiates the establishment of relics in the new terrain, beginning with a gift from the *nāgas*: the Veḷuriya throne, contested possession of which had brought the *nāgas* to the brink of war, is offered to the Buddha.[47] The *nāgas* together "placed the throne in the middle of the two islands. There, on that throne, the Light Maker, King of Truth, sat down."[48] By using the throne, the Buddha establishes it as a relic of use (*pāribhogika*). This suffusion of sacrality occurs at the request of the *nāgas* and in a liminal territory between their two warring camps. The *nāgas* offer food and drink to the Buddha on his throne, initiating and modeling the paradigm of support that qualifies one as Buddhist. The text's message is that giving to the Buddha in this way and to his relics in the future is the proper way to display gratitude for his ongoing compassion.

The story then tells of the *nāga* uncle Maṇiakkhika's pious invitation to the Buddha to return to the island one more time so that he can serve him (*Dīpavaṃsa* II.42–47). But the Buddha, Light Maker, withdraws to the center of the island to meditate. After this period of meditation, the Buddha again addresses the *nāgas*, telling them to worship the throne and the tree (from the Jetavana grove that the Buddha had used as a parasol during his visit) in his absence, and then he departs.

The Buddha's third and final visit to the island is said to occur in the eighth year after his enlightenment, which again locates it in a specific moment in his biography and its associated timeline. The Buddha returns in response to Maṇiakkhika's earlier invitation, and this time he brings with him a retinue of five hundred monks. The *nāgas* are seen to be dutiful Buddhist patrons as they prepare for the Buddha's arrival by constructing a jewel-encrusted pavilion. The Buddha and his *bhikkhus* are offered seats, and then the Buddha enters a meditative state, where his compassion once again is made manifest in terms of the way light travels beyond its emanator: "[The Buddha] entered into the attainment of benevolence [*metta*] and suffused all directions."[49] The Buddha accepts offerings from the *nāgas*, preaches to them, and then, accompanied by his *bhikkhus*, rises into the air for a tour of particular sites on the island. His next stop is briefly mentioned—the Dīghavāpi Cetiya—where he again descends, meditates, and enters a trance state. Then he alights at the future site of the bodhi tree in the Mahāmeghavana garden, which shows him as a node of connectivity with the buddhas of the past (the three previous buddhas are said to have stayed there as well) and with the textual (reading) community of the present (the time of the *Dīpavaṃsa*'s composition) because this site has a history: it is the first place given by King Devānaṃpiyatissa to Mahinda and his community of monks upon their arrival in Laṅkā.[50] The multilayered connection to the past is important within the text: the Buddha expresses that the very same site had hosted the bodhi trees of the three former buddhas of the era. His final visit occurs within the same garden, where he honors each of the three former buddhas by installing a throne and listing their meditative accomplishments. This declaration of buddha lineage anticipates the next narrative turn—the fourth chapter of the *Dīpavaṃsa* begins with an enumeration of kings and dynastic lineage that is at the supposed heart of the chronicle.

ANTICIPATING THE BUDDHA'S VISIT: *MAHĀVAṂSA*

In the *Mahāvaṃsa*, the story introducing the Buddha to the island of Laṅkā takes on a more potent force than it does in the *Dīpavaṃsa*. This may explain in part why so many commentators have overlooked the *Dīpavaṃsa* as a text with its own interpretive richness. In line with the critique waged in its proem that the *Dīpavaṃsa* is too long in some places and too abrupt in others, the *Mahāvaṃsa* follows the structure of the story but tells it at a much different pace. Umberto Eco asks a good question: "If, as we have noted, a text is a lazy machine that appeals to the reader to do some of its work, why might a text linger, slow down, take its time?"[51] Where the *Dīpavaṃsa* dives right into the account of the enlightenment event in order to ground the coming of the *dhamma* in the period of the Buddha's enlightenment, the *Mahāvaṃsa* begins even further back in the Buddha's biography.[52] In *Mahāvaṃsa* I.5, the then-bodhisatta desires to become a buddha so "he might free the world from *dukkhā* [disease]"[53] after seeing (coming in contact with) Dīpaṅkara, the current Buddha. The *Mahāvaṃsa* thus carries the impetus to create a refuge of Laṅkā further back in time to the bodhisatta's life as Sumedha, through whose life the basic format (or "Buddha Blueprint"[54]) is set up. Sumedha was a wealthy prince who became an ascetic but who was inspired to aspire to buddhahood through coming in contact with the Buddha of his day, Dīpaṅkara.[55] Projecting back through the Buddha's biography, his own *vaṃsa*, the *Mahāvaṃsa* reveals an underlying concern for its textual community—namely, that one must come in direct contact with the Buddha.

Could this narrative structure (the text) reflect the concerns of the textual community for sole authority at a time when rival *vihāras* made competing claims of legitimacy (the context)? In this account, the presence of the buddha of the current era is not enough to secure legitimacy—the *vaṃsa* projects the pattern yet further back into the past through many buddhas, where direct contact on the island of Laṅkā (or Oja, as the island was called in the time of the previous buddha) is possible. Furthermore, when contact happens, a primed and ready agent is rendered incapable of ignoring the Buddha's draw,[56] that attractive, penetrating light. That light is authoritative and reaches back through time. Indeed, the name "Dīpaṅkara" means "making light" or "illuminating." This reference to Dīpaṅkara in verse 5 not only adds legitimacy and legacy to the story but also foreshadows the metaphor of light that will come to dominate the chapter. The idea of *dhamma* as light, which was merely sketched in the *Dīpavaṃsa*, is here in the *Mahāvaṃsa* fully revealed and utilized in the retelling of the Buddha's three visits.

In the opening chapter of the *Mahāvaṃsa*, the narrative of the Buddha's three visits to the island of Laṅkā thrusts the island deeply into his conventional biography. All three visits are narrated structurally so that the stories of transformation of certain characters, the *nāgas* and *yakkhas*, parallel the transformation of the place, Laṅkā. The story is thus a didactic repository or, better, a vehicle for conveying the truths usually articulated by the physical presence of the Buddha (the often cited canonical formulation is "who sees the *dhamma* sees me").[57] The *dhamma* thus becomes transferable and the means through which Buddhism spreads and establishes itself in a new terrain; *dhamma* itself, conceived as light, functions as a mytheme. As a diffuser of *dhamma*-light, the *Mahāvaṃsa* pronounces an explicitly rendered "wish" of the Mahāvihāra textual community not simply to be incorporated into the Buddhist world but also to become the very center of it, transformed and sanctified by the Buddha's authoritative visits. The Mahāvihāra textual community asserts its claims to legitimacy and even supremacy at a time when spiritual and temporal authority conveyed through patronage by kings is being contested in Sri Lanka. The relocation of the Buddha's light from the homeland of India to the island of Laṅkā could have been a paradigmatic move that buttressed the Mahāvihāra's claims of centrality and authority.

Laṅkā, as envisioned by the *Mahāvaṃsa*, is susceptible, even prone, to the powerfully penetrating, border-destroying light of the *dhamma*. As in the earlier *Dīpavaṃsa*, the narrative opens with Laṅkā as the home to *yakkhas* (who must be expelled) and *nāgas* (who must be converted). As an island on the periphery of South Asia, an island connecting the *nāga* underworlds and the realm of the humans, Laṅkā is a liminal landscape. In spite of this position, or perhaps because of it, it becomes in the Buddha's estimation the ideal repository for the *dhamma*. Turning to the world envisioned by the text, and looking at how the narrative primes the reader for the full, enlightening impact of the transference of the *dhamma*, we see how the metaphor of *dhamma* as light aids in the transferral of the *dhamma* to a new landscape.

Even before the Buddha physically visits the new terrain of Laṅkā, he anticipates in luminous terms that it will be a fitting repository for the light of *dhamma*. As in the *Dīpavaṃsa*, the *Mahāvaṃsa* inserts this episode into the ninth month after the Buddha's enlightenment, which may be an intentional move to show just how soon after his enlightenment the Buddha's thoughts turned to the island of Laṅkā. Attributing a precise "date" to the event establishes authority beyond that of a disembodied (unplotted) event—dating the visit to Laṅkā firmly lodges it within the Buddha's biography. In verse 20, the Buddha (Gotama) is motivated to prepare the island of Laṅkā for the future reception of his *dhamma*: "For Laṅkā was known by the Conqueror as a place where the *sāsana* would shine, from Laṅkā, filled with the *yakkhas*, the *yakkhas* must (first) be driven out."[58] The reach (and very image) of the Buddha's influence (*sāsana*[59]) is conceived using a metaphor of radiant light.

In his first visit to the island to drive out the *yakkhas*, the Buddha employs his *iddhi* to fly through the sky, and then, hovering over the island, he takes away the light. This tactic is an especially effective attention getter: the *yakkhas* are terrified by the darkness. The Buddha then restores the light, thus restoring order, and takes a seat, thus grounding himself on this new terrain. The mat upon which he sits begins to smolder at the edges, frightening and pushing the *yakkhas* back toward the edges of the island, clearing the island for the Buddha at the center. Through his superpowers, the Buddha draws a neighboring island over to Laṅkā. By placing the *yakkhas* on it and removing them from Laṅkā, he "made this island worthy of men."[60] After this episode, the Buddha returns to his prior location in Uruvelā, an act that literally returns the Buddha to the established Buddha biography in process to pick up where he left off when he makes the aberrant visit to Laṅkā. Although for now Laṅkā is cleared of the *yakkhas*, the light does not quite remain situated in its new place.

As in the *Dīpavaṃsa*, in the *Mahāvaṃsa* the Buddha returns to Laṅkā in the fifth year of his buddhahood to intervene in the impending war between *nāga* families, which is more elaborately recounted here. The *nāga* Mahodara's hoards of supporters live in his extensive sea palace, described as five hundred *yojanas* in length; he is from under the sea, a different *loka* (world) than the battlefield. His nephew Cūlodara is a mountain *nāga*. These *nāgas*, coming from two different places, meet. The *nāgas*' emotional state, which is given prominence in the *Dīpavaṃsa*, seems less important in this text. In the sky over the battlefield, the Buddha once again applies the same technique that he used with the *yakkhas*—namely, the creation of darkness and then of redemptive light:

> The Leader was seated there in the sky over the middle of the battle; the
> dispeller of darkness produced awe-inspiring darkness for the *nāgas*.
> Consoling those tormented by fear, he revealed the light. Satisfied, and having
> seen the Well-gone One [*sugata*], they venerated the feet of the Teacher.[61]

After this powerful display, the Buddha teaches, alights on the contested throne, and accepts food and drink from the *nāgas*. From his station on the *nāgas*' own shared terrain, the Buddha then establishes in the refuges and precepts eighty million land and sea *nāgas*. He uses light to convert, rather than to expel, the *nāgas*.[62] The Buddha then takes his leave to return to the Jetavana grove (and hence rejoins his standard biography in media res).[63]

The third visit to the island does not continue the use of light imagery because the function of light has already been fulfilled—by this visit, the *nāga* inhabitants have already been converted. They are now fitting patrons of the Buddha and his retinue of five hundred monks. This time the Buddha does not manipulate light. He instead highlights the landscape of Laṅkā, indicating the various sites that will in the future become repositories of the Buddha's charisma (through placement of his bodily relics or through his association with the sites) and places of pilgrimage and devotion. In this visit, the transformative power of the light is unnecessary.

Thus, in all three postenlightenment, pre-*parinibbāṇa* visits depicted in the *Mahāvaṃsa*, the Buddha is an agent on the move over borders—he moves first from Uruvelā and then from his rains-retreat home in the Jetavana grove of northern India to the island of Laṅkā. The object at stake, the tool of transformation, is the *dhamma*—made manifest through the image of light, the bringing of the light to the island of Laṅkā. In other words, the Mahāvihāran authors are depicting the Buddha setting up the island of Laṅkā as a different kind of land—one far away from his own abode, a Buddhist place that has been transformed by the light of the *dhamma*.

The point of the *Dīpavaṃsa* is to argue for the compilers' rightful legacy and place in the Sri Lankan Buddhist landscape. By the time the *Mahāvaṃsa* was written, a more ambitious recentering of Laṅkā itself in the broader Buddhist landscape was at issue. Although there are several allusions to and descriptions of the Buddha's light-making capacity in the *Dīpavaṃsa*, the metaphor is more intentionally employed in the *Mahāvaṃsa*. Like any good story that grows and develops in the retelling, connections are made and symbolism, semantic charters, codes, and conventions are developed and augmented by the time of the compilation of the *Mahāvaṃsa*.

There is a big difference between the *Dīpavaṃsa* and *Mahāvaṃsa* accounts of the climax of the story. At the end of the Buddha's final tour of the island, and after a full recounting of his three visits, we get to the recapitulation of the fully transformed nature of this island. This recapitulation, too, capitalizes on the language of light that has been driving the chapter; hearers-readers would be primed for such a salient explanation of the previous stories.

Steven Collins translates the climax of the *Mahāvaṃsa* as follows: "So the Leader of boundless sagacity looked to the benefit of Lankā in the future, and saw the advantage to the crowds of Gods, snakes (i.e. *nāgas*) and the like in Lankā at that time. The Light of the World (*lokadīpo*), abounding in compassion, came to the good island (*sudīpaṃ*) three times, and therefore [or: through him] this island (*dīpo . . . ayaṃ*), radiant with the light [or: lamp] of the Dhamma (*dhammadipāvabhāsī*) became highly respected by (all) good people."[64] The recapitulation begins with the source of light, the Buddha, in the past. He sees benefit for other beings and is motivated to bring the light to the island; once his presence is established through his three visits over time, the *dhamma* becomes respected by the community of the good (the primed, the virtuous). In a provocative and lengthy footnote to this section, Collins explores the poetic work in the structure of this passage. He shows the modified chiasmus (A-B-B-A) in the Pāli verse: "Lokadīpo / sudīpaṃ / dīpo . . . ayaṃ / dhammadīpa" (Light of the World / good island / this island / light of the *dhamma*), and the pun involving the Pāli term *dīpa*, which means both "island" (Sanskrit *dvipa*) and "lamp" (Sanskrit *dīpa*). The verb *avabhasi* (*ava + bhasati*) means "radiant" or "shining," referring to *dīpa* as lamp, not island. The subject, the lamp of *dhamma*, does the shining, not the island itself.[65] This reading is corroborated by following the flow of the modified chiasmus, where the use of structured language—poetics—transfers meaning along with the dhammic light. The popular translation of the term *dhammadīpa* as "island of *dhamma*" thus does not in fact reflect the light (*dīpa*) of the *dhamma* that is grammatically suggested in the *Mahāvaṃsa* but instead imbues the term with anachronistic, nationalistic overtones.[66]

Dhammadīpa thus is the light of the *dhamma* that shines, not the island of the *dhamma* that shines forth. Also, the chosen epithet for the Buddha here is "Lokadīpo," or "Light of the World." As Collins remarks, it would make little sense to call the Buddha in this context "Island of the World."[67] Recapturing the sense of light as the metaphorical, transformative tool employed by the Buddha somewhat subdues the nationalist overtones that have clothed the term *dhammadīpa* since its first translation as "island of *dhamma*" (presumably for political purposes) in 1942. The contextually challenged translation of it as "island of *dhamma*" in *Mahāvaṃsa* I:84, then, is a modern misreading perpetuated opportunistically (intentionally or not) to advance certain political agendas. Challenging the conception of Sri Lanka as the land of *dhamma*, again in the relatively safe location of a footnote, Jonathan Walters writes: "As Steven Collins has pointed out to me, this idea appears nowhere in the Vaṃsas themselves. As far as I have been able to discern, the earliest published use of the term in its timeless sense occurred only in 1942, and the author quotes statements made by Lord Passfield in the House of Commons: Ven. Bhikkhu Metteye, 'Lord Buddha—The First Liberator of Slaves,' *Maha Bodhi Journal* 50 (April–June 1942), 178–79. I can only conclude that the Dhammadīpa was invented in the middle of the twentieth century as an ideologization of the [*Vaṃsatthappakāsinī*]/Okkāka world vision."[68] Although I am obviously in agreement with Collins's translation and analysis, and I fully support the destabilization of *dhammadīpa* as a claim for the island's inherent righteousness, I still have to wonder why the fifth-century Mahāvihāran community responsible for this text made this nuanced pun, especially considering that it occupies such a prominent place in the narrative that establishes the Buddha's *dhamma* on the island of Laṅkā. This question is particularly pertinent given that the term is established within the course of a text that self-consciously recenters the Buddhist world, making possible the Mahāvihāran Theravāda Buddhists' later hegemonic claims. It is important for modern polemics whether this authoritative source, the *Mahāvaṃsa*, makes an explicit claim that Laṅkā is an island of *dhamma* or not; looking back into a history of the island for an ideological foundation is a natural maneuver. But for the community of interpretation at the time of its composition, surely the dual meaning of *dīpa* was not only intentional but also skillfully employed, aiming for the ears, hearts, and minds of the primed "good people."

The Sanskrit terms *dvipa* (island) and *dīpa* (lamp, light) are conveniently and poetically collapsed into one Pāli term, *dīpa*, and the author-compiler of the *Mahāvaṃsa* astutely exploits this conflation of meanings. The semantic field of the term is multifaceted, which allows the text to enter the literary worklike rather than documentary mode. The important point is that light imagery has been utilized throughout the chapter, sensitizing or preparing the listener in a particular way. This leads us to posit the following reading:

The island, which is metaphorically like a lamp, has been primed by the Buddha. In this scenario, the Light of the World is an agent of transformation who is brimming over with compassion (like oil in a lamp). That this argument is made by a fifth-century Mahāvihāra text is no mystery; the text quite clearly identifies the people for whom it has been composed by the appearance of the same refrain at the end of each chapter: "composed for the anxious thrill [*saṃvega*] and serene satisfaction [*pasāda*] of good people," the people primed for his compassion to take hold. Reading or hearing the text, one becomes a participant in rendering its world wish. Who would want to be left out of the group of "good people" the text is claiming as its intended audience?

The text asserts a particular worldview—namely, Laṅkā's centrality in the recentered Buddhist cosmos—and a particular wish—that good people are primed and transformed by hearing it. The concluding pun plays on the Pāli homonyms *dīpa* (lamp) and *dīpa* (island) and capitalizes on the fact that the reader himself, a good person, has been "primed" for the dual resonance. Encountering the *dhammadīpa* (light of the *dhamma*) in this context means that the reader, like the island and like the *nāgas*, is being subjected to the Buddha's worklike, penetrating light.

The penetrating effect of the metaphor of light would not have been lost on an educated Buddhist audience of the fifth century; in fact, images of light abound throughout Pāli canonical texts.[69] But even in the canonical sources there is occasional ambiguity about which *dīpa* is meant: lamp or island? For example, Walpola Rahula considers an often-cited passage in the *Dīgha Nikāya*:

> *Attadīpa viharatha attasaraṇā* (D., p. 62). Some European scholars are inclined to translate this passage as "be ye lamps unto yourselves" (Rhys Davids' Dīgha Nikāya Translation, Vol. II, p. 108). But *dīpa* in this context means "island" and not "lamp." The [*Dhammapadātthakathā*] commenting on this word says: *mahāsamuddagataṃ dīpaṃ viya attānaṃ dīpaṃ patiṭṭhaṃ katvā viharatha*. "Live making yourself an island, a support (resting place) even as an island in the great ocean." *Saṃsāra* is compared to an ocean (*saṃsāra-sāgara*), and what is required in the ocean for safety is an island, and not a lamp. Cf. [*Dhammapada*] II, 5, *dīpaṃ kayirātha medhāvī yaṃ ogho nābhikīrati*; "the wise will create an island which the flood does not overwhelm." The idea of a lamp is, apparently, borrowed from the Bible.[70]

Although lamps (lit fires and candles) are used in many different religious traditions, both physically in rituals and metaphorically in literature, I do not agree with Rahula that the lamp is an imported, superimposed biblical image. It is abundantly clear that in the *Mahāvaṃsa* the *śleṣa* (double meaning) regarding *dīpa* as both island and lamp was intentionally employed for maximum poetic effect and delight for the reader-hearer.[71]

The *dhamma* is transferred to a good island (*sudīpaṃ*)—namely, an island that has been primed to receive the pervasive and penetrating light of the *dhamma*. Just as the *Mahāvaṃsa* itself has been "composed for the anxious thrill [*saṃvega*] and serene satisfaction [*pasāda*] of good people," so this statement makes a claim about the ethical propensity of the island's inhabitants. Just as a wick in a lamp must be primed and soaked in oil before it will accept the flame, so the lamp/island is primed to receive the *dhamma*, and so the fifth-century community is primed for transformation.[72]

◈ ◈ ◈

It is enlightening to read the opening chapter of the *Mahāvaṃsa* through the opening verses of the *Vaṃsatthappakāsinī*, a later commentary that reflects the concerns of its own textual community and interprets the concerns of the community responsible for the composition of the *Mahāvaṃsa*. Jonathan Walters calls the *Vaṃsatthappakāsinī* a "Mahāvihāran imperial project" that extends the claims of the *Mahāvaṃsa* by proclaiming Mahāvihāran supremacy (over the rival Abhayagiri and Jetavana sects and even over other countries).[73] The first verses of the *Vaṃsatthappakāsinī* claim to penetrate the true meaning of the *Mahāvaṃsa*, picking up on the leitmotif of the light of the *dhamma*:

> Having honored the lord of the world who ought to receive honors (*pūjā*)
> Who became the unsurpassed sun for tractable people-lotuses,
> Who illuminated the sky of the excellent solar clan with radiant energy rayed by the glorious teachings (*dhamma*),
> Who had vast majestic power in the dispersion of the darkness of delusion,
> And [having honored] his teaching and his disciplinary order, the mine of virtues,
> I shall give an explanation of the uncertain purpose (or meaning) of the verses of the *Mahāvaṃsa*:
> Pay close attention to it, excellent men![74]

My reading of the opening chapters of the Pāli *Dīpavaṃsa* and *Mahāvaṃsa* has led me to believe that these forms of religious textual production represent negotiations for power and claims for security in both the universal, "political" sense (Laṅkā as the new center of *dhamma*) and the personal, religious sense (the transformation arising from hearing or reading or both). Both texts are desperate, urgent attempts to reorder and reorient both self and place as exemplars of Buddhism. Both texts claim authority for their textual communities and transfer a center of power and legitimacy from the Indian homeland of Buddhism to a newly established center of authority. Both texts amplify the sense of *dhamma* as light, leading to a conclusion that they are as much chronicles of the light as they are chronicles of the island itself.

{3} *NĀGAS*, TRANSFIGURED FIGURES INSIDE THE TEXT, RUMINATIVE TRIGGERS OUTSIDE

WHY *NĀGAS*? Just as the conception of the other gives rise to a deepened awareness of self, the understanding of the *nāga* in the *Mahāvaṃsa* urges the reader to assume a certain understanding of himself or herself. The sense of self that is derived from reading this narrative peppered with *nāgas* is a temporally bounded one and ultimately provokes the reader into realizing his or her own immediate and urgent responsibility and agency toward his or her own moral development. As we saw in chapter 1, the proems of the two *vaṃsas* I focus on enunciate the reader's work in urgent, vocative tones (*suṇātha me,* "Listen up!") and press the reader toward a particular goal—namely, the cultivation of the requisite attitudes or emotions of *saṃvega* and *pasāda.* And as shown in chapter 2, literary devices work on the primed reader to effect transformation. The sense of self is thus dependent on the reader's agency and interest in and ability to cultivate such emotions in the here and now.

A sense of self is honed as it comes into juxtaposition with the narrative character of the *nāga*, whom the reader understands to be simultaneously fortunate and unfortunate—the *nāgas* are in a special, proximate relationship with the Buddha, even after his *parinibbāṇa* via his relics; but their spurious ontological nature and soteriological aptitude prohibits them from achieving the spiritual attainments that are possible for the text's human audience. It is through this awareness of otherness vis-à-vis the character of the *nāga* that the hearer-reader recognizes the rather urgent responsibilities of a human birth. This recognition is made possible by the sympathetic and empathetic imaginative modes that are engendered through the *nāga* stories.

The ideal reader-hearer of the *Mahāvaṃsa* (who has embraced the reading instructions given in the proem and recognized the role that the language of light has in effecting a transformation of the landscape both inside and outside the text) understands characters such as the *nāgas* in a different light. How do figures as seemingly low and innocuous as the ubiquitous *nāgas*, a fixture of the Indic landscape, function within this text to help drive home the desired emotional reactions and spur practical effects for the reader?

Nāgas are present in all Indic traditions as central and peripheral characters, as both agents and patients. As articulated in the *Jātaka* stories, the Buddha even lives as a *nāga* three separate times in his past lives in order to work out the perfections (*pāramī*) required to become a buddha. *Nāgas* are always seen to be in a special relationship with the Buddha, from bathing him at his birth to announcing that the time for a new buddha has come to protecting his relics after his death. They are present and active in the full range of Buddhist texts, from the canonical *Vinaya* (the collected text of monastic rules), the *Jātakas* (canonical and noncanonical stories of the Buddha's former births), and the *suttas* (doctrinal discourses of the Buddha) to the commentarial literature and extracanonical *vaṃsas* (chronicles of the Buddha, his relics, and lists of kings) that are under consideration here.

The significant role of *nāgas* in the Buddhist *vaṃsas* has largely been ignored or glossed over as a mythical or whimsical accretion to these otherwise trustworthy historical documents. Robert DeCaroli writes, "In the case of the Buddhist literature, the *yakṣas*, *nāgas*, and other beings more often than not serve as little more than narrative hooks that provide an opportunity for an explication of doctrine."[1] I strongly disagree with the characterization of *nāgas* as mere "narrative hooks" simply to grab the reader's attention. Rather, I argue that they stimulate actual ethical work on the reader's part; they are an intentionally employed trope to provoke the reader-hearer's imagination, a requisite practice in the cultivation of the very values[2] that are frequently extolled in Buddhist stories. As Charles Hallisey and Anne Hansen put it, "Far from being a cynical strategy to hold the attention of 'the popular mind,' the use of animal stories among Buddhists appears to be a sophisticated imaginative practice."[3] The *nāga* stories are fundamental to the functioning of the *Mahāvaṃsa* as a catalyst for emotional states conducive to the devoted practice of "good people" and *nāgas* are the rhetorical element that drives the narrative of the arrival, establishment, and proper veneration of the relics—which serve as the culmination of the *Mahāvaṃsa*'s narrative.

Part of the efficacy of the figure of the *nāga* lies precisely in its ontological status as something other than human. To empathize with the *nāgas* of the *Mahāvaṃsa* requires more of a leap of the imagination for the reader than if the characters shared more human qualities. They are a literary device that helps to create "interpretive openings," sites of active ethical negotiation of the text and the self.

Joseph Walser has considered plausible reading methods to apply to the more legendary or mythological aspects of Buddhist texts that may be fruitfully applied in an encounter with the *nāga* in the *vaṃsas*. In considering the best reading strategies for the copious legends surrounding the "historical" Mahāyāna character Nagārjuna, he suggests: "In order to interpret these legends, the most productive position is to assume that all pieces of information in the legends were included for a reason. The purposive element will be stronger for those elements of the story that occupy a prominent place in the narrative. For those who are uncomfortable with the 'intentional fallacy,' I will say merely that we must impute a purposefulness or a strategy to the text in order to interpret it in its historical context."[4] To interpret the *Mahāvaṃsa*, we cannot ignore the serpentine creatures that inhabit Laṅkā at the time of the Buddha and that respond to his presence with a radical shift in their behavior. What might the narrative of the *nāgas*' visceral experience of *saṃvega* and *pasāda* as provoked by the presence of the Buddha do in turn for the reader-hearer, whose objective is to experience those same emotional qualities? I contend that the presence of the *nāgas* is a part of the compiler's literary strategy to bring about the emotions called for in the *Mahāvaṃsa*'s proem.

Walser also offers some specific reading strategies to be able to pick out the reason for the incorporation of legendary materials into texts. He writes that, generally speaking, "hagiographers compose their stories with two purposes in mind, spiritual edification and institutional legitimation." Stories composed with the former purpose are easier to perceive as such because they "tend to echo or illustrate themes found in scripture, such as acts of altruism."[5] I would add that they are especially likely to be perceived and analyzed by the historian of religion, who is acutely attuned to anything smacking of religious or spiritual edification. In the case of the *Mahāvaṃsa*, the text is not squarely classified as a "religious" one, even though it was likely compiled by a monk (or monks) for other monks and was preserved by the monastic Mahāvihāra textual community until scholars became interested in it. In chapter 5, I consider how the earliest (Western) scholars and interpreters were interested primarily in the translated version of the *Mahāvaṃsa* and how they were followed by scholars and interpreters focusing on the historical veracity of this unprecedented (in South Asia) resource chronicle. The *Mahāvaṃsa* was thus ushered into the interpretive purviews of several disciplines in the social sciences, most especially history and anthropology. The elements that contribute to institutional legitimation have already undergone extensive scholarly scrutiny; as the *vaṃsa*s are encountered by scholars of religion, however, religious themes such as conversion and relic worship reorient the predominant reading. The reading given in this book builds on this accretion of religious readings and pays attention to the literary elements that make such a reading not facile but more productive.

Walser places the "elements . . . of institutional legitimation" into two categories. First, the protagonist is juxtaposed to "a person, place, or theme that is independently famous."[6] This is obviously the case in the *Mahāvaṃsa*, where the legitimating proximity to the Buddha takes center stage at the outset. The second category of institutional legitimation that Walser identifies is a bit more complicated; it is when the protagonist's fame and import is such that he then infuses places, people, and even events with legitimacy. In the case of Nāgārjuna, for instance, "once Nāgārjuna became famous, his association with pilgrimage sites lent an air of legitimacy (and antiquity) to those sites."[7] Even a cursory reading of the *Mahāvaṃsa* would suggest it is the Buddha who infuses Laṅkā with his authoritative presence. But I wonder if we can say that the *nāga*s themselves—who are created as model Buddhists at the outset of the text, striving for access to the Buddha and his teachings—are legitimized as carriers of the tradition's concerns? Does their indigenous presence on the island, which is poetically established prior to the Buddha's own visit, signify a special antiquity or legitimacy to the island itself, perhaps to indicate an a priori readiness of the island as a proper and fitting receptacle for the *dhamma* and *sāsana*? This reading might explain why their conversion story dominates the very first chapter of the *Mahāvaṃsa*. The prominence of the *nāga*s demands our attention both for the spiritually edifying reasons they crop up in this privileged position and for the two-way movement of legitimating influence they extend to (and from) the Buddha to (and from) the island of Laṅkā.

Claude Lévi-Strauss's apposite maxim that animals ("natural species") are "good to think" comes to mind in this context.[8] We might say that *nāgas* were good to think for the literary cultures that employed them in fourth- and fifth-century Sri Lanka and that they continue to be good to think now in terms of our modern understanding of how nonhuman, animal agents function in religious texts. The textual community receiving the *Mahāvaṃsa* is primed through the *Mahāvaṃsa* to expect and develop a heightened emotional response to it, which in turn creates the ethical behaviors fitting for a community of "good people." *Nāgas* are a good character to think with, to help individual hearers and readers navigate and work through this text, because of their radical transformation from selfish, bellicose creatures to model, devoted, relic-worshipping Buddhists.

Considering the ontological status, soteriological aptitude, and moral didacticism of *nāgas* as narrative characters in Pāli literature moves a reader. The use of *nāgas* is extensive in all genres of Pāli literature, often appearing in didactically and practically important stories at critical junctures. Indeed, *nāgas* were an accepted and effective trope in the Pāli Buddhist "tropics of discourse."[9] Here I focus primarily on their use in the opening story of the *Mahāvaṃsa* and in one particularly salient *Jātaka* tale.[10] Becoming aware of the ontological status and soteriological aptitude of *nāgas* helps interpreters of the *Mahāvaṃsa* understand the *nāgas*' role in conveying ethical lessons for the hearers-readers. Understanding the work *nāgas* elicit from readers-hearers is, in turn, critical for our understanding of the *Mahāvaṃsa* as a piece of multivalent transformative literature rather than singularly as a historical chronicle. It is crucial that we think through the fertile cultural sphere reflected in early Sri Lankan Pāli Buddhist chronicles, where in some cases *nāgas* have significant relationships with the Buddha (both as a live teacher and through his post-*parinibbāṇa* relics) and in other cases the bodhisatta has taken *nāga* form on his way to buddhahood.

A particularly salient *Jātaka*, the *Bhūridatta Jātaka*, and the opening chapter of the Pāli *Mahāvaṃsa* read together can help flesh out the meaning of the character of the *nāga* for fifth-century interpreters. Stylistically, the *Jātakas* share an element of narrativity with the *Mahāvaṃsa* (both are good stories). There is also a didactic dimension to the *Bhūridatta Jātaka*, and it exhibits a more transparent moral dimension than the *Mahāvaṃsa*'s first chapter (especially when it is read without the benefit of the proem). Finally, the *Jātakas* overtly appeal to the legitimizing presence of the Buddha, who is both the narrator and the protagonist. In terms of content, both stories are about the interstices of time and ethics. The *Jātaka*s are iterations of the extensive former lives of the Buddha and tell vignettes that illustrate his cultivation of *pāramitā* (the perfections), so the fact that he took a *nāga* birth on his journey to Buddhahood is significant. *Vaṃsa*s are also unequivocally about the passage of time, spanning from the *nāga*s' inhabitation of early Laṅkā to their holding on to the cache of Buddha relics for future use to the *nāgarāja* (*nāga* king) named Kāla (Time). It is reasonable to assume that the *Bhūridatta Jātaka* and the *Mahāvaṃsa* might have been encountered on similar terms within a monastic setting; a member of the textual community of the *Mahāvaṃsa* would likely have a general and practical familiarity with both episodes. Also, I argue that these stories, taken together, flesh out the creativity of the articulation of a particular, ethically imbued worldview or "world wish" that can be understood in distinctly religious rather than primarily political terms.

Although slippery to grasp, *nāga*s provide us with a lens to observe what is happening ethically and didactically in the core texts of the Sri Lankan literary tradition. *Nāga*s craftily wind their way through different genres, eras, languages, and local and translocal religious traditions. They are omnipresent physically in the Indic landscape, both as imagined and as experienced. So what might they tell us about the nature of being, the innate proclivities for buddhahood in certain individuals (including *nāga*s themselves), and the operative ethical structures in a medieval Buddhist imagination?

INTRODUCTION TO THE *BHŪRIDATTA JĀTAKA*

The *Jātaka*s are a collection of stories that loomed large in the medieval Buddhist imagination. These stories served didactic purposes: as fodder for localized, vernacular folktales, as a basis for ritual or liturgical practices, and as subjects for representation on the *stūpa*s that visually articulate the Buddhist landscape. But the *Jātaka*s were also, like the *Mahāvaṃsa*, open and fair sites of active negotiation by interpreters or, in other words, vehicles for constructing and projecting particular worldviews and wishes as well as for recording and interpreting them. Jonathan Walters explains:

> Virtually all Indian Buddhists maintained versions of the Buddhist "canon," the Tipiṭaka/Tripiṭaka. Parts of these canons—certain texts of the Vinaya and Sutta/Sūtra Piṭakas—were "closed," and disciplinary orders, especially

> the "Hīnayāna," maintained roughly similar versions of these texts, even though minor differences in the various monastic disciplinary rules (*vinaya*) often functioned as hooks upon which doctrinal disputes were hung, and the interpretation of these shared texts by philosophers and commentators varied widely. However, other portions of these canons, especially the texts of the Khuddaka/Kṣudraka or "miscellaneous" division of the Sutta/Sūtra... were "open."[11]

The *Jātakas*, contained as they are in the *Khuddaka Nikāya*, were among the "open" texts that different textual communities would read and interpret according to their individual concerns. The Pāli *Jātaka* collection as we have received it is the result of the Mahāvihāra's legacy of textual practices; according to tradition, it had been recorded, preserved, and passed down within the same textual community that was purportedly responsible for the *Mahāvaṃsa*. Walters notes: "My own work on the Pāli Vaṃsas makes it clear that these 'open' divisions of the canon became key sites for the disputes of 'medieval' Indian Buddhists. The 'miscellaneous' literature included all the elements that in their various ways constituted the 'philosophies of history' of the various orders, that is, their own versions of the *Jātakas*, narratives about the successions of the Buddha's lives and Apadāna/Avadāna, stories about the nature of the cosmic polity he instituted."[12] It is productive for us to see these open sites as negotiating a vast network of literary images, tropes, techniques, and expectations and to examine how these texts deliver their message. It is helpful to pair an "open site" such as the *Bhūridatta Jātaka* with the story of the Buddha's initial impact on the *nāgas* of Laṅkā in the *Mahāvaṃsa*.

Variations, retellings, and commentaries on *Jātaka* stories abound in the Pāli tradition, indicating their openness. Different monastic orders maintained their own versions of the *Jātakas*, each version with a slightly (or vastly) different ordering of the stories. The depiction of the *nāgas* in each version is, by extension, similarly diverse. Fascination with and proliferation of *Jātaka* tales in art and architecture survive even today. Individual *Jātaka* tales occur in the Sutta and Vinaya Piṭakas, which compose the core of the Buddhist canon.[13] Abbreviated versions of the stories and commentaries about the *nāgas* Bhūridatta, Campeyya, and Śaṅkhapāla also make a canonical appearance in the *Cariyāpiṭaka* of the *Khuddaka Nikāya*. The *Cariyāpiṭaka* includes thirty-five stories grouped together as illustrative of various perfections (*pāramitā*), with most focused on *dāna pāramitā* (perfection of generosity), *sīla pāramitā* (perfection of morality), and *nekkhamma pāramitā* (perfection of renunciation). All three stories of the bodhisatta's *nāga* births are classified as stories about *sīla pāramitā*.[14]

The pre-Buddha is born as a *nāga* only three times in the *Jātakas*, although *nāgas* are involved in several of the stories as subordinate characters. In Viggo Fausbøll's seminal edition of the Pāli *Jātakas*, the *Bhūridatta Jātaka* is number 543 of the 547 Pāli *Jātakas*, a placement that takes on significance when one considers that the *nipāta* (books) of the *Jātakas* are arranged according to the number of *gāthā* (verses) within each story.[15] The final *nipāta* contains the longest, most substantial *Jātaka* stories, and this is where we find *Bhūridatta Jātaka*, the third longest in the entire collection and only a few removed from *Vessantara*, the story of the penultimate birth of the bodhisatta and arguably the most significant and popular *Jātaka*. The frame story for the *Bhūridatta Jātaka*, recounting the reason given for the Buddha to have the opportunity to tell the story of his former birth, is of the Buddha at Sāvatthi preaching a discourse to *upāsaka* (laity) on the importance of keeping the fast day. The moral of the story is that one should strive to vigilantly uphold one's precepts and practice (especially because one is lucky to have been born a human). The Buddha then illustrates his lesson on *sīla* (morality) and perseverance with the story of his former birth as the *nāga* Bhūridatta.

The frame story here works like the proem of the *Mahāvaṃsa* insofar as it renders transparent the didactic aims of the story that is about to be told. Where the *Mahāvaṃsa* tells the story of the coming of the Buddha and his relics to cultivate emotions in the hearts of an ideal audience, the purpose of the *Jātaka* is the opportunity to remind the *upāsaka* to be vigilant and to practice correctly. In both texts, the presence of the Buddha lends even more legitimacy to the importance of the lesson to be conveyed. And in both stories the *nāgas* are the crucial agents who effect these perceptible changes in the audience.

In the particular *Jātaka* story I have selected, the bodhisatta actually takes birth as a *nāga* while perfecting himself on the long path to eventual buddhahood. Several *Jātakas* incorporate *nāgas* in their narrative, sometimes as prominent agents in the story, but, as noted earlier, the bodhisatta is born a *nāga* only three times in the *Jātakas*, as the *nāgas* Campeyya and Śaṅkhapāla as well as the *nāga* Bhūridatta. My reason for choosing the Bhūridatta story over the other two is simple: it is the longest and most layered and developed of the three accounts. The Campeyya narrative recounts an almost identical, although pared-down, tale, with a *nāga* aspiring to shed his *nāga* existence by practicing austerities and vows on an anthill in the realm of humans. Campeyya, like Bhūridatta, was enticed to the human realm as the only place to practice purity and self-control, requisite aspects of the *sīla pāramitā* (perfection of morality) that would ensure his progress on the path toward *nibbāṇa*. Śaṅkhapāla's story is rather brief; we see a *nāgarāja* again observing austerities in the realm of humans, and he is beaten by a band of villagers (which is fine with him—to die, especially while observing moral practices, would bring him to a better birth). A sympathetic passerby saves him and then joins him for a while in the *nāgaloka* (subterranean *nāga* world)[16] as a cherished guest before returning to be a storytelling ascetic. The *Śaṅkhapāla Jātaka* does not have an obvious underlying moral lesson.

I have selected the story of Bhūridatta here because I want to figure out just what a *nāga* birth entails,[17] so that when we see the *nāgas* of Sri Lanka encountering (and being converted by) the Buddha, as recounted in the *Mahāvaṃsa*, we can have some prefatory understanding of what is at stake for people hearing and participating in the text and what the ethical implications of these characters or lessons might be. What are the implications for imagining the bodhisatta near buddhahood taking a *nāga* birth? If we understand what it may have meant for the writers and hearers-readers of the *Mahāvaṃsa* to imagine the bodhisatta undergoing a *nāga* birth in a well-known *Jātaka* tale, we will be better prepared to reflect on the work that *nāgas* in the *Mahāvaṃsa* elicited from fifth-century hearers-readers.

BHŪRIDATTA: TRANSFIGURED

The Bhūridatta story invokes the power of familial love. It begins with the marriage between the prince of Benares and a *nagīnī* (female *nāga*) and moves through the marriage of their daughter Samuddajā[18] to the *nāgarāja* Dhatarāṭṭha and on into the lives of their four sons, who are described as being "of watery nature."[19] The hero of the story is the second of Samuddajā's sons, Bhūridatta, who is in fact the bodhisatta himself taking a *nāga* birth in his cultivation of the *pāramitā* (perfection) of *sīla* (morality).

Bhūridatta vows to observe a fast each night in the human realm, where this practice will cultivate great religious consequence (merit).[20] Bhūridatta is a large, supernatural snake being; he must transform into the more naturalistic cobra for his temporary ascetic practices in the human realm. Every evening he assumes the form of a giant snake and lies on top of an anthill, the natural abode of great snakes. Each morning as he transforms back into a heavenly body, *nāga* maidens serenade and ornament him and accompany him back to the *nāgaloka*.[21]

After some time, Bhūridatta is discovered by a Brahmin hunter, who asks him what kind of being he is: A *sakka* (god), a *yakkha*, or a *nāga*?[22] He is in the midst of observing the fast, so he is compelled to tell the truth because to lie while cultivating morality, even to save your life, is anathema.[23] He invites this Brahmin together with the Brahmin's son to the *nāgaloka*, where they live happily and lavishly for a year until they grow restless and leave. Bhūridatta gives them a special protective jewel (as we will see in the next chapter, *nāgas* are hoarders of such valuables), but when the two men stop and strip to take a bath on their way home, the jewel sinks into the earth and returns to the *nāgas*' abode.[24]

Later, a group of *nāgas* who are carrying that same jewel in the human world are frightened into dropping the jewel by the Brahmin Alambāyana's anti-*nāga* spell, and Alambāyana attains possession of it. Alambāyana is a forest hermit who learned this special spell from the head ascetic at a forest ashram to frighten *nāgas* and bring forth wealth. The head ascetic had learned it directly from the *garuḍa*, an eaglelike natural enemy of the *nāgas* whom we will meet again later in the story. The Brahmin who had been a houseguest of the *nāgarāja* immediately sees the jewel and recognizes it as having been the gift from the *nāgarāja* given to him and his son as they left the *nāgaloka*. He tries to convince Alambāyana to give it back to him and finally succeeds when he agrees to show Alambāyana the place where the *nāgarāja* comes nightly to observe his fasting precept. (The Brahmin's son, by the way, is so disgusted by his father's duplicitous and morally reprehensible actions that he runs off to be an ascetic in the Himālayas.)

Betrayed by his Brahmin friend, Bhūridatta allows Alambāyana to capture him; he knows he cannot fight back or show anger toward Alambāyana while he is observing his fast, or his own moral character would be compromised. As Alambāyana tosses the jewel to the Brahmin as a reward, it falls to the ground and is once again swallowed up by the earth and transported back to the *nāgaloka*. The Brahmin is left with nothing. Meanwhile, Alambāyana chews special herbs, utters his spell, and then pounds the *nāgarāja* Bhūridatta into submission (although it is gratuitous for him to demonstrate such violence toward the snake because Bhūridatta has accepted his fate and does nothing to protest or defend himself).

Alambāyana then puts Bhūridatta to work performing as a captive snake for the entertainment of crowds for some time, although Bhūridatta continues to observe his fast, eschewing any food offered to him for "fear of not being released from his captivity."[25] The snake charmer plans a special performance for the king of Benares (who is, in fact, Bhūridatta's own uncle, unbeknownst to everyone present).

Meanwhile, at the same time Bhūridatta is abducted, his mother has a dream foretelling her son's capture.[26] After waiting yet another month for her absent son to return home (he is the most dependable of all her sons, the most regular of her visitors), she breaks down, cries, and convinces her eldest son, Sudassana, that something wicked has befallen Bhūridatta. Sudassana enlists the help of his two other brothers, and each proceeds to a different world. Sudassana takes the appearance of an ascetic, and when his sister Accimukhī insists on accompanying him, she takes the form of a frog that hides in the ascetic's hair. They travel to the human world, see Bhūridatta's blood on the anthill where he had been fasting, and follow the trail of blood, asking people along the way about the snake charmer's whereabouts. The two enter the palace just as the snake show is beginning. The snake charmer lets Bhūridatta out of his basket to survey the crowd. Bhūridatta immediately spots his brother (*nāgas* can see through disguises): "The Great Being [bodhisatta], as he looked, beheld his brother in another part of the crowd, and, repressing the tears which filled his eyes, he came out of the basket and went up to his brother. The crowd, seeing him approach, retreated in fear and Sudassana was left alone; so he [the Great Being] went up to him and laid his head upon his foot and wept; and Sudassana also wept. The Great Being at last stopped weeping and went into the basket."[27]

The snake charmer is nervous because from the tears he assumes Sudassana has been bitten. But Sudassana proclaims that in fact the snake is harmless and cannot bite. The snake charmer is offended at Sudassana's assertion that he has been cajoling his audiences with a less-than-fierce specimen and accepts a wager to see who is more powerful. Sudassana calls forth from his matted hair his sister in frog form, and she deposits an extraordinarily virulent poison into his hand. He then announces that there is no safe receptacle for it and that it will destroy the land, the sky, the water, even the entire earth upon contact. Only a ritual disposal of it into three specially dug holes—one filled with herbs, one with cow dung, and one with "heavenly medicines"—will suffice. When the poison is placed in the middle hole, a fire erupts, turning Alambāyana into a leper. Terrified, he agrees to set the *nāga* Bhūridatta free (who only then assumes a nonsnake form!). Sudassana then reveals to the king of Benares that the king is in fact their mother's brother, hence their uncle, which sets up the penultimate chapter of the text, a massive family reunion that I will not recount here.

In the final chapter, another brother comes across the Brahmin who had initially betrayed Bhūridatta. The brother is about to kill him out of revenge but then decides instead to bring the Brahmin to the *nāgaloka* to see what the other brothers would recommend. This narrative twist allows for an extensive discourse on the folly of sacrificial Brahmins, the impotency of Vedic ritual practices, and the alternative Buddhist emphasis on the primacy of the *dhamma*, especially right practice (following the precepts and observing fast days, as Bhūridatta does), over Brahminical rites.[28]

The centrality of *nāga* characters in the *Bhūridatta Jātaka* and especially the bodhisatta's birth as a *nāga* to attain the perfection of morality (*sīla pāramitā*), when he is so close to completing the cultivation of the ten perfections, demand our attention. The *Bhūridatta Jātaka*'s frame story depicts the Buddha teaching laity about perseverance in upholding precepts and practice. The Buddha then illustrates his lesson with the story of his former birth as the *nāga* Bhūridatta.

Perhaps the frame story works in a similar way as the proem of the *Mahāvaṃsa* insofar as it renders transparent the didactic aims of the story that it is about to tell. Where the *Mahāvaṃsa* tells the story of the coming of the Buddha and his relics for the cultivation of emotions (agitation and satisfaction) in the hearts of an ideal audience, this *Jātaka* introduces the premise for the storytelling as an opportunity to remind the *upāsaka* (laity) audience to be vigilant and to practice correctly. Setting it in the voice of the Buddha lends even more legitimacy to the importance of the lesson to be conveyed. As a didactic text, the *Jātaka* provides a useful mechanism by which avid lay practice could be maintained because it was in the best interest of the *saṅgha* (monastic community) to develop a strong and supportive laity. Likewise, the imperative of the *Mahāvaṃsa* is to initiate or bolster requisite emotional attitudes that engender the proper practice (namely, relic veneration). In both stories reviewed here, the *nāga*s are crucial agents in effecting perceptible change in the audience.

Shifting our focus from the metaphor of light explored in chapter 2 to the character for whom that light was powerfully persuasive and transformative, we have to ask, What has the light of the *dhamma* exposed about the prominence of the *nāga* within the narrative? As we have seen, the *Mahāvaṃsa* begins with a story of *nāgas*. What is this *nāga* story doing at the very outset of a text frequently characterized as "a mythicized history (or [*H*]*eilsgeschichte*) of Buddhism in India and Sri Lanka"?[29] What does it mean for a text that imagines itself to be participating in a translocal Buddhist holy history, linking this *Heilsgeschichte* to the local reigns and accomplishments of Buddhist kings, to begin with *nāgas*? It seems particularly significant that the *Mahāvaṃsa* opens with a *nāga* story of monumental importance situated in the Buddha's lifetime. He converts the *nāgas* by inculcating fear and then satisfaction, but he dismisses the *yakkhas* entirely. What, then, is the relationship between the Buddha and the *nāgas*, and what does this relationship convey to the reader about the *nāgas*' ontological status and soteriological capacity? Most importantly, what does this special relationship between the Buddha and the *nāgas* do for the reader-interpreter? Now that we are familiar with the *Bhūridatta Jātaka* and the *nāgas* in the first chapter of the *Mahāvaṃsa*, we can more closely examine the ontological status, soteriological aptitude, and moral didacticism of *nāgas* as particularly salient literary features.

THE *NĀGAS*' ONTOLOGICAL STATUS

The *nāgas* in the *Mahāvaṃsa* and the *Bhūridatta Jātaka* are obviously related. They all are *nāgas*, which are special snakes and classed as *bhūta devatā* (divine beings),[30] distinguished from *sappas* (Sanskrit, *sarpas*), or common snakes. The narrative function of *nāgas* undergoes a subtle shift between the *Mahāvaṃsa* and the *Bhūridatta Jātaka*. In the first chapter of the *Mahāvaṃsa*, the Buddha himself comes in contact with the *nāgas* and actually forms relationships with them, individually (such as with Maṇiakkhika, who invites him back to the island for his third visit) and collectively (the Buddha converts multitudes of *nāgas*—eighty *koṭis*, an unthinkably high number—en masse upon his arrival to Sri Lanka). Bhūridatta, in contrast, *is* the Buddha-to-be, albeit in a previous life. Elsewhere in the *Mahāvaṃsa*, stories of the *nāgas* entail conversions by *theras* (monks) in borderlands, the introduction of the *dhamma* to new territory, and relationships with the relics of the dead and departed Buddha initiated and sustained by the *nāgas*. These stories stress both the expansionist strategies of the *sāsana* and the sustained relationship between the Buddha and this particularly slippery category of being.

In contrast, in the *Jātakas* we find a plethora of both common snakes (*sarpas*) and majestic *nāgas* who ultimately are interpreted in relation to the Buddha (as the Buddha himself puts it when he explains who is who at the conclusion of each *Jātaka*). The Buddha himself takes a *nāga* birth three times, so it is clear that such a low and detestable birth as that of a *nāga* does not prevent someone destined to become a buddha from attaining his goal but in fact helps him along. So why might the Buddha have taken a *nāga* birth? Was there something peculiar to this kind of existence that primed him for buddhahood in a unique way?[31]

Although both of our sources are saturated with clues as to the embodied nature of the *nāgas*, such as references to their abodes, habits, and practices, it is still relatively unclear what exactly they *are*. The word *nāga* is imprecisely translated into English by a variety of suggestive concepts: "snake," "snake being," "serpent," even "dragon." Stepping back from these two texts to consider the nature of *nāgas* in the broader Indic context, I am struck that we do not see other animals or gods or beings with a defined snakelike form such as that found in Sri Lankan Buddhist texts. Gaṇeśa may have an elephant head, but he does not have an explicitly elephant nature—he has a new head out of necessity, and it is an elephant's head because of happenstance. *Yakkhas*, *apsaras* (beautiful, supernatural, nymphlike female beings), *asuras* (power-hungry, morally neutral, but more often than not challenging subdeities), and *devas* (deities) are all cosmological, ontological categories, but none of these "births" is described with reference to a particular natural, animal form. So are *nāgas* naturalistic animals or supernatural beings or even a group of humans who have assumed such lore and characteristics through years of being defined as the "other"?

As for the ontology of the *nāga*, the fifth-century virtuoso translator and commentary producer Buddhaghosa includes *nāgas* in the animal realm: "the animal generation is indicated by the mention of *states of loss*; for the animal generation is a state of loss because it is removed from the happy destiny; but it is not an unhappy destiny because it allows the existence of royal nāgas (serpents), who are greatly honoured."[32] At least by the fifth century, in Sri Lankan commentarial literature *nāgas* are squarely located in the animal realm, although it is not as bad a birth as that of other animals; one might be fortunate enough to be a *nāgarāja* and thus have a very comfortable and rich life.

Within the Theravāda tradition, that *nāgas* might be considered animals and not just animal-like is significant on many levels. Animals are sentient beings, viable agents in the ever-operative, world-ordering karmic drama; they are able to be saved by a good-intentioned bodhisatta or, in fact, *be* that bodhisatta. But animals are not humans and can therefore be used in allegorical ways in the literature. *Nāgas* benefit from a familiarity factor: people in early India and Sri Lanka regularly saw snakes, so it is no wonder that snakes loomed large in the literary imagination. The *nāga* is envisioned to be a sort of supersnake, with all the attributes of common snakes plus superpowers such as the ability to shape-shift and to kill by a mere glance or puff of poison breath. There may be some basis in nature (natural snakes) for the particular powers a *nāga* is assumed to hold. For instance, watching a snake glide effortlessly across the ground, disappearing through small cracks in the earth, one might be inclined to imagine some shape-shifting capacity as well as a subterranean home (*nāgaloka*). Likewise, snakebites can be poisonous, so it is easy to imagine why a *nāga*'s breath would be considered particularly virulent.

On a cosmic scale, it is good that classifying nonnatural animals is so difficult because it reminds humans that categories are permeable even within their lifetime (one's neighbor might be a *nāga*), let alone through the course of several lifetimes. The relationship between humans and animals becomes more significant when viewed from a karmic, *longue durée* perspective.[33] An animal is never simply just an animal; an animal might have been one's mother in a past incarnation—what Christopher Chapple has referred to as "an ever-changing game of cosmic musical chairs."[34] The *nāga*, therefore, has a particular valence as a "ruminative trigger" for compassion because one's own mother, daughter, father, or son or even oneself could have been a *nāga* in a past life.

Thinking about how other characters within the stories view animals, especially the *nāgas*, may help to define the nature of the *nāga* for interpreters outside the text. Chapple writes that "animals in the *Jātaka* tales are seen not so much as animals but as potential humans or as animals that can teach humans a lesson."[35] We must also consider the added dimension that the "main animal" in the *Bhūridatta Jātaka* is none other than the bodhisatta himself, the ultimate teacher, and that he is in fact the narrator of the story as well. Philip Kapleau makes an excellent point about the underlying karmic system when he says that "the Buddha himself, narrator of these tales, regarded his own animal incarnations as no less meaningful than his human ones."[36] This sentiment directly problematizes the widely held perception ingrained in the karma system that an animal birth is to be detested. It is true that Bhūridatta (as well as other *nāgas* throughout the *Jātakas*) strives to overcome his animal nature, observing rigorous practices to cultivate merit for a better rebirth, yet the Buddha, recalling his past lives, does so with respect for this station of birth.

In the *Mahāvaṃsa*, the first chapter is concerned less with a physical depiction of the *nāgas* and more with their actions vis-à-vis the visiting Buddha. They are ontologically different than the *yakkhas*, which is clear from the fact that they are able to be converted by the Buddha. In later chapters of the *Mahāvaṃsa*, to which we turn in the next chapter, they are seen living in an underground palace; they can curl at the base of Mount Meru (which means they are immense and snakelike); and they have particularly long bodies. Considering that the first chapter might have been culled from sources different from those for the later chapters may explain the various representations of the *nāgas*. But we may also argue that these differing portrayals were intentional, keeping the reader in the imaginative mode and the *nāgas* salient, malleable characters to work (think) with in the narrative.

DeCaroli writes, "The difficulty of the authors in finding a consistent framework within which to locate these spirit-deities is a testament to the mercurial and often contradictory natures of these illusive beings."[37] *Nāgas*, though, are always *nāgas* in form and function, even when they are shape-shifting; serpent beings thus seem to be of a different sort of being than the *yakkhas*, *guhyakas* (attendants of Kubera, deity of wealth), *gandhabbas* (typically flying musician deities), and so on, who do not have a more stable, recognizable ontological status, stylized depiction, or naturalistic animal connection. *Nāgas* even have their own articulated *nāgaloka*, with its capital Poṭala. Of course, they are variously represented as fully snake, partially snake, or even an entirely other sort of being altogether when in their shape-shifting modes—for example, Bhūridatta's sister Accimukhī, who appears as a frog—but as a default status they are always serpentine.

At the heart of the nature of the *nāga* is its liminality. The *nāga* seems to be neither entirely human nor entirely snake nor entirely god, but some sort of being that transcends earthly categories, even emic Pāli categories. Throughout Indic literature, we frequently see a mysterious visitor being asked, "Are you a *nāga*?" This mystique gives the *nāga* a peculiar sort of power. Heinrich Zimmer notes that for South Indian dynasties, to have a *nāga* or *nāgini* in one's family tree "gives one a background." Indeed, several notable Indic dynasties, in particular southern ones, trace their lineage back to a *nāga* or *nāgini*.[38]

In a broad, cursory survey of Pāli sources, we see *nāgas* as shape-shifters, transforming themselves into whatever form is most appropriate to their circumstances. For example, the *nāga* Mucalinda transforms into a giant snake who is able to wrap his coils seven times around Gotama as he meditates under the Mucalinda tree.[39] In canonical and extracanonical stories, *nāgas* classically change into Brahmin youths to be able to approach the Buddha or be ordained into the *saṅgha* so they can hear the *dhamma* being preached. Their serpentine nature is inevitably revealed, and they are ridiculed and punished for their deception (or perhaps just for being snakes).

In the plastic arts, *nāgas* are treated with a range of representations, from the fully serpentine Mucalinda to completely anthropomorphized *nāgarājas*, such as those depicted at Amarāvatī. They are shown attending relic enshrinement ceremonies with their wives and are identifiable as *nāgas* only by the stylized, turbanlike headdresses they wear, which feature a frontal, cobra-hood-like protuberance, indicating the *nāga*'s polycephalous nature. In both the *Jātaka* and *Mahāvaṃsa* accounts, although it is clear that *nāgas* are figures in the stories, the actual physical form they take is unclear. In the first chapter of the *Mahāvaṃsa*, the status of *nāgas* as a group seems more salient than the exact type of body they may possess. No references in the first chapter indicate any particular interest on the part of the author-compiler as to what physical form the *nāgas* take. However, as we will see in chapter 4, *nāgas* are decidedly serpentine when in the *nāgaloka* in the *Mahāvaṃsa*'s later chapters.

In contrast, the *Jātakas* are filled with stories of the *nāgas*' shape-shifting powers. We see much shape-shifting in the *Bhūridatta Jātaka* alone, which for me begs the question of what is the default status or resting nature of the *nāgas* when they are not in disguise. Interestingly, references to appendages (arms and trunks) abound when the *nāgas* are situated in the *nāgaloka*. For example, Bhūridatta's *nagīnī* wives flail their arms in distress when he is discovered missing in the human realm.[40]

Nāgarājas typically take one of two primary forms, one fully snake and the other anthropomorphic, so regal in countenance and accoutrements that this form is compared to the god Sakka. *Nāgas* take a human form frequently, and they seem to live quite comfortably with it. The emphasis that Buddhist texts place on the act of taking a human form suggests that the default form of a *nāga* is, in fact, that of a snake. For example, when the *nāgarāja* Dhatarāṭṭha wants to fool his bride Samuddajā (who, remember, is the daughter of a human prince and a *nagīnī* and later is Bhūridatta's mother) into believing she is in the world of men, not the *nāga* realm, he orders by official proclamation that all inhabitants must not reveal their snake form to her.[41] All residents of the *nāgaloka* hide their "true form" in this elaborate scheme. Later, one of Samuddajā's own children (Bhūridatta's brother Ariṭṭha) decides while nursing from her[42] to reveal his true *nāga* body to her by letting his long tail hit her foot. Rudely awakened from her breastfeeding, she is so shocked she pierces his eye with her fingernail.[43] Bhūridatta chooses between a regally adorned princely body worthy of Sakka and a simple (albeit impressive) cobra body. He assumes the form of a snake (literally, "a body consisting of head and tail only") resting on top of an anthill in a natural way, as a "real" snake would, in order to observe his fast in the human realm, saying, "Let who will take my skin or muscles or bones or blood."[44] He assumes this form knowing full well that he may fall prey to humans, but this possibility is no deterrence because any abuse he suffers in his ascetic practice might further him on his goal. And his sister takes the form of a frog to hide in another brother's hair when he takes the form of an ascetic Brahmin man.

In several Indic texts, we see the perennial tension between the *garuḍa*, an eaglelike bird, and the *nāga*, its main source of food. In the *Bhūridatta Jātaka*, the story of a *nāga* whisked away for food dangling from the *garuḍa*'s talons makes a psychological and physical imprint on the landscape of men. As the *garuḍa* rests in a banyan tree, holding his prey after a successful hunt, the *nāga* wraps its tail around the tree. When the *garuḍa* flies off, the *nāga* pulls the tree right out of the ground. The ascetic Brahmin recluse living at the ashram where this happens uses it as an opportunity to discuss karma (the *nāga*, he says, accrued no negative karma because he did not intend to uproot the mammoth tree).[45] What we can ascertain from this story is that the *nāga* in fact does have a snake body.

When Alambāyana beats Bhūridatta into submission, we see that the latter is most certainly in a snake form and that in this form he is mortal. Alambāyana holds the snake upside down by the tail and forces him to vomit; he crushes the snake's bones and rolls him into a basket to carry him.[46] And then, of course, Bhūridatta is forced to perform as a snake at the snake charmer's will. Even if Bhūridatta is so assiduously following the precepts, once night is over (marking the end of the fasting period, when he usually turns into a princely figure for his return to the *nāgaloka*), why doesn't he escape? He can effortlessly turn into any number of beings, and it seems that *nāgas*, like the jewels they covet, can slip readily into the earth. Yet Bhūridatta stays in his snake form to suffer under his oppressive and selfish master, and in doing so he presents the reader with a moral character so assiduous in his right practice that the reader is compelled to amplify his or her own understanding of morality. Charles Hallisey and Anne Hansen write about the use of animal characters in moral narratives: "Nor do animals in the *Jātaka*s exhibit what we would take to be their biological instincts: moral snakes in the *Jātaka*s do not bite. . . . [T]he use of animal stories among Buddhists appears to be a sophisticated imaginative practice, one which is a creative response to the social patterns that Buddhists shared with their non-Buddhist neighbors."[47]

Just as Bhūridatta's expedient choice to submit to his tormenter suggests his own "creative response" within the text, so the inclusion of morally endowed *nāga*-agents in the texts indicate the Buddhist writers' imaginative response to an expanded vision of the world and history. Considering why the Buddha might have taken a *nāga* birth engages the reader in worklike ways. Certainly, he was able to prime himself for buddhahood by taking this birth. But outside the text, for the reader, that the Buddha himself was born in the lowest of the low forms to best cultivate *sīla* (morality) becomes a lesson for deep reflection. The reader must ask, If Bhūridatta, handicapped by a snake birth, could act with such moral sophistication, how much more so should I be able to, blessed as I am with a human birth?

THE *NĀGAS*' SOTERIOLOGICAL APTITUDE

Closely related to the *nāga*s' ontological status is their soteriological aptitude. The idea of soteriological aptitude relates to the operative ethics within the stories—namely, how the *nāga*s' snake-beingness affects the way they live their current lives and how it influences their decisions for the next life. The ethics operate within the story as motivation for and explanation of characters' behaviors and thoughts. The ethical dilemmas negotiated within the text produce related ethical implications for the reader-hearer outside the text as the *nāga*s draw the reader-hearer into a participatory relationship with the story and the agents of the text itself.

That there is tension regarding the *nāga*s' soteriological aptitude is evident in both the *Bhūridatta Jātaka* and the *Mahāvaṃsa*. We must remember that in the *Jātaka*, it is the Buddha in his former life who *is* the *nāga*, making the level of soteriological aptitude abundantly clear—a *nāga* can aspire to become and actually become the Buddha! In the *Mahāvaṃsa*, too, the

Buddha himself legitimates the *nāgas*' soteriological potential: they are brought into the *saṅgha* as the first converts, and the Buddha explicitly accepts alms from them, initiating the reciprocity that leads to a better birth. And yet *nāgas* are ill prepared to reach enlightenment in their current state of existence. They, like the *yakkhas*, are bodhi challenged.[48]

However, the *nāgas* (liminal characters that they are) are also considered to be able to deal with sensitive, deep material that even humans might not be ready or able to deal with.[49] In the *Bhūridatta Jātaka*, personal cultivation of morality (*sīla*) motivates Bhūridatta to pursue a better rebirth. Bhūridatta is so set on attaining a better rebirth that he does not defend himself when the snake charmer challenges him. He does not try to escape, either, choosing instead to submit to another's will so as not to accrue undue *pāpa* (demerit or negative karmic value) that would jeopardize his plans for a better rebirth. He even refuses to allow himself to feel anger toward his friend who has betrayed his confidence by leading the snake charmer to Bhūridatta's anthill: "if I were angry at him for his treachery, my moral character would be injured. Now my first of all duties is to keep the fast-day in its four periods—that must remain inviolate; so whether Alambāyana cut me to pieces or cook me or fix me on a spit, I must at all events not be angry with him."[50] Even as Alambāyana poisons him with herbs and beats him up, Bhūridatta keeps his sights fixed beyond his current birth: "The pure-natured *Nāga* king did not allow himself to feel any anger through fear of violating the moral precepts, and though he opened his eyes did not open them to the full."[51] Opening his eyes fully could be disastrous; the gaze of a *nāga* could be deadly, and Bhūridatta is intent on keeping his precept of doing no harm. Although Bhūridatta could do something in his defense, he chooses not to. This exercise of agency indicates his eventual soteriological aptitude in spite of his present low birth and low nature. By seeking to actively follow the precept of nonharm, Bhūridatta assures himself a future that will be closer to the Buddha and the *dhamma*.

Even if *nāgas* follow the precepts and are moral exemplars, the tradition is explicit that they are incapable of reaching enlightenment in their corrupt birth station. One must be human to aspire to enlightenment. In some Pāli sources, the *nāgas* are not in fact classed specifically as animals; the parameters of their classification are somewhat malleable, especially in the *Mahāvaṃsa* and *Bhūridatta Jātaka*, as we have seen. Their ontological status seems less important than their fervent expression of agency and their self-engineered soteriological transformation from unworthy to worthy, but they must wrestle with their *nāga* status nonetheless. Continually stressed is the depravity of *nāga* status, which is so powerfully felt by particularly morally striving *nāgas* that they yearn for proximity to the Buddha or at least for a human birth, where actions may lead to a better rebirth. A reader, then, encounters the *nāga* as a particularly provocative character, inciting him or her to be imaginative or even grateful for his or her good fortune not to have been born with the same soteriological handicap. If even one so low as a *nāga* such as Bhūridatta can strive for the perfection of morality, how much more should I, born human, do the same?

THE *NĀGAS*' MORAL DIDACTICISM

The *nāgas*' murky ontological status and limited soteriological aptitude within Pāli narrative literature provokes the reader's ability to be imaginative and bolsters the text's ability to effect powerful changes in the reader. These stories are told to elicit certain effects. The "plan" announced by the proem of the *Mahāvaṃsa* is enacted through the emotionally provocative narrative about the *nāgas*. The trope of the *nāga* works on the reader-hearer didactically as well as emotionally to elicit emotions such as fear, gratitude, and even pity. The reader's empathy is key for the story to engender the transformative effect. About the creative, imaginative aspect of empathy, Hallisey and Hansen write:

> As is probably well known, both experientially and theoretically, to all readers, through narrative we are able to imagine ourselves in the place of another. It might also be said that when, in reading, we leave aside our own social location, with its constitutive cares and perspectives, and enter imaginatively into the experience of a character in a narrative, we cultivate capabilities that are necessary to all moral agency. Since it is the case that "when people think about other people, they think about them in a certain way, as having thoughts, plans, ambitions, and knowledge like themselves" . . . it is equally important that they also cultivate a sub-ethical capacity to recognize that the "thoughts, plans, ambitions and knowledge" of others are also quite different from their own. As Lynn Tirrell has said in her essay "Storytelling and Moral Agency," "the essence of morality is a 'going out of our nature' or a lack of self-centeredness that is common to nearly all views of morality," and the sub-ethical conditions for this other-directedness are generated in narrative.[52]

In other words, *nāga* stories are crucial fields for the emotional and moral development of the characters within the *Mahāvaṃsa* and *Bhūridatta Jātaka* as well as for the audience outside the text. The hope, then, is that the reader-hearer will be able to carry the heightened sensitivity she has learned through engaging with the *nāgas* in texts to her own situation in the human community. Hallisey and Hansen suggest that the incongruity of the world inside the text with the world actually inhabited by the reader-hearer is no detraction from the stories' imaginative function and effect: "The comparison with Dr. Doolittle, although misleading in terms of the content of many *Jātaka* stories, does suggest that their significance lies in their ability to enable us to appreciate the ethical significance of our coexistence with other humans, even as they portray a world that is quite dissimilar to our ordinary experience. More particularly, the *Jātakas* may be understood as acts of social imagination, playing a role analogous to the role of utopia and ideology in the modern West."[53] The *Mahāvaṃsa* envisions a world that does not look like the fifth-century textual community's world. But this disconnect serves to heighten, rather than obviate, the fostering of "acts of social imagination."

Why might the author-compiler of the *Mahāvaṃsa* have employed the narrative trope of the *nāga*? In a text that ostensibly catalogs the history of the island from the initial visits of the legitimating Buddha to the reign of Mahāsena, beginning chapter I with the *nāgas* may be a move to suggest that this text is more than mere chronology. The *Mahāvaṃsa*'s author-compiler knew that the text's audience would be familiar with the *nāgas*' range of behaviors and aptitudes, which suggests that he believed that the ideals and intentions spelled out in the proem—to produce *saṃvega* and *pāsada* in the readers—could be supported through the use of this narrative trope.

As indicated in the historical survey in chapter 1, different social strata were clearly divided and yet mutually dependent in the world that spawned the *Mahāvaṃsa*. The textual community of the *Mahāvaṃsa* likely depended on royal patronage. In that light, stories about animals, who are removed from the human hierarchical schema, are especially significant for the audience, whether a monk, layperson, or the king himself: "Using animals as ethical exemplars," state Hallisey and Hansen, "provides a way of discussing generic moral virtues—gratitude, generosity, loyalty—without any misleading references to specific social locations. That is, the use of a human exemplar would inevitably run the risk of obscuring the proper perception of moral action, and of the causes and effects of that action, because there would be the possibility that a reader or listener would interpret that action within the local social framework."[54] As we have seen, the *nāgas*' ontological status as beings of nonhuman birth does not diminish their soteriological aptitude, consisting of an intense desire to be near the Buddha, his relics, and his *dhamma*. It is clear that this status does not diminish the *nāgas*' moral didacticism either.

Evidence of this claim can be seen in tales of the *nāgas*' intense desire to join the *saṅgha*. In some such tales, the *nāgas* go undercover, assuming human form, even though their inclusion in the *saṅgha* is prohibited in the *Vinaya*. The *Vinaya* story of the *nāga* who fools the *saṅgha* in order to have access to the *dhamma* is frequently retold. A *nāga*, ashamed of his *nāga* status, wants to gain (or regain) human status. The sight of renunciants leading chaste lives and practicing the *dhamma* inspires him. He takes the form of a Brahmin youth, asks to be initiated into the *saṅgha*, and is eventually ordained. One morning his roommate wakes up early to practice walking meditation outside of the cell. The *nāga* feels secure that his roommate is gone, and so, when he falls back asleep, he reveals his true, natural, default *nāga* form. The roommate, of course, returns to find snake coils pouring out of the cell. His screaming wakes the *nāga*, who resumes his human form and then has to explain his motivations to the community of monks. The monks bring the case to the Buddha, who proclaims that *nāgas* cannot advance by spiritually practicing the *dhamma* and *vinaya* (the monastic rules themselves) but that they can observe ritual fasting and the Uposatha (special observances on quarter days of the lunar calendar) to secure a better rebirth. The Buddha forbids the ordaining of animals, even stating that if one is ordained by accident, he should be expelled.[55]

This story shows that although the paths toward spiritual attainment available to humans are not open to *nāgas*, *nāgas* ultimately do have access to a path, albeit a longer one. This story is part of the *Vinaya* and thus anticipates a monastic audience. In fact, it is located at the very outset of the *Vinaya*, at the threshold to the rest of the text.[56] A reader must practically enter the text through the *nāga* story, just as a reader of the *Mahāvaṃsa* does. This is also a significant story with ongoing practical effects for the monks; in the *upasampadā* ceremony, when novices undergo higher ordination, even today the simple question is asked whether the monk-to-be is in fact a *nāga* or not.[57] DeCaroli says that this practice is "a good case of a monastic rule based on the acceptance of spirit-deities as a reality."[58] I would add that underlying this reality is the urge to be in proximity to the Buddha and the teachings and that a monastic reader might be inclined to feel a sense of gratitude that he finds himself fully human and thus capable of pursuing the Buddhist path. As we saw in chapters 1 and 2, the more a reader-hearer is made to feel special in the text, privileged to be among the "good people" to whom the text is directed, the more compelled he or she is to change behaviors and become a better monk.

Nāgas are interesting to a human audience and useful as teaching devices because of their human characteristics. The *nāgas* we encounter in Pāli texts sometimes appear in human forms, but even when they take on the commonplace physical characteristics of snakes, they still talk, act, and think very much like humans. *Nāgas* share many human qualities, such as the desire to be close to the Buddha for moral edification as well as the less-desirable inclinations toward covetousness and the tendency to cling. In this way, the human audience can sympathize with the *nāgas*. For example, a reader of the *Bhūridatta Jātaka* sympathizes with the beaten *nāga* Bhūridatta rather than with any of the human characters in the story. This arousal of sympathy might be what Hallisey and Hansen refer to as a "sophisticated imaginative practice," a means by which the hearer-reader is transformed through a mental experience by the text's otherwise whimsical material. The emotion resulting from the arousal of sympathy is real, felt, and able to be acted upon by the audience, just like the *saṃvega* and *pasāda* aroused through a reading of the *Mahāvaṃsa*.

In the end, however, the *nāga* is not human, and the emotional crescendo of both of these stories depends on this fact. *Nāgas* cannot, in their current form of existence, pursue the most direct path toward buddhahood—entering the *saṅgha*—but instead must resort to other, more indirect means such as practicing the five precepts diligently, fasting, and undertaking the triple refuge in order to aspire to a better birth in the next life. The *nāga* is an altogether different character who desperately wants to pursue the righteous life but who is limited by his birth. The "sophisticated imaginative practice" of empathizing with the distinctly "other" *nāga* may thus result in a sense of urgency regarding one's own practice and moral conviction. The relationship of the human audience to the *nāga*, then, is multivalent, predicated simultaneously on the sympathy generated when the human can recognize himself in the *nāga*'s emotions and exploits in the narratives as well as on the empathy aroused by the human's awareness of the *nāga*'s inherent otherness. Both responses to the *nāga* depend on an engaged and sophisticated imagination.

However, this facile bifurcation (readers are interested in *nāgas* because of similarities; readers are interested in *nāgas* because of differences) is problematized when it is understood through the Buddhist conception of time—the very understanding of time that is made central in the *Mahāvaṃsa* through its focus on the relics and chronicling history and in the *Jātakas* through the representation of the multitude of the Buddha's past lives. In Theravāda Buddhism, one does not have just a single life to live in order to perfect oneself. One follows a long and arduous path on one's way to buddhahood. This fact is reiterated at the very outset of the *Mahāvaṃsa*, right after the proem, in verses I.5–11, where we see the bodhisatta declaring his intentions to attain buddhahood in front of all twenty-four previous buddhas, all the while attaining each of the *pāramitās* through various births over a vast swath of time. The cultivation of ethics (here indicated by the bodhisatta's cultivation of the perfections) is thus coordinated with the passage of time. The passage of time is "textualized" in our two sources and is, in fact, the "ultimate referent."[59]

As we can see, even in the canonical material the *nāgas* are depicted as striving for better births and to participate in the Buddha's *dhamma*. The *nāgas* are not simply chthonic, indigenous animist elements that infiltrate the orthodoxy, nor are they beings of strictly local concern. Quite the opposite, *nāga* characters are literary devices employed by orthodox textual producers in even the most "closed" sections of the canon, such as the *Vinaya*. They occupy a position of prominence in the texts and in the very practices that literally make monks. Their slippery nature provides the storyteller with an ideal character through which questions of ethics and orthopraxy may be addressed.

But in the *Vinaya* story about the *nāga* who tries to be initiated into the *saṅgha* by disguising himself as a Brahmin, the deception is not what prevents the *nāga* from remaining a part of the *saṅgha*; it is his actual birth status that undermines his good intentions and the efficacy of his actions toward his goal. In the *Bhūridatta Jātaka*, we see that the virtuous snake undergoes humiliation and torture at the hands of his oppressor when he might be able to, on his own effort, escape with a simple change of shape. Why does the *nāga* willingly endure such degradation? Perhaps it is to live to the extreme of his vows, concentrating his effort instead on the accumulation of merit to escape the *nāga* status by remaining, in fact, a snake. What might this choice convey to a textual community? It may suggest that one needs to work with what one has or that the harder one has it in life, the sweeter the result. This lesson echoes the relationship between *saṃvega* and *pasāda* in the *Mahāvaṃsa*, where the resulting serene satisfaction is worth the stress of the initial agitation.

The point is that regardless of one's current birth status, it takes multiple lifetimes to morally develop oneself and to achieve the set of perfections requisite for all buddhas before one may actually become a buddha. Each lifetime, each particular birth, leads to the development of a particular *pāramī* (perfection). The fact that the bodhisatta takes *nāga* births on his way to becoming the Buddha Gotama precisely because the *nāga* status can teach him something or even develop something within him requisite to his successful achievement of buddhahood, has a major impact on the way we read the story of Bhūridatta.

In the *Jātaka*s, *nāga*s consistently aspire to better births in order to progress along the *dhamma* path. This portrayal is different than how they are portrayed in the *Mahāvaṃsa*, where they have immediate and personal access to the Buddha, so much so that when the *nāgarāja* Maṇiakkhika asks the Buddha to return to Sri Lanka for a third time, he does. Of course, in the *Jātaka*s a *nāga* is sometimes the Buddha himself in a pre-Buddha birth, which indicates a different sort of proximity to and affinity for *nāga*s.

◈ ◈ ◈

We began this foray into *nāga* nature with Lévi-Strauss's oft-cited dictum that "natural species . . . are good to think." In the Buddhist context, the *nāga* is a natural species, one that operates according to the natural laws of cause and effect (karma), just like humans, frogs, and gods. I believe that the reason for the *nāga*s' very existence in these texts is that they are "good to think" on several levels for their special functions vis-à-vis the Buddha's *dhamma* and his bodily relics. A *nāga* is the ultimate liminal creature in the Buddhist cosmos: inhabiting his own world and a frequent visitor of the humans' realm; full of magical power and yet soteriologically impotent; protector and thief of the Buddha's bodily relics; shapeshifter, poison-exhaler, gaze-killer, and agent in some of the raciest love and war stories inside and out of the Buddhist canon. The *nāga* simply *is* good to think, and in the next chapter we will see how effectively the author-compiler of the *Mahāvaṃsa* employs him to draw a certain kind of attention to what is important in his text.

The *nāga*s are, in short, an effective rhetorical tool, a narrative trope, *and* a ruminative trigger to provoke certain associations and inclinations through engaging the reader-hearer's imaginative process. Insofar as they are nonhuman, they evoke simultaneously a sense of pity (because they are soteriologically challenged by Buddhist standards) and a sense of urgency regarding the hearer-reader's own religious practice. The stories of the *nāgas* serve to underscore how privileged a status a human birth can be if one makes full use of it. The *nāgas* thus stimulate a sense of gratitude and responsibility for the practitioner. And even though I refuse to demote the *nāgas* to mere narrative hooks in these stories, they do draw a reader in. Because they are nonhuman and thus outside the bounds of social realities, the reader-hearer must perform an imaginative act to make relevant connections between the *nāgas* and his or her own situation. The text cultivates this moral and intellectual exercise.

Nāgas are both model worshippers and unworthy hoarders of relics, and in the next chapter I ask if these functions are necessarily contradictory or if there is room for subtle gradation in the ethical framework implied in the texts or if perhaps the role of the *nāga* evolves as the literature imagines new uses for these liminal characters. That the textual community for the *Mahāvaṃsa*, self-consciously choosing to write about the *nāgas* in the translocal language, Pāli, in this case was unaware of, overlooked, or purposely wrote over these snake-beings' soteriological ineptitude seems remarkably significant to me. We might challenge the dominant perception of *nāgas* as morally deficient and spiritually inept beings by using Pāli *vaṃsa* accounts of the relationships of *nāgas* with the relics of the Buddha. Are *nāgas*, as snake-beings, located outside the realm or scale of human morality? Are they to be understood allegorically? Are they stand-ins or models for human agency, easy to identify within narrative literature because as nonhumans they are removed from rigid social structures such as caste or ethnicity? Clearly, *nāgas* have been "good to think."

[4] *NĀGAS* AND RELICS

As LIMINAL characters, the betwixt and in-betweeners, *nāgas* mediate the dark and the light. They are characters precisely poised to be interpreters for the outside reader-hearer through the text. As we have seen, *nāgas* often act as attention getters within the text, functioning as red flags to denote important passages, but that is not all they do. In the previous chapter, we saw *nāgas* in close proximity with the living Buddha. In the case of Bhūridatta, this proximity is in fact a shared ontology of sorts and a window into the eventual soteriological aptitude of even the lowest born—the *nāga* Bhūridatta is in fact the bodhisatta developing himself on the way to buddhahood. The *nāgas* of the *Mahāvaṃsa*'s first chapter are also exceptionally close to the Buddha—it is their impending war that drives the Buddha to visit the island of Laṅkā, and the *nāgas* are depicted as the first and the model converts on the island he determines to be ideal for his *sāsana*. In both cases, we see the Buddha imagined as living and active in a distant past and the *nāgas* imagined as naturally included in the same world the Buddha inhabits.

In Buddhist literature, *nāgas* are considered to have a very special bond with the relics of the Buddha. Relic veneration distinguishes Buddhist practices from those of the other religious traditions in the Indic landscape, and so the common pan-Indic trope of the *nāga* shifts in meaning as it is used and interpreted by Buddhist texts.[1] In pan-Indic representations, the *nāga* is always depicted as a hoarder and protector of treasures, but in the Buddhist world the *nāgas* also protect, care for, and demonstrate proper veneration of the greatest treasure of all, the Buddha, both during his life and after his death and *parinibbāṇa* (final extinguishing) in the form of his relics. *Nāgas* reveal what is important, whether it is a treasure or the Buddha himself, to help orient devotees to the proper objects and mode of veneration.[2] *Nāgas* determine the value of relics; they locate and guard relics; they are simultaneously model worshippers and unworthy hoarders of relics; and they mark time and recall the Buddha. As a literary trope, then, *nāgas* demand that we pay attention to them if we are interested in the Buddha, dead or alive, whom they worship.

The textual community of the *Mahāvaṃsa* envisions the world without the living Buddha as being still saturated with his enduring presence. Within the text, relics are a viable technology developed by a community seeking continuous proximity to the Buddha, and the *nāgas* are utilized as particularly salient characters to facilitate an ongoing connection with the Buddha via those relics. There is a clear relationship developed in the *Mahāvaṃsa* between the *nāgas* and the relics of the departed (post-*parinibbāṇa*) Buddha, especially in the transportation of relics to the island and the procurement of relics to enliven *stūpas* as sites for human ritual interaction. Relics notably seem to need to pass through the possession of the *nāgas*, especially through their hands and stomachs, to arrive at their respective proper resting sites and to validate the *cetiyas* (sanctified places that provoke memory of the Buddha).

What is the place of relics in the tradition that created and sustained the *Mahāvaṃsa*? Relics bring legitimacy and a story that further supports the legitimacy, and they constitute a productive trigger for the remembrance of the Buddha. How does the position of the literary character of the *nāga* vis-à-vis the relics initiate a worklike dimension for the reader? And does the tripartite classification of relics operative in the early medieval textual community responsible for the *Dīpavaṃsa* and *Mahāvaṃsa* as articulated in the *Kalingabodhi Jātaka* have an impact?[3] Beginning with the typology of relics articulated by none other than the authenticating voice of the Buddha himself found in this *Jātaka* text, we might envision how the *Mahāvaṃsa*'s textual community understood these relics.

Particularly curious is the *nāgas*' relationships to *pāribhogika* relics (relics of use) in the *Mahāvaṃsa*. The arrival of the bodhi tree to the island of Laṅkā was a significant moment in enacting the transplantation of the *dhamma* circumscribed by the light imagery in *Mahāvaṃsa* I. The bodhi tree is designated the best type of relic to use while the Buddha is alive. It is also the first relic to be transported to the island for the newly converted king Devānaṃpiyatissa because the first three visits left incidental relics such as the jeweled throne and parasol that are functional only for ritual use by the *nāgas*.

But *nāgas* also maintain a relationship with the corporeal relics of the Buddha (*sarīrika*), as we will see in the Soṇuttara story (about a novice monk's procurement of the requisite bodily relics from the *nāgas* for enshrinement by King Duṭṭhagāmaṇī). This story is especially interesting if we consider the literary maneuvers of the *Mahāvaṃsa* in light of the simplicity of the *Dīpavaṃsa*. The Soṇuttara story is entirely absent in the *Dīpavaṃsa*, but in the *Mahāvaṃsa* it is prominent, the culmination of the entire "Duṭṭhagāmaṇī epic." It is significant that the supernaturally gifted novice Soṇuttara is himself classed a *nāga* (novice monk), so that the story presents a *nāga* who is sent to outwit a *nāga* who has been hoarding the relics. Here, all transactions (of value, of power) occur in liminal regions, regions of easy access for the two kinds of *nāgas*, both of whom are liminal characters. How does reading or encountering this narrative of the gift of relics predestined for Laṅkā (according to the deathbed prognostications of the Buddha himself, at least as formulated in the *saṅgha*'s version of the story) inspire a charged sense of confidence or faith and a layer of obligation in the reader-hearer that might effect a moral or ethical transformation?[4]

Finally, the sole example of *uddesika* relics (representation or image relics), appearing in a salient story embedded in the Asoka cycle (*Mahāvaṃsa* V), demands our attention. A *nāga* represents the image of the Buddha! King Asoka honors the image as if it were the Buddha himself, which provides an interpretive community the opportunity to explore issues of the Buddha's absence and presence as well as the role of the *nāga* in negotiating or mediating the chasm between the temporally distant Buddha and future generations of Buddhists.[5] This story also allows for an exploration of the Buddhist concept of time and space, as the *nāga* (here named Mahākāla, or "Great Time") has lived to see all four buddhas of this aeon. As conceived in Theravāda Buddhism, one is spatially and temporally removed from the intercession of a historical Buddha; *nāgas* function as intermediaries to bring images and relics forth for the ethically motivated connection to the Buddha. For the primed interpreter, encountering the *nāgas* in the narrative and being susceptible to the imaginative work provoked by that encounter result in a satisfying experience (*pasāda*) conducive to intensified religious practices such as relic veneration.

READING RELICS: RUMINATIVE RECEPTACLES TO ENSHRINE IMAGINATION

The term *vaṃsa* covers a rich and multivalent semantic field; it can mean everything from "history," "chronicle," and "lineage" to "node of bamboo" or even "hollow bone" or "spine."[6] This matrix of meanings expands yet further when we consider the historical situation of many interpreters (both of the term *vaṃsa* and of the *vaṃsa* genre of literature) and how the *vaṃsa* genre itself has accreted meaning for interpretive communities—the *Mahāvaṃsa* can be and has been read as a charter for the political aspirations of relatively contemporary Sinhalese Buddhists. It can also be read as a charter or, better, a manual that outlines proper royal duties and authority, and in this way it leads to confirm or provoke value judgments regarding good Buddhist kingship. It can be read as a chronicle of the establishment and subsequent *paramparā*, or teacher–student succession, of the monks who sustain and perpetuate the Buddhist tradition. Finally, it can be read, as I do in this chapter, as a text that provides the appropriate pedigree for the relics that are so central to ritual practices of the *Mahāvaṃsa* textual community and of the *saṅgha* to this day. The *Mahāvaṃsa* can be viewed as each of these things: a history of the island, a chronicle of kings or of the lineage of the *saṅgha*, and a substantiation of the development of the cult of relics. It chronicles the vicissitudes of power both inside the narrative—that of the *saṅgha* and the royalty, both "historical" and imagined—and outside the narrative—the latent, transformative power unleashed through the reading or hearing of the text itself.[7] What it does with the most conscientious agency and rhetorical force, however, is chronicle the full transplantation of the *dhamma* to the island through narratives of the enshrinement of relics.

The *Mahāvaṃsa* begins and ends with stories about *nāga*s and relics. It opens with the coming of the Buddha himself to the island, where he sets up a *pāribhogika* relic and designates the future sites for his relics. And it concludes with a full epic narrative of the great hero-king Duṭṭhagāmaṇī, his ceremonial building of the Mahāthūpa, and the enshrinement of the *sarīrika* relics within. By opening with a story of the Buddha himself, the *Mahāvaṃsa* locates its beginning in a particular time. But the maneuver from the Buddha's living presence to his relics allows the text to put forth an open-ended telos. The Buddha's presence in the future is both implied and perpetual because it is contained in his relics. A new aeon is ushered in and a new buddha is possible only when his relics are no longer worshipped. Relics are, in short, concrete purveyors of Buddhist eschatology. The main narrative arc of the *Mahāvaṃsa* is thus based on the establishment of the relics and the concomitant expectation that the proper sentiments conducive to proper behavior are stimulated by hearing their story.

Based on this orientation, a new reading of the *Mahāvaṃsa* is warranted. Other studies have relegated the relics to an ancillary role, suggesting that they validate, legitimate, or corroborate the authority of a ruler (secular king or head of the *saṅgha*). For example, in a provocative article Alice Greenwald treats the relic mounted on Duṭṭhagāmaṇī's spear as a legitimating device for his actions.[8] As the *Mahāvaṃsa* tells it, after killing many people on the battlefield, Duṭṭhagāmaṇī feels guilty and struggles with his worthiness; he is then educated by eight *arahants* ("worthy ones," enlightened beings) that he is indeed a good person.[9] But what if the focus of the Duṭṭhagāmaṇī epic in the *Mahāvaṃsa* is not, in fact, Duṭṭhagāmaṇī? What if it is not essentially a story about a great king but instead a story about the great relics that require a good and righteous king—and an encounter with the *nāgas*—to finally enshrine them? If we consider the *Mahāvaṃsa* primarily as a history of the coming of the relics and *sāsana* to the island (as claimed explicitly in the the *Dīpavaṃsa*'s proem) and as a vehicle for the cultivation of heightened emotional states for the reader-hearer (as claimed in the *Mahāvaṃsa*'s proem), how does our understanding of the compiler-author's rhetorical strategy change?

This trajectory complements my focus on the poetic aspects of the *Mahāvaṃsa* over and against but not supplanting the political, literal, or historical aspects. When King Devānaṃpiyatissa asks Mahinda how he can see the Buddha who has already passed into *parinibbāṇa*, Mahinda explains, "When you see the relics, you see the Conqueror."[10] In other words, to experience emotional satisfaction and the quelling of agitation, one must have imagination. It is a mental condition that an adept and experienced senior *thera* (monk) such as Mahinda comprehends; he has cultivated the imaginative process necessary for the worship of relics. Likewise, for the hearer-reader of the *Mahāvaṃsa* to become the good, virtuous person called forth by the text, he must cultivate the imaginative ability to equate the relics with the Buddha.

Having been primed first by the reading instructions contained in the proem, and having bolstered our reading technique through the examination of metaphor in the first chapter of the *Mahāvaṃsa*, we are ready to consider the relics in a new light. I would extend Mahinda's maxim in the following way: when we see the relics, we see the *nāgas*, and vice versa. The *nāgas* loom large in the lightened landscape of the *Mahāvaṃsa*. Why? Keeping in mind the type of reading called for in the proem, having honed our lenses to adjust for the glare of the light of the *dhamma*, we should perceive that the *nāgas* reveal something about the work of imagination in reading religious literature.

The fact that the *nāgas* are markers of important events and locations and even of value in the "life" of the relics has for the most part been overlooked in previous studies of Buddhist relics.[11] The *nāgas* are such familiar characters in Indic contexts that for many scholars they seem at best to recede into the background or are otherwise cast aside or treated as part of a generalized mythic topos rather than as significant agents in religious and historical texts. My project has been to pay attention to the poetic elements of the *Mahāvaṃsa* to see what aspects of the text provoke the desired ethical and emotional responses in the reader—in other words, to highlight the *nāgas* in the *vaṃsas*. As I have suggested in earlier chapters, we should consider the production of the *Dīpavaṃsa* and *Mahāvaṃsa* to be the constructive "world wishes" of their ambitious fourth- and fifth-century textual communities. The stories of the pedigreed relics are essential to these texts' respective arguments for and visions of Laṅkā's premier placement in the Buddhist world; the prominent position given to the stories of *nāgas* procuring and protecting said relics suggests that these fourth- and fifth-century monks were employing an established, powerful literary strategy.

NĀGAS' WORK ON RELICS

Relics and relic worship are critical in the living tradition instigated by these fourth- and fifth-century Mahāvihāra monks, and in the *vaṃsas* they produced, the *nāgas* can be seen as model agents regarding relics.[12] First, *nāgas* determine or attribute value to the relics. As Patrick Geary suggests of the Christian context in his book *Furta Sacra*,[13] the value of relics can be determined by their theft, and the relics in the *vaṃsas* are habitually being stolen by the *nāgas* (especially when they are en route to an enshrinement in Laṅkā), even if only temporarily. This motif is so important in the *vaṃsas* that I am inclined to think that a trip through the hands of the *nāgas* is requisite before a relic is of full use or value.[14] The bodhi tree, having been established by Ānanda (the Buddha's principal disciple) to be the most suitable substitute as a relic of use for the Buddha in his absence,[15] endures a baptism or consecration by *nāga*s as it is whisked away to the *nāgaloka*. For the textual community of the *Mahāvaṃsa*, by this function of value attribution the *nāga*s help to determine where the practical, ritual focus should be—on the relics.

Second, often simply (though uncritically) designated by scholars as "chthonic deities," *nāga*s also serve to ground, locate, and guard various kinds of relics.[16] In the *Dīpavaṃsa* and *Mahāvaṃsa*, *nāga*s guard relics of all types. Bodily relics, both bones (internal body parts, available only after the Buddha's bodily death) and hair and teeth ("dead" parts of the Buddha that might be given by the Buddha during his lifetime, such as the hair and nail relics given to Tapassu and Bhallika[17]), are important because they viscerally connect the present worshipper with the Buddha. Relics of use appear frequently in the *vaṃsa*s; for example, according to the first chapter of the *Mahāvaṃsa*, the Buddha gave to the *nāga*s the tree that was used as a parasol to shade him and the throne upon which he sat during his second visit to Laṅkā. *Nāga*s also oversee the places designated by the Buddha as *cetiya* in his second and third visits to the island[18] until they receive their intended bodily relics in the future. Relics are equipped with some sort of homing device, so that *nāga*s are led to those that have been abandoned or that are not receiving adequate human attention. *Nāga*s are thus naturally inclined to find and guard the relics of the Buddha, and it is a convenient trope in the Pāli narrative tradition that they consider any relics that have been buried in the ground or washed out to sea as their rightful property. This crucial behavior captured in narrative form provides the tradition with a perpetual source of relics for future installations. For instance, in the *Mahāvaṃsa*, a *doṇa* (measure) of Buddha *sarīrika* (bodily relics) is kept guarded in the *nāgaloka* until King Duṭṭhagāmaṇī needs them to be established in the land of Sri Lanka.[19] We see that a portion of relics kept in the hands of the *nāga*s allows for potential future enshrinements. That the *nāga*s always retain a reliable source of relics leads the audience of the *Mahāvaṃsa* to feel gratitude upon reading or hearing about them.

Third, *nāga*s model ideal veneration of the relics. As we saw in chapter 3, *nāga*s are of dubious soteriological aptitude; there is tension in the tradition regarding the relationship of relics to *nāga*s. *Nāga*s are simultaneously cast as ideal worshippers of the Buddha and as karmically incapable of receiving the full benefit of their veneration.[20] In the *Mahāvaṃsa* account of the novice monk Soṇuttara, who is sent to the *nāgaloka* to retrieve the relics kept there in order to install them for King Duṭṭhagāmaṇī in Sri Lanka, when the *nāgas* are outwitted by the novice and divested of their precious relics, they argue that they are actually better equipped than humans to lavishly worship the relics.[21] The *nāgas* (as nonhuman) are located outside the social framework, and yet they challenge that framework in an eminently Buddhist way (it was the Buddha, after all, who said that behavior, not one's birth station, determines virtue and potential).[22] The *nāgas* are depicted as ideal worshippers of the Buddha's relics, and yet they are thieves, in direct violation of one of the five fundamental moral precepts in Buddhism (namely, *adinnādāna*, or "taking what is not given"). Yet as we saw in the first chapter of the *Mahāvaṃsa*, the Buddha himself converts the *nāgas*, who undertake the precepts and who are thereby bound to honor them. They seem to provoke pity from the reader-hearer, perhaps even jealousy, insofar as they have immediate access to relics. *Nāgas* as portrayed in narrative literature are especially susceptible to the power of relics, and they are in the enviable position of having access to them in spite of their soteriological ineptitude. How much more urgent, then, is the focused attention and veneration from the reader outside the text, who is in a much better position to benefit from right behavior?

In the broader Theravāda Buddhist conception, relics function at the junction of ethics and time. Relics point back to the good deeds performed by the Buddha on behalf of his future community and engage the imagination of their audience in "re-presenting" the Buddha through remembrance of those good deeds. Relic veneration is a central act or, as Kevin Trainor succinctly calls it, a "technology of remembrance and representation."[23] In other words, relics simultaneously carry the presence of the Buddha into future times and to future receivers and remind practitioners of the Buddha's eventual complete absence. I would expand Trainor's definition of the function of relic veneration to include inspiring the worshipper and increasing his or her capacity to receive the *dhamma*, so the process of relic veneration fully activates the relic itself. The compilation, recitation, and reading of these *vaṃsas* and attention to the texts' focus on relics and their pedigrees become strategies first for reception and then for "remembrance and representation" of the Buddha. Relics literally cement the tradition: when enshrined (whether physically contained or textually located), a relic provides a focus for practice and a tangible site for connection with the Buddha.[24] In this secondary level of the "technology of remembrance and representation," narratives, with *nāgas* at their center, teach why the relics are important.

As discussed in chapter 2, *dhamma* is conceived metaphorically as light. This same light pervades the relics. As described in the Pāli *vaṃsas*, relics frequently exude the six-colored rays that the Buddha himself cast as a visible reflection of power. The relics typically generate and emanate these rays at the moment of enshrinement to inspire *saṃvega* and the feeling of awe and to instill *pasāda* in the hearts of humans, confirming the relics' potency and efficacy. *Nāga*s are likewise tempted and empowered by these rays. In short, it is through the relics that the *dhamma* extends its penetration into the world of human, ethical agents; the light of the *dhamma* attracts and energizes its viewers' imagination.

Relics are the means by which Buddhist time is measured. Relics transcend the usage of a single generation and serve to link a community of practice over time and hold the community together through focused practice. The *Mahāvaṃsa* marks the passage of time in its narrative; by reaching into and depicting the past, it creates a future for relic veneration. There could not have been relics until there was a Buddha, and there cannot be a new Buddha until all the relics of the recent Buddha have disappeared.[25] The textual tradition narrating the importance and effects of relic veneration further serves to link the community through time; the narrative itself links successive textual communities. The literary character of the *nāga* similarly spans generations, both in its relevance and utility within the narrative and in its function vis-à-vis the interpreter outside the text.

Just as the *sarīrika* (corporeal) and *pāribhogika* (usage) relics span vast swaths of time, *nāga*s have exceptionally long lives, which makes them particularly useful characters in narratives because they have been firsthand witnesses of the Buddha. They can even be called upon to become relics themselves; by taking on the image of the Buddha, *nāga*s in essence become the third classification of relics, *uddesika* (image), so that worshippers who are unable to view the countenance of the Buddha himself during his lifetime might still view a glimpse of his magnificent being. Later in this chapter, the image of the Buddha as assumed by a *nāga* is considered to be a manifestation of his very real presence and as a potent indication of the special nature of the *nāga*. This manifestation functions to bring the reader-hearer into proximity with the Buddha himself in spite of the passage of time. Of course, the process is dependent on the text character's imaginative ability to utilize the image manifested by the *nāga* and on the reader-hearer's imagination upon envisioning the image.

RELIC TYPOLOGY IN THE *MAHĀVAṂSA* AND THE *KALINGABODHI JĀTAKA*

Narratives allow the absent Buddha to be made present for a textual community that is temporally and spatially removed from his ministry. Part of the way this temporal and spatial distance is mediated is through the use of *adhiṭṭhāna*, determined resolutions and prophetic proclamations made in the authoritative voice of the Buddha himself. In the *Kalingabodhi Jātaka*, we find one such explicit lesson delivered by the Buddha to his disciple Ānanda that legitimates the practice of relic veneration. The *Kalingabodhi Jātaka*[26] thus perhaps represents an effort by the developing Buddhist community to attribute the popularity of relic veneration and typology to the prophetic, didactic, and authoritative vision of the Buddha himself.

Generally speaking, both the *Jātaka* tales and the *vaṃsa*s are about the presence and absence of the Buddha through time. They are also, to some degree, about the succession of presences of the Buddha in this world and how the aporia is negotiated through narrative as a technology of representing the absent Buddha.[27] The *Mahāvaṃsa* begins with the legitimating force of the Buddha's presence and then illustrates how strategies of access and proximity are developed through the technology of relic veneration, effecting the transfer of the light of the *dhamma* to the land of Laṅkā. In the same way, the *Jātaka*s deal with the legitimating presence of the Buddha in each frame tale, where the Buddha explicates a former life for the edification of the audience inside and outside the text, collapsing the distance between the teacher Buddha and his pupils, who span generations. The *Kalingabodhi Jātaka* establishes a paradigm that helps the Buddhist community negotiate the Buddha's absence from that community after his *parinibbāṇa*.

In the *Kalingabodhi Jātaka*'s frame story, Ānanda wishes to have a substitute for the Buddha so that when the Buddha is temporarily away from the Jetavana monastic complex, his disciples might have recourse to an appropriate receptacle for flower offerings and the like. The Buddha asks Ānanda how many kinds of *cetiya* there are, and Ānanda answers that there are three—namely (1) *sarīrika*, those of body; (2) *pāribhogika*, those of association; and (3) *uddesika*, those "prescribed."[28] The Buddha concludes that while he is still alive, only a bodhi tree is a fitting recipient of veneration in his temporary absence.[29]

The scenario reads like a trial run for the Buddha's imminent *parinibbāṇa*. In the relatively safe confines of this narrative, "absence" ostensibly refers to the times when the Buddha is away from the monastery, but we know that soon after his death, he will be completely and permanently away (*parinibbāṇa*). These strictures will hold and help guide the community in lieu of his live, physical, charismatic presence. Early on, then, we see the tradition seeking to establish through narrative an explanation of the different types of relics, with recourse to a tripartite divisional scheme. Practically speaking, once the Buddha is really gone, all three categories become viable objects of relic veneration. The threefold schema is significant in Sri Lanka, and it has penetrated into contemporary practice, as Richard Gombrich reveals in the following Pāli verse, which he says is "known by heart by most villagers and recited by the most pious laymen who take the Eight Precepts at the temple on *poya* days": "I worship always every shrine, standing in every place, the bodily relics, the great Bodhi tree, and every image of the Buddha."[30]

Relic veneration is still a key practice in the present day, just as it was for the textual community of the *Mahāvaṃsa*, where the establishment of the relics is at the core of the text. The focus on the relics in the *Mahāvaṃsa* could have been an argument for a nascent practice, but it could also have been a deliberate adoption of an orthodox veneer, a proclaimed assumption of practices without which attention and patronage could have shifted away from the Theravāda monastic practices. We cannot know exactly what practices were au courant for the textual community of the *Mahāvaṃsa*, but we can pay attention to the text's dominant focus on the relics of the Buddha as the concrete purveyors of Theravādin eschatology and the presence of the Buddha and as the catalyst for the emotional reception by the audience. Significantly, the *nāga*s closely relate to each of the three types of relics and thus warrant our attention.

NĀGAS AND *PĀRIBHOGIKA* RELICS

As we saw in chapter 2, when the Buddha returns to India, he leaves the bejeweled Veḷuriya throne behind in Laṅkā, the object that had in fact been the catalyst for the unrest that was the very reason for the Buddha's intervention and presence on the island. Previously an object of contestation between groups of *nāga*s, the throne is transformed by his use into a relic and established by the Buddha as an object of veneration, even though he used it for only a short time. The Buddha also leaves behind the parasol (tree) that his companion, the god Sumana,[31] had brought from India and that had been used to shade him during his stay in Laṅkā. The *Mahāvaṃsa* begins with both of these relics of use, illustrating the importance that relics exert on the religious practices established in the narrative for the textual community of the *Mahāvaṃsa*. This text is not a simple "history" of the Buddha's visits to the island but instead a provocative vision of the Buddha leaving behind concrete items to inspire and incite the emotional responses that would drive future communities' religious practices.[32]

The Veḷuriya throne, simultaneously representing both the Buddha's presence and absence, and the parasol-tree, presaging the centrality of the bodhi tree, are meant explicitly for the *nāga*s to worship after the Buddha has left the island. It is understood that after the Buddha leaves, the *nāga*s will remain behind to cultivate themselves by fostering good practices such as relic veneration. In a similar way, the narrative inspires an intellectual and moral connection, even obligation, to the practice of relic veneration and inspires the outside reader-hearer to behave like a good Buddhist. From the beginning, the *Mahāvaṃsa* establishes the centrality of relic veneration as a means to achieve *saṃvega* and *pasāda*, which in turn inspires veneration's continued practice.

The narrative then presses forward to a time where the people (humans) of Laṅkā have yet to be made aware of the Buddhist way of life. The good king Devānaṃpiyatissa of Laṅkā encounters the monk Mahinda, who has been sent forth at the behest of the *thera* Moggaliputta of India at the end of the Third Council to convert people in "the adjacent countries," the borderlands.[33] Just as *nāga*s occupy an inauspicious birth situation, so the borderlands are considered unlikely locations for the *dhamma* to thrive. Yet the king of Laṅkā is easily converted by the *thera*, and soon his entire retinue wants to be included in the movement. A narrative that dwells on the efficacy of the *dhamma* to take hold in such liminal beings and places surely underscores the power and persuasiveness of that *dhamma*.

The structure and pace of the narrative as well as its plot illustrate the expected transformation of the audience. If chapter I of the *Mahāvaṃsa* is an introductory lesson on how to be Buddhist—namely, to set up the paradigm of *saṃvega* and *pasāda* and the focus of worshippers on the relics left behind—chapter XIV illustrates the basic questions a community generates as it accepts the doctrine: practical questions such as what kinds of seats the *bhikkhus* might like, when food can be served to them, and so forth. One of the most vocal of the nascent Buddhists, Queen Anulā, Devānaṃpiyatissa's queen, would like to seek ordination. When the king asks Mahinda to ordain her, Mahinda explains that a *bhikkhunī*, or female monk (nun), must perform the ordination and that his own sister, Saṅghamittā, would be the one to come from India to oversee the ordination of the women of Laṅkā, thus establishing another layer of the transference of the *dhamma* to Laṅkā.

As recounted in *Mahāvaṃsa* XIX, *nāgas* were among the various classes of beings appointed by Asoka to watch over the bodhi tree prior to its voyage to Laṅkā.[34] A scion of the bodhi tree has a supernatural voyage to Laṅkā; the sea stands still for a surrounding circle with a radius of a *yojana* (about seven miles), while flowers and music envelop the tree. Even though some *nāgas* are among the beings charged with the protection of the tree during its travels, other *nāgas* in the ocean are overwhelmed with the desire to possess and worship it and seek to take it by magic.[35] As they are just about to steal it, the *bhikkhunī* Saṅghamittā (the daughter of Asoka and sister of Mahinda), by her own great supernatural powers, takes the form of a *garuḍa* to try to scare off the *nāgas*. Terrified, the *nāgas* first take the graft of the bodhi tree down to the *nāgaloka* to pay reverence to the relic for seven days and seven nights before returning it to Saṅghamittā.[36] This is a case of a relic of the Buddha actually being taken (by force) to the *nāgaloka* for worship before it becomes an active site for veneration in Laṅkā: "Trembling, the great snakes begged the great Theri [to stop scaring them]; thereupon they carried away the great Bodhi to the snake realm. Having worshipped it with manifold venerations and with the kingship of the *nāgas* for seven days, they brought it back to the ship and had it set up there. Thus, on the same day, the great Bodhi came here to Jambukola."[37] Significantly, one week is the proper amount of time for relic veneration and for establishing a new Buddha image by investing it with power and the story of the Buddha.[38] The week-long sojourn in the *nāgaloka* could similarly invest the bodhi tree graft. The layover at least confers upon it a good story, a pedigree of value. What happens to relics when in the *nāgas*' possession? Why is there a need for a cosmic layover or virtual baptism in the narrative? Even before this *pāribhogika* relic is established in Sri Lanka, it must first receive this special attention from the *nāgas*.

According to the *Kalingabodhi Jātaka*, the bodhi tree was the most fitting relic to venerate during the life of the Buddha. We can see that it has special importance after his death as well. Saṅghamittā is a liminal character of sorts (a woman, a *bhikkhunī*, a shapeshifter-*garuḍa*), presaging the other liminal figures we will meet in other relic-procurement stories (the novice Soṇuttara, who claims *sarīrika* relics from the *nāgas*, and *nāgas* with the *uddesika* relic of the Buddha). To get the relic to Laṅkā requires a trip over the ocean, a liminal territory (just as Soṇuttara travels through the earth and the *nāgas* "travel" through time). The pattern of retrieval is an important feature of the narrative, and it is repeated both internally (it happens more than once in a story) and externally (it happens in multiple stories in Pāli texts).

Even the stalling of the relic serves to heighten the suspense; in some ways, perhaps this interlude is included precisely to change the pace of the chronicle and add to the emotional effect on the reader-hearer. By being a member of the textual community that is sustained by the relic veneration narrated by the text, the reader-hearer knows the outcome of the *Mahāvaṃsa*'s suspenseful relic procurement stories even before they are told.[39] The story of the *nāgas* taking the bodhi tree to their abode attests to the value and temptation of the relics, and for the reader-hearer outside the text it instantiates a certain gratitude that the relics described therein are so readily accessible.

The first stories of the *Dīpavaṃsa* and *Mahāvaṃsa* establish the connection between the Buddha himself and the *nāgas*, a connection that hinges on relics. The *nāgas* use relics in their pursuit of a better Buddhist life (ideally for rebirth as a human). What is salient for us here is the idea that objects of the Buddha's use (throne, parasol, tree) become objects fit for use as relics to be venerated in order to stimulate and sustain the newly converted *nāgas*' religious practice. The *pāribhogika* relics are not only accessible to humans but are also used by the *nāgas*. In the story, then, having the *nāgas* so focused on the relics draws the reader-hearer's attention likewise to the centrality of the relics.

NĀGAS AND *SARĪRIKA* RELICS: THE STORY OF SOṆUTTARA

Although *pāribhogika* relics are a fitting focus for veneration because they connect to the Buddha's presence through his use of them, once a buddha has died, a new category of relics becomes available for division, dispersal, enshrinement, and veneration. In this section, I explore the relationship between the *nāgas* and the corporeal relics (*sarīrika*) of the Buddha through the development of the Soṇuttara story (the procurement of the requisite relics for enshrinement by Duṭṭhagāmaṇī) from its absence in the *Dīpavaṃsa* to its prominence in the *Mahāvaṃsa*. The *Dīpavaṃsa* does not include the Soṇuttara narrative and only briefly references King Duṭṭhagāmaṇi. The Duṭṭhagāmaṇi epic is very important to the *Mahāvaṃsa*, however, and the *nāgas* are instrumental in the dispersal and enshrinement of the Buddha's *sarīrika* relics at the story's culmination. This story cycle represents an explicit turn by the *Mahāvaṃsa* compiler to focus on different material and provides us with an opportunity to think about how this new material may function to engender the desired response of agitation and religious satisfaction in good people. And it is the *nāgas* who help facilitate this goal.

According to the *Mahāparinibbāṇa-sutta,* after the Buddha's corporeal relics were divided into eight portions after his cremation, the portion that was enshrined on the banks of the Ganges at Rāmagāma washed out to sea in a flood.[40] Anything that haphazardly finds its way into the sea becomes fair game for the poaching, hoarding ways of the *nāgas* who inhabit the water, and the relics come into their possession. This story serves the later relic-centered Sri Lankan tradition—ever concerned to preserve the impression of its status as preordained by the Buddha himself—in that it allows for a significant portion (one-eighth) of *sarīrika* relics to be brought to the island in the time of Duṭṭhagāmaṇī, two centuries before the Common Era.[41] This cache of corporeal relics is entrusted to the *nāgas*' guardianship.

The supernaturally gifted novice Soṇuttara is himself classed a *nāga*, as all novices are until they have undertaken full ordination. The story thus presents a *nāga* (novice) who is sent to outwit a *nāga* (supersnake), and all transactions (of value, of power) occur in liminal regions, regions easily accessed by both kinds of *nāgas*. How might reading or encountering this narrative of the gift of relics predestined for Laṅkā, according to the deathbed prognostications of the Buddha himself, effect a moral or ethical turn for the hearer? A focus on the impact on the audience, however, is not to argue explicitly against the more conventional reading of the Soṇuttara story as a model for the nascent state–*saṅgha* relationship in that the Mahāvihāra expresses its unique and ideal situation to procure the relics that fulfill the requirements of *stūpa* building.[42] That this story does not exist in the *Dīpavaṃsa* provides us with an opportunity to think about how it may function in the later *Mahāvaṃsa* as a critical means to engender a desired response, the text's poetic aim.

Relic theft is a tantalizing topic. Unlike in other religious traditions, such as the Roman Catholic, where relic theft is confined to the human realm and human agents, the Pāli *vaṃsas* maintain that thievery happens between worlds and is perpetrated primarily by nonhuman agents. What all of these traditions have in common, though, is that the perpetrators (here, the *nāgas*) may not be motivated by greed but rather by extreme piety and the desire to serve and worship the relics appropriately. Following Patrick Geary's ideas about relic theft in the Christian context,[43] I suggest that thievery points to the extreme value of the relics and even generates additional value. I argue that thievery also heightens the imaginative involvement the reader-hearer of the *Mahāvaṃsa* has with the story. For the textual community, much is at stake regarding the theft of relics. It is really no surprise to hear of the theft because the story is narrated expressly to attribute a pedigree, a *vaṃsa*, an authoritative link to the Buddha himself. In the case of Soṇuttara, stealing relics is an essential part of the establishment ritual, of the bringing of the relics to the new land of Sri Lanka. Passing through the hands, bellies, or coils of the *nāgas* seems a requisite layover before a relic can be activated in the landscape proper and enshrined for human veneration. Thievery occurs in liminal spaces, in the betwixt and between worlds; it happens as relics are in transmission from their original location to the island of Laṅkā; one might even say that relic theft happens during the in-between times as well.[44]

As the story goes, King Duṭṭhagāmaṇī prepares the preordained site for the Buddha's corporeal relics, the Mahāthūpa at Ruvanveli, with great pomp and circumstance. The *stūpa* is built, the ceremony is under way, and the crowds have gathered before anyone seeks to retrieve the one-eighth portion of the Buddha's corporeal relics that had been in "storage" in the *nāgaloka* for this very (legitimizing) occasion. The king depends on the specialized skills of the *saṅgha* to procure the essential ingredient to enliven his *stūpa*. The *nāgas* had grown quite attached to the relics in the intervening centuries, however, and are reluctant to part with their charge. The novice monk Soṇuttara, on account of his highly developed *iddhi* (meditative superpowers), is dispatched to recover the relics from the *nāgas*. He enters into meditative states conducive to the sort of intra-world travel he needs to do, and when he hears the music in the city indicating that the ceremony has begun, by means of his *iddhi* he enters the earth to reach the *nāgaloka* (*Mahāvaṃsa* XXXI.45).

After being greeted respectfully, Soṇuttara explains to the *nāgarāja* the purpose for his visit. The *nāgarāja* motions to his nephew Vāsuladatta, who takes the hint, swallows the relic casket, and hurries off to the base of Mount Meru, where he coils up in an immense circle.[45] In a desperate attempt to outwit the visitor, the *nāgas* behave in a most *nāga*-like way: one of them steals away with the treasure, here the relics of the Buddha, and lies at a mound, here none other than Mount Meru itself, the very center of the Buddhist universe, as if it were a safety zone. But Vāsuladatta is no ordinary snake; he creates various other regular snakes through his own superpowers (*mahiddhi*), the same type of special powers that Soṇuttara has. The image conjured is that of a snake pit, a seemingly safe place to hide a treasure, encircled as it is by treacherous snakes. Vāsuladatta's hiding act is far from discrete, however. It attracts the attention of many onlooker *nāgas* and *devas*, who approach the site, thinking, "We will witness the battle of both *nāgas*."[46]

Meanwhile, the *nāgarāja* explains to Soṇuttara that he has no relics. Soṇuttara responds by recounting the story (pedigree, *vaṃsa*) of the relics and explaining how they are destined to be enshrined in Laṅkā on that very day. The *nāgarāja* tries another tack: he points out the superiority of the gem-encrusted *cetiya* in the *nāgaloka*, contending that human worship is far less lavish and sumptuous than the veneration paid by the *nāgas* and that it would not do to move the relics from such a high place to such a low place.[47] This logical argument, that "we can provide better service than you can," following right upon Soṇuttara's recapitulation of the story of the relics, suggests that hearing Soṇuttara's account only further entrenches the *nāgarāja* in his proprietary position. Soṇuttara then argues with the *nāgarāja* over who is in a better position (soteriologically) to benefit from worshipping the relics and who can provide better veneration of them, veneration that is actually conducive to bearing out the Buddha's intentions that relics can be used to help shed *saṃsāra*, the cycle of birth, life, death. I consider the *nāgas*' debate with Soṇuttara a narrative device that engages the reader-hearer in the tension.[48] The reader-hearer, just like the multitude of *nāgas* and *devas*, is privy to a fundamental debate of worthiness, and reading this provocative passage prompts his or her imagination. For the fifth-century textual community, the winner of the debate is already known, and the feeling of gratitude toward Soṇuttara and the *saṅgha* of the past and even toward the wily *nāgas* who had to release the relics may set in.

True to his trickster nature, the *nāga* king tells Soṇuttara that he may have the relics if he can see them, thinking that they are well hidden and that the novice has no chance of finding them. But Soṇuttara uses his *iddhi*-empowered vision to detect the whereabouts of the hidden relics and then causes his arm to become very skinny so he is able to slip it down into the belly of Vāsuladatta to retrieve the relic casket. Soṇuttara shouts, "Stay, *nāga*!" (*tiṭṭha nāga*), and then returns successfully to the ceremony already taking place in Sri Lanka (*Mahāvaṃsa* XXI.66–68). While the *nāga* spectators lament the loss of the relics, the *devas* who had assembled there celebrate the victory of the "*nāga* among *bhikkhus*" (*bhikkhunāgassa*) (*Mahāvaṃsa* XXXI.72). Soṇuttara is a *nāga*, a novice, but he also behaves like a *nāga*, a snakelike being, by tricking the *nāgarāja* and his nephew, fashioning a snakelike arm to retrieve the relic casket, and moving between the *nāgaloka* and the world of humans above it.

In a sympathetic postscript to this story, the *nāgas* disregard Soṇuttara's command to stay behind and instead, grieving, complain to the *saṅgha* about the loss of their relics.[49] Out of compassion and in an illustration of true goodness and generosity, the *saṅgha* gives a few relics back to the *nāgas*, and the *nāgas* then bring treasures to Sri Lanka as offerings and thus participate in the enshrinement ceremony (*Mahāvaṃsa* XXXI.73–74).

In this story, the sacred space is already primed; the enshrinement ceremony is already under way before the relics arrive as final confirmation. The relics are venerated in various locations in the cosmos and by various entities (which is allowed by Buddhism's extensive cosmological formulation). The authenticity of the relic is proven by the fact that it was in the care of the *nāgas* and by the fact that the *nāgas* were extraordinarily reluctant to give it up. To accommodate the tradition's penchant for keeping a reserve portion of relics in the hands of the *nāgas* for possible future use, the narrative acquiesces to the *nāgas*' petition for some relics to be returned to the *nāgaloka*. Of course, in the story this gesture is seen to be an act of generosity and compassion on behalf of the *saṅgha*, not a selfish act to ensure the *saṅgha*'s future access to a store of relics.

The Soṇuttara story is nowhere included in the *Dīpavaṃsa*, so it illustrates the type of literary turn the *Mahāvaṃsa* compiler makes. The story of the procurement of the relics, with the exciting "battle" between the *nāgas*, is a particularly salient story that showcases the type of ethical lessons that arise from a good reading of the *Mahāvaṃsa*. According to the logic of this text, the procurement of the relics by Soṇuttara is absolutely not a theft, but a legitimate act, simply confirming the prognostications and actualizing the intentions of the Buddha himself.[50] Delivering the relics from the *nāgaloka* to Laṅkā is thus seen to be a legitimate act and draws the reader-hearer's imagination into a realization that the Buddha has done so much that even after his passing he affects the world. For the audience outside the text—the *Mahāvaṃsa*'s textual communities who might be looking right at Great Stūpa Ruvanveli—this story is included precisely so that it will engender *saṃvega* and *pasāda* in them.

NĀGAS AND AN *UDDESIKA* RELIC

There is a sole example of an *uddesika* relic (representation or image relic) within the *Mahāvaṃsa*. It is not an ordinary *uddesika* image, manufactured by human hands and sanctified by its likeness to the Buddha or its ability to stimulate the memory of or faith in the Buddha. Instead, in the *Mahāvaṃsa* account we find a particularly salient story embedded in the Asoka cycle of a *nāga* representing the image of the Buddha. Asoka honors the image as if it were the Buddha himself, which provides the opportunity to explore issues of absence and presence as well as the *nāga*'s role in negotiating or mediating the chasm between the temporally distant Buddha and future generations of Buddhists.

The story of the *uddesika* relic occurs in the midst of the account of the Third Buddhist Council in *Mahāvaṃsa* V, where we see Asoka's faith developing. Just before the story of the *nāga*, Asoka is depicted as increasing his contributions to the *saṅgha* in response to his developing faith.[51] Everything changes when he hears about the powerful *nāgarāja* Mahākāla, who has lived through the eras of the previous four Buddhas and therefore has seen each of them. Mahākāla is brought before King Asoka, who asks him to make manifest the image of the Buddha. The *nāgarāja* then "made by miracle the delightful form of the Buddha, endowed with the thirty-two major signs and blazing with the eighty minor attributes (of a Buddha), encircled by a fathom-long halo and shining with a garland of light beams."[52] The king's response after seeing him is *vimhaya* (astonishment) and *pasāda* (religious satisfaction)—the same emotional qualities that the reader-hearer is expected to experience upon hearing this particular story. Then Asoka exclaims, "By him [Mahākāla], this image is such like the form [of the Buddha], how much more so then the form of the Tathāgata [himself]!"[53] After his viewing of the *uddesika* relic (courtesy of the *nāgarāja*), Asoka is "increasingly struck by the emotion of joy."[54] The viewing lasts for seven days, where the great king of great power keeps the great festival named the Akkhipūja (Veneration by the Eyes).[55] Just as the *nāgas* commandeered the bodhi tree en route to Laṅkā and worshipped for seven days, here we see a *nāga* as the Buddha worshipped for seven days and nights. Providing an image that responds to the faithful Asoka's religious needs within the text, the *nāga* also thus offers the reader-hearer outside the text an image to provoke the right emotions.

◈ ◈ ◈

In historical narratives, *nāgas* are seen to be in relationship with the Buddha's relics. In the *Mahāvaṃsa*, *nāgas* are beings that inhabit their own subterranean world, the *nāgaloka*, but they also have significant interactions in the human world. As we saw in chapter 2, *nāgas* first interact with the Buddha himself in his postenlightenment visits to Sri Lanka described in *Mahāvaṃsa* I. After the Buddha's passing away, the *nāgas* maintain a relationship with him as they interact with his relics. Even though the texts portray *nāgas* as ideal, devoted servants and worshippers of the Buddha, due to their nonhuman ontological status they are soteriologically incapable of benefiting directly from their proximity to him and his relics. But this limitation does not seem to sway the *nāgas*' devotion, as depicted within the text, or affect their utility to the reader-hearer outside the text. *Nāgas* function in the texts as connective characters between the relics of the Buddha and the Sri Lankan landscape, connecting the audience with the Buddha as proximately as possible.

In the Sri Lankan Theravāda tradition underlying the *Mahāvaṃsa*'s textual community, sacred space is preordained; it is established by the Buddha in his pre-*parinibbāṇa* visits to the island. Relics serve in a confirming capacity rather than a sacralizing one and are brought into the landscape through the *nāgas*. Relics are brought to the island of Sri Lanka to provide viable outlets to the light of the *dhamma*. The *Mahāvaṃsa*, then, is ultimately about rendering the absent Buddha accessible. When we consider the centrality of the relics in the *vaṃsas*, we might further be able to destabilize the reified notion of the *dhammadīpa* as the "island of *dhamma*" (or "righteous isle" in Ananda W. P. Guruge's translation[56]), replete with nationalistic overtones. Applying our reading of *dīpa* as "lamp" and understanding that a lamp requires priming before it can receive the transferred light, we can understand the landscape of Laṅkā as having been made ready by the Buddha for his relics so that future communities might have access to his presence.

Corporeal and use relics are distributed and enshrined throughout the land to actualize the Buddha's predictions articulated in the *Mahāvaṃsa*'s initial chapter. The stories of their establishment via the *nāgas*' nascent Buddhist practice suggest that relics must make a prerequisite trip through the "hands" (bodies) of the *nāgas* to become charged and viable objects of veneration. And not only must the relics themselves pass through the "hands" of the *nāgas* to become charged, but the Buddha must interact with the *nāgas* to establish the future location for those relics, as we saw when the Buddha quelled the battle of the *nāgas*. The textual tradition thus develops a narrative strategy whereby the *nāgas* are hoarders and protectors of relics, safeguarding repositories to be used in the future to continue the tradition of Buddhism in Sri Lanka. Finally, *nāgas* can even assume the image of the Buddha to assuage the need of worshippers (that is, Asoka within the text as well as the fifth-century textual community outside it) to be in the presence of the Buddha, a presence that stimulates feelings of amazement and religious satisfaction.

Nāgas are conveyors, thieves, hoarders, guarders, and representers of relics, at once linking relics with the landscape and determining their value through their desire to acquire them. They are used to assist in the *vaṃsa*'s aim, to engender the intended effects that the reading of these stories should have for good people. *Nāgas* are thus more than a simple "narrative hook." Although they do engage the reader as interesting characters to develop, they also facilitate the text's practical aim—namely, to build a sense of a community around the shared emotional response of *saṃvega* and *pasāda*, felt during and after reading the text and experiencing the relics. The *nāgas* in the first chapter of the *Mahāvaṃsa* prime the reader in a visceral way for how to understand the *nāgas* later in the text. The readers-hearers are not inclined to revile the *nāgas*; rather, they are compassionate and empathetic, recognizing the advantages and concomitant responsibilities of their own superior soteriological location to these poor characters. These ethics are underscored in the Soṇuttara story when the narrative ensures that the *nāgas*, dejected over having lost their relics, do not return to the *nāgaloka* empty-handed.

The *nāgas* point to relics as sites capable of provoking intense emotion. This connection is viscerally captured by Vāsuladatta's and the *nāgarāja*'s angst when the relics are taken away. Relics are appropriate and potent vehicles for one's religiosity and one's patronage, time, and energy. In the text, then, the *nāgas* are model worshippers—thankful, confident, devoted, loyal, and emotional. They serve to indicate the potency of relic veneration for the reader/hearer outside the text as well. The effective worship of the relics provides them the means to escape the *nāga* birth, in some sense proving that veneration of relics is a powerful spiritual tool. *Nāgas* are literary characters employed to evoke pity and an emotional response from the imaginative and compassionate audience. And yet because some relics are left behind in their possession, and there is the possibility that long-lived *nāgas* may conjure the form of the Buddha for future viewing, the textual community is simultaneously thrust into a position of gratitude toward these otherwise pesky characters. As humans, we have a relationship with the *nāgas*, whom we rely on to get relics in the future and to show us the Buddha.

Considering the *nāgas*' dubious soteriological aptitude, discussed in chapter 3 and illustrated in the Soṇuttara story here, a reader-hearer must feel the text's imperative. If the *nāgas* are so unworthy and yet strive to be close to the relics and be dutiful worshippers, how much more so should the human reader-hearer, who is in the right place (soteriologically and geographically), strive to become the "good person" envisioned by the *Mahāvaṃsa*? As the *nāgas* of the first chapter of the *Mahāvaṃsa* illustrate the cultivation of the prerequisite emotions of *saṃvega* and *pasāda*, so the *nāgas* at the culmination of Duṭṭhagāmaṇī's enshrinement of the relics demonstrate the proper attitude of gratitude and the criticality of proximity to the Buddha's relics. These stories generate a palpable sense of urgency, an awareness and recognition that because the relics are accessible to the *Mahāvaṃsa*'s textual community, the reader-hearer should feel grateful toward Soṇuttara and toward the *nāgas* for accomplishing a task in the past for the continued benefit of Buddhists in the future.

The exemplary devotion paid by the *nāgas* to the Buddha during his life is not just matched but surpassed after the dispersal of his relics. Something shifts within the narrative when the focus of the *nāgas*' devotion transforms from being the live, walking, talking Buddha to being the transportable, compact (able to be held, swallowed, hoarded), highly desirable relics. This tension exists for humans as well, and we see that the initial division of the relics upon the Buddha's cremation, as told in the *Mahāparinibbāṇa-sutta*, becomes a time for looming competition among tribes of people all wanting the same thing, just as the *Mahāvaṃsa* opens with the *nāgas*' impending war. While the Buddha was alive, his ministry tended to emphasize unity, and his peripatetic wanderings served to spread his teachings far and wide, making them multilocated. Upon his death, a new paradox was engendered: although the Buddha can be dispersed through his relics, those relics must be enshrined and therefore fixed and located. So although it may seem that relics geographically amplify the Buddha's *dhamma*, in fact they peg it down to particular locations.[57] The *nāgas*' locative nature, chthonic or not, is significant to the relic tradition, especially as it is conceived and voiced by the fifth-century textual community of the *Mahāvaṃsa* in its claims of legitimacy and even primacy.

[5] HISTORICIZING (IN) THE PĀLI *DĪPAVAṂSA* AND *MAHĀVAṂSA*

As histories, the *vaṃsas* are explicitly concerned with linking the "good people" of the textual community to the Buddha through both narratives and the actual presence of relics. The Pāli *Mahāvaṃsa* is at once historical and literary—the former because it was written in a particular cultural and temporal moment about other events in the deep recesses of the collective imagination or inherited cultural memory of its community of production; the latter because it employs devices such as metaphor and plot development to tell that story to its audience. But the categories "history" and "the literary" are far from mutually exclusive; a rethinking of the Pāli *Mahāvaṃsa* reveals how very dependent on narrative and "the literary" the early Buddhist textual community in Sri Lanka was in formatting and arguing its own "history."[1]

Hayden White has extensively analyzed the structure and processes of history writing and examined how the rhetorical choices made by the historian in the presentation of his or her material prefigure the range of audience responses, much like the intentional fabrication concocted by the literary author.[2] Dominick LaCapra extends the discussion of the intentionally fictive dimension of history writing and interpretation to claim that in narrative "worklike" elements engage the audience in imaginative and interpretive acts that move beyond mere "documentary" representations of the past.[3] Paul Ricoeur, too, has extensively examined the aesthetic and ethical effects of narrative, whether classed as historical or fictive in nature.[4]

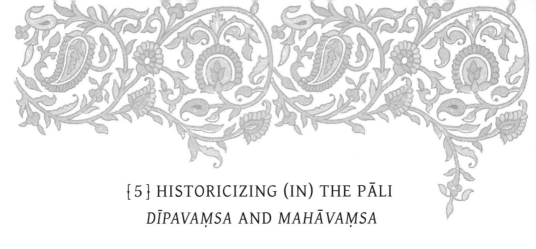

In her argument for renewed appreciation for a vibrant and productive Buddhist literary culture in medieval Tamil areas, Anne Monius argues that certain "literary works" are agents of religious community formation and imagination: "Ornate poetic narrative, even poetic theory itself, draws attention to various kinds of cultural practices in the absence of archaeological or inscriptional evidence and offers fresh insight into the long and complex historical processes of debate, selection, transmission, and recreation that constitute religious community."[5] This assertion may appear at first the converse of Gregory Schopen's recommendation for the Buddhologist (and, more broadly, the historian of religion) to eschew the "Protestant presuppositions" inherent in the study of religious communities, whereby the text is privileged over concrete sources of historical information that can be excavated, literally, through archaeology and epigraphy.[6] But in fact both Monius and Schopen call for a new way of reading those textual, "historical" sources. In the absence of definitive sources from material culture to employ as a corrective to the overly textual orientation of the historian of religion, and in the face of the continued (or new) emphasis on the centrality of the *Mahāvaṃsa* in Sri Lankan Theravāda Buddhism, rethinking Buddhist histories such as the Pāli *Mahāvaṃsa* in explicitly literary terms becomes a fruitful corrective to the common "documenting history" or "establishing a political charter" readings that are more typically performed. My method for reading does not undermine the utility of prior readings but rather extends the possible interpretations of the *Mahāvaṃsa* to include the kind of personally and communally transformative literature that creates and sustains a religious, textual community.

Reading the *Mahāvaṃsa* as a literary work rather than exclusively as a historical source requires us to change our expectations regarding the value of the text or the possible effect it has had or will have. We simply cannot be sure of the veracity or objectivity of any of the claims in the *Mahāvaṃsa* when it is read as a source for social history. We have no concrete evidence outside of our texts, except for brief epigraphical donative inscriptions, to confirm or corroborate the timeline of events—the "history"—presented therein.[7] Thus, we should approach these sources with the hermeneutic of suspicion;[8] these texts are ideological in nature, not documentary resources through which a reasonable facsimile of the events and circumstances of history may be constructed. They may be arguments, agendas, and ideological treatises or self-conscious attempts at rendering good local literature into Pāli for particular religious or aesthetic aims or both. We may never know the precise sociohistorical situation of the textual communities responsible for the Pāli *Dīpavaṃsa* and *Mahāvaṃsa*, but I suspect we can know something about their literary concerns. I contend that one of the primary concerns for the fourth- and fifth-century Mahāvihāran monks responsible for compiling these two *vaṃsas* was to provide a vehicle for the continued presence and proximity of the Buddha through evocative, transformative literature—a narrative unfolding through the course of time as recounted in the text.

The *Dīpavaṃsa* and *Mahāvaṃsa* do operate in a recognizably historical mode, in chronicle form, establishing an implicit timeline as they construct a narrative of a series of events over time, from an ancient and mythically infused past to the historical present. By extending the narrative into the historical present, the text manufactures a *vaṃsa* (lineage) that directly connects the present community with the past presented in the text. The further back the narrative goes, the more transformed the environment becomes, to where the island of Laṅkā in the time of the Buddha is populated with *yakkhas* and *nāgas* instead of with people. Certainly this is mythologizing about the past, but we must not misunderstand it as an error by the compilers or a substitute for missing data for events too far removed for historical rendering. It is instead a purposeful narrative technique—while it emphasizes how removed we are from the Buddha, temporally and physically, it simultaneously connects the reader with the Buddha's presence. Narration of the distance through time is an effective connecting technique that, for the primed reader, roots an experience of the mundane present in a glorious history. The texts and the narratives within them act as connecting devices to a meaningful origin, and the means through which the connection is established is a strategic (and literary) use of time.

TEXTUAL COMMUNITIES: WRITERS AND READERS IN CONTEXT

Much of how contemporary scholars of Buddhism, Sri Lankans, and Buddhists have understood the *Mahāvaṃsa* to date is predicated upon the particular cultural and historical situatedness of our own interpretive abilities, lenses, and inclinations.[9] We also encounter texts through the various ways they have been interpreted in the past. This is particularly true for a text such as the *Mahāvaṃsa*, which has later extensions as well as a medieval commentary on it. Can we ever escape who we are and how we have learned to think about texts long enough to allow for a text to work upon us on its own terms? Does a text even have its own terms, and can a contemporary reader connect with a text directly, without intervening interpretive layers coloring the experience? Just as our own historical and cultural circumstances delimit the ways we interpret texts, so the circumstances of the fifth-century Mahāvihāra author-compiler of the *Mahāvaṃsa* colored his reformulation of the narratives in the *Mahāvaṃsa*.

The primary key employed to unlock the hidden meanings of the *Mahāvaṃsa* and for fleshing out the scanty data available about its historical context is its medieval commentary *Vaṃsatthappakāsinī*. The exact date of composition of this text is unknown. The earliest it could have been written would have been after the reign of Dāṭhopatissa II (659–667 C.E.).[10] It is referred to in other texts by the thirteenth century. Whereas *Mahāvaṃsa* editor and translator Wilhelm Geiger dated the *Vaṃsatthappakāsinī* to 1000–1250, based on his assumption that the text references the tenth-century *Bodhivaṃsa* in its present form,[11] G. P. Malalasekera dates it much earlier, citing the fluid nature of texts prior to critical editions. He suggests that it was written in much closer temporal proximity to the *Mahāvaṃsa*, believing that there is evidence in the text to suggest that the "original sources" for the *Mahāvaṃsa* "were still being studied" while the commentary was being written. As Malalasekera writes, "Since Mahānāma [the author-compiler of the *Mahāvaṃsa*] is generally believed to have lived in the sixth century [C.E.], it would not, I feel, be too early to assign the author of the MṬ [the *Vaṃsatthappakāsinī*] to about two or three centuries later, the eighth or ninth century. This would also allow sufficient time for variant readings to develop in the [*Mahāvaṃsa*] text."[12] Whether we follow Geiger or Malalasekera's dating, we know that the *Vaṃsatthappakasinī* was written at least a few centuries after the *Mahāvaṃsa* and thus represents the concerns of an entirely different community than that which produced the *Mahāvaṃsa*. The *Vaṃsatthappakasinī* follows the narrative of the *Mahāvaṃsa* quite closely, although it chooses to elaborate on some sections far more than others. Both early translators, George Turnour and Wilhelm Geiger, used the commentary to read and translate the *Mahāvaṃsa*. The commentary does elucidate otherwise hard-to-render passages of the *Mahāvaṃsa*, but it nonetheless represents later concerns and values used to interpret the text and not necessarily the concerns and values of the *Mahāvaṃsa* itself.

Likewise, reading the later section of the *Mahāvaṃsa*, or what Geiger called the *Cūlavaṃsa*, alters the overall effect of reading the *Mahāvaṃsa*.[13] Each time the *Mahāvaṃsa* was continued, the concerns of the new interpretive community were inserted into the text; and even if a past section was not altered, the document as a whole was nevertheless affected. The later section further reorients the text as it brings the history of the island to the modern period; its inclusion in a reading of the *Mahāvaṃsa* results in a sense of this text as history. The first part of this later section begins in the fourth century with the arrival of the tooth relic, a key event in the history of Theravāda Buddhism, and then spans centuries to culminate in a narration of the twelfth-century reign of the influential king Parākramabāhu I.[14] The compilation of this section is claimed by the monk Dhammakitti in the twelfth century. The material may have gradually accumulated, making Dhammakitti only one hand among many making editorial decisions, but the ultimate form that the first part of this later section takes certainly reflects the concerns of the twelfth-century Mahāvihāran community. The next installment continues through the arrival of the British in 1815, which segues into the more recent interpretations (and, in fact, to the continuation of the *Mahāvaṃsa* to the present day). Here in this book we are singularly concerned with the first section of the *Mahāvaṃsa* that concludes with the thirty-seventh chapter, entitled "King Mahāsena," and ends with the simple subscript, "Mahāvaṃso niṭṭhhito" (The *Mahāvaṃsa* has ended).

The *Mahāvaṃsa* is thus layered with accretions, with each new textual community subjecting it to a new layer of interpretation. Any stratum we might isolate to undergo historicizing scrutiny bears the marks of the interpretive community of the era in which it was created.[15] As R. G. Collingwood observes, "The historical past is the world of ideas which the present evidence creates in the present. In historical inference we do not move from our present world to a past world; the movement in experience is always a movement within a present world of ideas."[16] Of course, textual communities through time are hardly as distinct and bound as layers of an onion, with each new understanding of a text revealed as we peel back intervening interpretations. Nor are they necessarily monolithic, although a singular, unified interpretive vision is the general idea the *vaṃsas* intend to provoke. The text of the *Mahāvaṃsa* acts as the central cohesive unit for such a textual community at the time of its production, but later communities of interpretation are in constant evolution, especially as they begin to produce commentarial material that attaches successive and sometimes disparate layers of meaning to the original cohesive text.

The modern interpreter must use his or her imagination and a study of history to arrive at any understanding of the community. Even the most thorough of investigations will result in conjecture at best, not "fact." As Brian Stock says,

> The analysis of textual communities—whether these consist of religious sects, political groups, social movements, or relations between authors and audiences—requires a combination of literary and historical techniques. Both are cognitive activities. The historical is not so isolated from the literary as fact and representation. The two aspects of textual experience are multidimensional, and the objectivity of the alleged events spills over into the alleged subjectivity of the records, perceptions, feelings, and observations. . . . One cannot, therefore, like Derrida, wholly neglect the world outside the text, or reduce it to aspects of internality, since the recodification of behavior by someone consciously reliving an earlier text constitutes a new text, which . . . appears as meaningful activity before it is transcribed and passed on in written form.[17]

Jonathan Walters concurs with this situated reading of the textual communities when he recommends that we read Pāli texts as "actions within the sociohistorical circumstances of their production rather than as passive transmitters of neutral information."[18] If we pay attention to the active, constructive, worklike elements of the text, whether explicitly rendered as messages to an intended audience (such as "good people") or subtly conveyed through rhetorical devices, we may be able to better understand how the texts have been interpreted through the centuries. We may also discover that we have no recourse to "actual history" within these texts; they may indicate much about the textual community responsible for their production, but even this information comes to us in a highly manufactured form. All written histories play with the persuasive powers of text and demand that the reader-hearer follow along the trajectories they set, accepting even the most fanciful of situations in service of maintaining a narrative arc that leads to the present.

Hayden White reflects on the tension between the reader's present activities and the past as presented by the text: "The historically real, the past real, is that to which it can be referred only by way of an artifact that is textual in nature. The indexical, iconic, and symbolic notions of language, and therefore of texts, obscure the nature of this indirect referentiality and hold out the possibility of (feign) direct referentiality, create the illusion that there is a past out there that is directly reflected in the texts."[19] The *Mahāvaṃsa* in particular requires a new reading, one that pays attention to the material of the text and how it may be a window onto the particular concerns of the textual community of its production, so often assumed to be the fifth- or sixth-century manifestation of the Mahāvihāra. But it also begs to be read as a literary text, full of self-proclaimed good poetry and emotionally evocative material, which happens to find a "historical," chronologically organized narrative the most effective framework for transmission.

Buddhist histories are a particular genre of literature produced and consumed first and foremost to assert the ideas of their textual communities, recasting prior material and claiming pride of place in the lineage extending back to the Buddha, to help in the ongoing project of self-definition and autonomy. *Vaṃsas* project into future communities the particular ethical and aesthetic concerns of the communities responsible for their production in a narrative wish for future "good people." These ethical and aesthetic concerns may intrude into the political realm (as they inevitably do), but the political dimension or any underlying ideological agenda is but one facet of this multifaceted type of text. To hone in on the political to the exclusion of other readings (or workings) of the text as literature misses its richness and its inherent value to its various interpretive communities, both the textual community that created it and successive communities of Sinhalese Buddhists.

THE *DĪPAVAṂSA* AND *MAHĀVAṂSA* AS "CHARTERS"

Secondary scholarship to date has discussed the *Mahāvaṃsa* mainly as a political charter, a repository for the Duṭṭhagāmaṇī epic, or at best a narrative of the coming of the relics and *sāsana* to Sri Lanka and the recentering of the Buddhist cosmos. Scholars interested in postcolonial self-awareness have recently begun to consider how the *Mahāvaṃsa* in particular has come to be understood as a charter for the modern nation-state of Sri Lanka. As the long period of colonial occupation drew to a close in the 1940s, people looked to indigenous sources for a nascent independent identity.[20] When contemporary scholars tentatively challenge the nationalist usurpation of the text, they tend to perpetuate certain elements conducive to a nationalist and reconstructivist reading. Even the critique of the perception of the *Mahāvaṃsa* as a nationalist charter inevitably perpetuates that very idea. Most scholars read and rely extensively on Geiger's translation of the text without reading the original

Pāli. This is not to say that Geiger's translation is exceptionally flawed; it is quite good. But it was informed by his concerns, as our readings of it are inescapably informed by our own and readings to serve Sinhalese Buddhist nationalists are informed by their own.[21] Rhetoric derived from the *Mahāvaṃsa* fueled the discourse and the violence sustaining the more than quarter-of-a-century-long civil war in Sri Lanka. I contend that this rhetorical phenomenon points more to the efficacy of language than to the ideological or political power of the text as a charter.

Because much of the *vaṃsa* literature chronicles the successive reigns of kings, it is commonly read through a political lens. Any attempt to simplify the explanation of the complex relationship between the *saṅgha* and the ruling power leads to oversimplification and to the bias toward a politicized reading of the *Mahāvaṃsa*. Heinz Bechert writes:

> The authors of the chronicles were [Theravāda] Buddhist monks. It is surprising at first sight that *bhikkhus* should have been the propagators of a state ideology, when we recall the rule of the Order. We know, however, that religious ideas always have occupied an important place in the traditional state ideology of a Theravāda Buddhist kingdom. The king was customarily described as a *cakravartin*, i.e., as a universal monarch as described in canonical Buddhist works. He was also identified as *bodhisattva*, i.e., a Buddha-to-be, and his Buddhist legitimation was bound to his function as a promoter and protector of orthodox Theravāda Buddhism.[22]

In this reductive assessment, the reason for the *vaṃsa* compilation is entirely a political one; the *bhikkhus* (monks) are rendered "propagators of a state ideology," and religious ideas become subservient to the "traditional state ideology."

There are several problems with this argument, most obviously the anachronistic use of the term *state*.[23] Nonetheless, the parallel *vaṃsas* (lineages) of the *saṅgha* and the king are present in both the *Dīpavaṃsa* and the *Mahāvaṃsa*. Ample fodder exists for the interpretation of the lineages as "a model of and a model for the Sinhalese Buddhist identity. . . . The resultant stereotypes are one element in the Sinhalese Buddhist world view."[24]

Richard Gombrich asserts that "the *Mahāvaṃsa* is the charter of Sinhalese Buddhist nationalism,"[25] but framing the *Mahāvaṃsa* as a nationalist charter is an anachronistic and self-serving interpretation and a politically legitimizing usurpation of a multivalent literary text.

By stating that the *vaṃsas* constitute "the sacred history of a people destined with a sacred mission, namely, to maintain the purity of the *Dhamma* in a world of impermanence and self-seeking," Bardwell Smith comes closer to the sort of interpretation I advocate.[26] "Sacred history," or *Heilsgeschichte*, operates beyond the mere reportage of events; it is a theological and ideological claim.[27] In the *Mahāvaṃsa*, we read such a claim in the proem, and it is repeated in the stock phrase at the end of each chapter that no matter how banal the subject may be, it was "made for the anxious thrill and serene satisfaction of good people." However, key words in Smith's argument, such as *sacred*, *destined*, and *purity*, oversimplify the impact of this text and add a layer of interpretation because of his word choice. "Purity" and "destined" are concepts never explicitly used in the text in reference to the *dhamma*, but the text's modern interpreters nevertheless read them as implicit.[28]

Smith's assessment is also employed by scholars working in other fields to further their own arguments even though they may not have read the *Mahāvaṃsa*. For example, political scientist David Little concludes that "the chronicles have a mythical aspect. Historical facts are embellished in various ways to lay the foundations for the 'charter' of an ideal social order."[29] Why privilege the "historical" as the basis upon which "mythological" embellishments accrue? Couldn't the *Mahāvaṃsa* just as easily be read as a mythological text to which historical "facts" are added to suggest the idea of charter? After all, the text begins not with a "historical" event but in the mythical realm, with the Buddha's three visits to the island.

Alice Greenwald, too, categorizes the *Mahāvaṃsa* as a charter, but in a broader sense than a specifically political charter. She almost claims the converse of Little's statement: "[A] [c]harter is conceived of in the Malinowskian sense as that which, through the medium of myth (or, in this case, religious historiography), both engenders and substantiates a cultural self-consciousness."[30] The *Dīpavaṃsa* and *Mahāvaṃsa* are charters in this latter sense insofar as they both generate and validate a "cultural self-consciousness" by and for the textual communities that compiled them. They are the texts that form the fulcrum for the textual community, the reason for its very existence.[31]

I disagree that the *vaṃsas* are charters for contemporary political purposes. I understand the *Mahāvaṃsa* in particular as a charter for an internal conversion experience or a deepening of faith for the audience, individually or collectively. After all, this text was compiled by and for monastics and became available to a secular audience only because it had been preserved in monastic settings. If its proem is to be believed, it certainly did not set out to chart new territory or political agendas for the twentieth- or twenty-first-century Sinhalese; the narrative focus is on the past and the particular sentiments generated when one reads or hears it. The *Mahāvaṃsa* does claim superiority over what it deems to be lesser expressions of the same material, but this claim is made in literary (and not overtly political) terms.

One could argue, however, that the *vaṃsa*s do chart the religious and ethical aspirations of communities in the future. In that sense, they are as much about the future as about the past, but only insofar as they reach out to the future reader and implicate that reader in participating in the text's religious dimension.[32] For example, we find in *Mahāvaṃsa* XXXII an adaptation of the standard formulation the Buddha reveals at the end of every *Jātaka* story ("At that time, I was so-and-so," "Ānanda was so-and-so," etc.). This formula comes to be anticipated by the reader of the *Jātaka*s, who becomes increasingly aware of the interwoven relationships that transcend individual births. It is this "group karma" encountered in the paradigmatic *Jātaka*s that is mimicked in the *Mahāvaṃsa*, but not with reference to the past birth of the Buddha. It instead appears in the context of the future—namely, the anticipated birth of Duṭṭhagāmaṇī in the time of the Buddha Metteyya, the future Buddha. In the scene of Duṭṭhagāmaṇī's death, replete with a chariot from Tusita heaven to carry him away, circling the Mahāthūpa three times in the air, we see the narrator conclude the story with the observation that "Great King Duṭṭhagāmaṇī, he who is worthy of the name king, will be the first disciple of the blessed Metteyya; (Metteyya's) father (will be) the king's father, his mother the mother, (Duṭṭhagāmaṇī's) younger brother Saddhātissa will be his second disciple. But the son of the king Sālirājakumāro will be the son of the blessed Metteyya."[33] If this particular portion of text is working as a charter, it is a religious—not political—one.

Another problem with the classification of the *Mahāvaṃsa* as a political charter is that its proem explicitly declares its religious function—namely, to arouse *saṃvega* (awe, religious agitation) and then *pasāda* (serene joy, peace). The primary aim for a political charter typically is not to arouse specific emotional or ethical effects in a reading audience. The proem makes it clear that the *Mahāvaṃsa* is a charter only insofar as it circumscribes a certain textual community (of "good people," *sujana*), a community that it seeks to create.

Thus we can see that the term *charter* does not easily apply to the *Mahāvaṃsa*, in spite of its common use in politicized readings performed for specific political agendas. The modern reception and categorization of the *Mahāvaṃsa* as a charter nonetheless has had an impact on Sri Lankan Theravāda communities of the present. H. L. Seneviratne refers to the dominant Sinhalese Buddhist understanding of the island's history as the "*Mahāvaṃsa* view,"[34] and Tessa Bartholomeusz refers to it as the "*Mahāvaṃsa* mentality,"[35] a bellicose one at that.

The *Mahāvaṃsa* is best read by suspending the type of reading that has been informed by state-building, identity-reifying political rhetoric. Although the document attests to the struggles for power through the ages, jumping straight to that conclusion (of preauthorized, even mandated and sacralized Sinhala hegemony) overlooks the work of the text. Eschewing recent rhetoric that espouses the "*Mahāvaṃsa* view" or the "*Mahāvaṃsa* mentality" as a singularly hegemonic political ploy, we open ourselves to the text's more literary function and to what may have been at stake for the community that inspired the fifth-century composer.

IF NOT A CHARTER, IS IT HISTORY? IF HISTORY, A HISTORY OF WHAT?

To fully appreciate the literary qualities of the *vaṃsa*s, however, we must situate these works, in particular the *Mahāvaṃsa*, in the community responsible for generating them and for whom the literary maneuvers were crafted. Herein lies a methodological dilemma that has plagued (but not impeded) all prior research into the historical era responsible for the earliest Pāli *vaṃsa*s. The primary source for the historical information reported in the plethora of secondary sources is the *Mahāvaṃsa* itself. The object of our literary study is thus also the main informant on the social history of the time. It is certainly possible that the text can reveal significant information about the period in question, especially when one reads between the lines and accepts the chronology and implicit argument of the text's author-compiler. But there remains an inescapable tension between what we think we can be certain about and how we have derived what we know from the text that is the object of our study. This inscrutable tension between methods and genres must inform a new evaluation of the *Mahāvaṃsa*.

In the medieval West, "histories" come in several forms, one of which is the chronicle, a form that adds depth and detail to the basic temporal sequence of the annals. As Hayden White explains,

> The annals form lacks completely this narrative component, since it consists only of a list of events ordered in chronological sequence. The chronicle, by contrast, often seems to wish to tell a story, aspires to narrativity, but typically fails to achieve it. More specifically, the chronicle usually is marked by a failure to achieve narrative closure. It does not so much conclude as simply terminate. It starts out to tell a story but breaks off *in media res*, in the chronicler's own present; it leaves things unresolved, or rather, it leaves them unresolved in a storylike way.[36]

Structurally, then, the *Mahāvaṃsa* and *Dīpavaṃsa* could be classified as chronicles because, at least in the case of the *Dīpavaṃsa*, they do trail off into the compiler's present. Yet the designation *chronicle* is complicated; it may attenuate a fuller comprehension of the text and unhelpfully inform the modern reader about what to pay attention to and what to mentally edit upon its encounter. This designation divests the first story cycle of its narrative strength. The very designation of these texts as "chronicles" in the minds of their interpreters, who have been infected by modern standards and methods of historiography, seems to have triggered a certain mode of interpretation that consciously overlooks the ethical dimension of the act of reading or receiving the text and that edits out the historically challenging aspects of the narrative (such as the miracles surrounding the relics and the *nāgas*). The problem exists in calling the text a chronicle and thus exporting medieval European expectations (or, more appropriately, modern scholars' and historiographers' notions) about what a chronicle conveys.

The structure and content of the first chapters of both the *Mahāvaṃsa* and the *Dīpavaṃsa* seem to be closely related to the genre of Sanskrit *purāṇa*.[37] Both open with the construction of a mythic landscape in a timeless time, through which the narratives of the lineages of kings are to be interpreted. Acknowledging the assertively literary qualities of the *Mahāvaṃsa* and based on his reading of the five elements (*pañcalakṣaṇa*) of *purāṇa* writing, Steven Collins concludes that the *Dīpavaṃsa* and *Mahāvaṃsa* have much in common with Indic *purāṇa* literature. As he suggests, "We see the Pāli chronicles in this perspective as a part of the literary genre of the *purāṇa* in the widest sense, listing the genealogy and deeds of the lineage of the Buddha and his heritage."[38] Sequence, *paramparā* (lineage), legitimacy, and security in being connected to authoritative sources (whether the Buddha or the deities of the *purāṇas*) are themes that tie the *vaṃsas* and *purāṇas* together. Considering the *vaṃsas* as *purāṇa* is by no means an original observation by Collins; in fact, Buddhaghosa himself refers to the *Dīpavaṃsa* as "the Purāṇa."[39] But just as the term *history* can never fully translate the term *purāṇa*, so I contend that it is also an insufficient translation of *vaṃsa*—and yet many scholars translate it this very way.

Stephen Berkwitz argues that because the term *chronicle* is a similarly insufficient translation of *vaṃsa*, we should call this genre of text "Buddhist histories." Following arguments by Stephen Greenblatt, Keith Jenkins, and Hayden White, he concludes that "historical writings are 'fictions' in the sense of being made or fashioned, things shaped by human imagination and the available resources of narration while still referring to actual events believed to have taken place apart from its description." Recognizing that Buddhist histories, with their abundant stories of miracles and fanciful landscapes and characters, may challenge a historian's reading—even one attuned to the artfully manufactured quality of history—Berkwitz argues that in comparison to modern Western historiography, "Buddhist *vaṃsas* are more transparent with their 'fictive' qualities and revel in the creative potency that is ascribed to their narratives."[40]

The term *history*, of course, comes with its own semantic baggage. A proper history assumes a firsthand witness as source. Classicist Carolyn Dewald discusses the origins of the classification "history" as a titular creation by Herodotus as he sought, a full forty years after events had transpired, to uncover the reasons why the Greeks, not the Persians, had won the great war in 481 B.C.E.:

> [*History*] was a noun formed out of a very old Indo-European stem *vid-* meaning sight, or knowledge gained through sight. We have its cousin words through Germanic Old English in wit, or wisdom, and through Latin, another cousin language, we have vision, and video. In Greek very early, before Homer, the digamma or w-sound was lost, and the stem came in as the verb *idein*, to see, and in its noun of agency, a *(w)istor*, or *histor*, a witness, a man who knows things because he has seen them. In the *Iliad*, a text written three hundred years or so before Herodotus, a *histor* is in one passage a judge of a horse race, waiting at the end goalpost to declare the winner, and in another passage he is one of a group of judges gathered to weigh the evidence and determine the outcome of a manslaughter trial.[41]

The *vaṃsas*' chroniclers were not alive to witness the Buddha's three visits, the landing of Vijaya, the coming of Mahinda, and the rise of Duṭṭhagāmaṇī. In fact, the narrative telos for the *Dīpavaṃsa* is the description of the end of King Mahāsena's reign, a fact that has been interpreted to mean that the writer of the *Dīpavaṃsa* had thus reached his (or her) contemporary period. But the first cycle of the subsequently written *Mahāvaṃsa* ends with this same event, which suggests that it is simply a retelling of the content of the *Dīpavaṃsa* (whether the *Dīpavaṃsa* itself was the source or not). Given the commonly accepted dating of the *Mahāvaṃsa* as about one hundred years after the *Dīpavaṃsa*, why wouldn't the *Mahāvaṃsa* compiler have had the confidence to continue the narrative to his own time? (After all, he asserts in the proem such confidence in his poetic ability!) One possibility is that the two texts are, in fact, more contemporaneous than evidence suggests. The evidence that separates them, however, is compelling. Buddhaghosa mentions the *Dīpavaṃsa* by name but does not mention the *Mahāvaṃsa*. This seems to set Buddhaghosa's period of production between the two documents, unless Buddhaghosa was residing with monks who were preserving the lineage and claims of the *Dīpavaṃsa*, and the *Mahāvaṃsa* was being written by another faction within the Mahāvihāra. The contentious, assertive proem of the *Mahāvaṃsa* would then make sense; the *Dīpavaṃsa* represents a lesser work by a lesser contemporaneous community. Could the assertions of the *Mahāvaṃsa* author have been an attempt by a separate faction of the Mahāvihāra brethren to curry the court's favor or to lay claim to the authentic *paramparā* (lineage) of the Buddha through Mahinda by utilizing the successful rhetorical strategies employed by the compiler of the *Dīpavaṃsa*?

Although previous attempts at dating the texts have attempted to do so on stylistic ground alone, I am unconvinced that the crude form of the *Dīpavaṃsa* necessitates an earlier composition date.[42] After all, poor poets exist in every generation. Several scholars have suggested that the clumsiness of the poetry was due to a lack of confidence on the author's part in the new idiom, Pāli. It is true that there are several awkward passages in the text, but this awkwardness could have easily been due to the compiler's aspirations to preserve variant traditions in the text. Of course, as Walpola Rahula asserts, it may also be simply due to multiple authors: "The rugged nature of its language and style, its grammatical peculiarities, its many repetitions and the absence of any plan or scheme in its narrative convince the reader that the *Dīpavaṃsa* is not the continuous work of one individual, but a heterogeneous collection of material like ballads of some unskilled versifiers who lived at different periods in different parts of the Island."[43] Whereas the *Dīpavaṃsa* may have been about collating and documenting important stories of lineage (and especially connections to the Buddha through the monks and nuns and to Asoka's court through the coming of Mahinda to Sri Lanka), the *Mahāvaṃsa* is about provoking an emotional response in primed readers.

HISTORICIZING *VAṂSAS*: THE *DĪPAVAṂSA* AND *MAHĀVAṂSA* AS "BUDDHIST HISTORIES"

According to previous scholarship, the *Mahāvaṃsa* springs from Sri Lanka of the fifth century, specifically from the Mahāvihāra monastic complex in Anurādhapura, which was at the time the seat of the monarchy and the center of political and cultural production. All scholars are in agreement that the textual community responsible for the *Mahāvaṃsa* inherited a set of source material contained in the Sinhalese (or Eḷu, Old Sinhalese) *Sīhaḷaṭṭhakathā*. Although no such text is extant today, several references found in later texts attest to its prominence and influence at that time. The *Mahāvaṃsa* proem refers to an older version of the *Mahāvaṃsa* "made by the ancients" (*porāṇehi kato*), which remains unnamed there. The medieval commentary *Vaṃsatthappakāsinī* explains that this source text was written in Sinhalese prose interspersed with Pāli verse.[44] It also states that monks of the Mahāvihāra were responsible for writing the *aṭṭhakathā*.[45] Malalasekera comes to several conclusions about this early compilation of texts:

> It is generally agreed that there was preserved in the Mahāvihāra in Anurādhapura an old commentary to the *Tipiṭaka*, which was generally referred to as the *Aṭṭhakathā*. This work was written in Sinhalese prose, interspersed with Pāli verses. Oldenberg has suggested that the *Sīhalaṭṭhakathā-Mahāvaṃsa* . . . formed a historical introduction to the dogmatic part of this *Aṭṭhakathā* of the Mahāvihāra fraternity, much in the same way as the historical introduction to Buddhaghosa's *Samantapāsādikā*. Geiger disagrees with this view and expresses the opinion that the "*Mahāvaṃsa* of the ancients" was an independent chronicle, which the dwellers of the Mahāvihāra carried down to Mahāsena, and certainly would have continued further had not the Mahāvihāra been destroyed and depopulated and their peaceable work

> disturbed by the violence of Mahāsena. . . . It is quite probable that originally this chronicle formed a sort of historical introduction to the Canonical commentary and dealt only with the 13 subjects mentioned in the proem of the *Dīpavaṃsa*. Later, however, it burst its framework by the incorporation of a great deal of extraneous information and developed into an independent compilation, whose custodians were the Mahāvihāra monks.[46]

Scholars such as Hermann Oldenberg, Wilhelm Geiger, E. W. Adikaram, G. C. Mendis, and G. P. Malalasekera are in relative agreement that there were texts (*porāṇa, aṭṭhakathā*) in circulation (oral or written) that formed the source material for the *Dīpavaṃsa* and *Mahāvaṃsa*.[47] Oldenberg considers the *porāṇa* to be a historical preface to the *aṭṭhakathā* (or to *Sīhalaṭṭhakathā-Mahāvaṃsa*).[48] Geiger seems to consider the *aṭṭhakathā* and *porāṇa* as "one and the same." Adikaram and Malalasekera seem to be in agreement that the *porāṇa* refer in a general way to "teachers of old."[49]

Although the *Vaṃsatthappakāsinī* states that the *Mahāvaṃsa* (there named *Padyapadoruvaṃsa*) presents a faultless version of the *Sīhālaṭṭhakathā-Mahāvaṃsa*, which was riddled with *dosa* (defects), it also states that "they are not really *dosa*, but they make the work difficult to understand and remember. It is only these 'difficulties' that the Mhv. [*Mahāvaṃsa*] had tried to avoid."[50] But this source, too, is dated centuries after the *Dīpavaṃsa* or *Mahāvaṃsa* would have been compiled. We cannot be certain of the exact nature, provenance, or even the existence of the source texts for the *Dīpavaṃsa* and *Mahāvaṃsa*, but we can at least question why the authors of both texts would have explicitly claimed in their proems that they were revising older materials if such source texts did not exist (*Dīpavaṃsa* I.4; *Mahāvaṃsa* I.2). Reading the *Dīpavaṃsa* and *Mahāvaṃsa* together, we can be fairly certain that each text followed some manifestation of an urtext rather closely because whole story cycles are repeated (sometimes practically verbatim) in both texts.

Both texts begin with the ultimate legitimating persona, the Buddha of this (our) era. We can be fairly certain of one thing: in the Buddhist milieu during Gotama Buddha's life, there was a central authority that could ensure, to some degree, the continuity and coherence of the religious order known as the *saṅgha*. Following Max Weber's understanding of the "routinization of charisma,"[51] we can assume that in the social life of the *saṅgha* in the period immediately following the Buddha's corporeal death (*parinibbāṇa*), considerable attention was paid to the systematization of institutional resources and policies to ensure the longevity of the Buddha's vision for his community. Much is said in the canonical sources to explain the necessity to preserve the sermons (*suttas*) and the rules of the order (*vinaya*). Maintaining continuity with the Buddha's own *saṅgha* became an imperative of the developing and expanding Buddhist community, so much so that new techniques to appeal to the legitimacy and authority of the Buddha were utilized by all communities, ancient and nascent, seeking legitimization.[52] Authenticity became paramount in claims of legitimacy, especially in light of variant readings of literature and various traditions that all claimed a spot in the Buddha's *paramparā*. In this context, the designation "Theravāda" (Doctrine of the Elders) can be seen and evaluated as carrying with it an argument about legitimacy.

This is not the place to delve into the morass of scholarship and speculation on early Nikāya Buddhism (that is, the period after the Buddha's *parinibbāṇa* when several variant traditions and communities of interpretation arose). Nonetheless, we may want to destabilize the familiar yet problematic categorization of a monolithic Theravāda as the sole form of early Buddhism and the most legitimate heir to the Buddha's *sāsana*, even though this is the position that the Pāli *vaṃsa* texts vociferously argue. Indeed, this destabilization should penetrate even the designation "Theravāda" itself; disparate *vihāras* (monastic complexes) competing for limited sources of patronage show that the Theravāda then, as now, was hardly a monolithic institution in spite of its periodical councils and purifications and otherwise convincing rhetoric.

The *Dīpavaṃsa* and *Mahāvaṃsa* imagine that the island itself was primed to receive the *dhamma*. A timeline is constructed in the text to support this argument: the Buddha visits, and upon his *parinibbāṇa* Vijaya arrives. These two events mark the beginnings of the lineages, both religious and royal. The *Dīpavaṃsa* and *Mahāvaṃsa* maintain that Buddhism was brought to the island by the missionary monk Mahinda during the reign of Devānaṃpiyatissa (247–207 B.C.E.). Could it be that this event is portrayed in the early *vaṃsas* for rhetorical force and to legitimize a particular strain or inheritance of the Mahāvihāra? K. M. de Silva suggests that given the degree of trade and traffic between Laṅkā and mainland India, early Buddhist influences are likely to have been imported to the island before Mahinda's mission: "Once again the *Mahāvaṃsa*'s account of events conceals as much as it reveals, and what it hides in this instance is the probability that Buddhists and Buddhism came to the island much earlier than that."[53] The monastic institution granted by the Sinhalese king to this proselytizing monk from India was the Mahāvihāra, so the text claims, thus establishing—at least for the purposes of the narrative—a named community with a definitive beginning. Considering that it is this very named community that preserves and recasts the narrative through the *Dīpavaṃsa* and *Mahāvaṃsa*, we may think critically about just what the term *vaṃsa* in this context means, especially given Collins's definition: "Bamboo grows by sending out one, and only one, shoot: unlike our concept of a genealogical tree, therefore, a *vaṃsa* genealogy allows one legitimate successor at a time. Thus the term not only describes a line of transmission, but at the same time ascribes to the members of the *vaṃsa* a specific status and authority as legitimate heirs of that transmission."[54] Thus, we may wonder if the *vaṃsa* genealogies of the competing monastic institutions, the Abhayagiri and the Jetavana, might have contained similar originary tales highlighting the central position of their own lineage. We cannot know for sure; the resurgence of the Mahāvihāra after a period of persecution resulted in reciprocal persecution of variant sects and the burning of these *vihāras*' texts by the queen's command.[55] When writing alone was not powerful enough to ensure hegemony, physical force was used.

If the timeline of the series of events in the *Dīpavaṃsa* and *Mahāvaṃsa* is to be believed, the Mahāvihāra itself was not established until Mahinda brought Buddhism to Laṅkā during Devānaṃpiyatissa's reign, which would put the founding of this school in the third century B.C.E. Even if, as many have speculated, Buddhism was a known entity on the island prior to Mahinda's arrival, the designation of actual space for the establishment of the *saṅgha* marks the institutional commencement. The very identity and self-understanding of the Mahāvihāra community responsible for writing the history is contingent upon direct, fundamental association with Mahinda. What is important to consider here is the representation of that founding—in the *Dīpavaṃsa* and *Mahāvaṃsa*, the Mahāvihāra is understood to be the legitimate heir to the *sāsana* and the king (here Devānaṃpiyatissa, the first convert) its patron. The founding of the Mahāvihāra also comprises the third discreet narrative cycle in the litany of events recounted in the text, the first being the Buddha's three visits and the second being the arrival of Vijaya.[56]

Following the chronological temporal structure, the *Mahāvaṃsa* urges us on to the narrative about Duṭṭhagāmaṇī. According to the text, the reign of the famed Duṭṭhagāmaṇī (101–77 B.C.E.) resulted in a massive building campaign for the Mahāvihāra. As we will see, so much of the

Mahāvaṃsa is devoted to the epic narration of this king's deeds that its story cycle can be referred to as the "Duṭṭhagāmaṇī epic," and narratively it can stand apart from the rest of the *vaṃsa*. In the *Mahāvaṃsa*, the "Duṭṭhagāmaṇī epic" is expanded significantly from the abbreviated form found in the *Dīpavaṃsa*—the Duṭṭhagāmaṇī cycle constitutes ten of the thirty-seven chapters that make up the first section of the *Mahāvaṃsa*, more than one-quarter of the entire text. And yet this king is virtually absent in the *Dīpavaṃsa* account.

How each text represents this king's reign could be a clue regarding its textual community's motivating concerns. That the *Dīpavaṃsa* barely mentions Duṭṭhagāmaṇī by name may suggest that the *Dīpavaṃsa* is, as several scholars have argued, a faithful, documentary reconstruction of previous source materials, an assemblage of various texts, many of which were likely in oral circulation, and its aim was to set down and preserve as much as possible of those earlier texts. The reign of this king was secondary in importance to the spiritual lineage that garners greater focus in the *Dīpavaṃsa*. By contrast, the aim of the *Mahāvaṃsa* appears not to record the story but to amplify it and develop it poetically. The historical hero-king Duṭṭhagāmaṇī provides the *Mahāvaṃsa* with an ideal protagonist and the opportunity for a good, inspiring story.[57] A narrative about a king is the medium for many of the composer's most effective poetic flourishes. Kings are certainly important in this text, but Duṭṭhagāmaṇī here is depicted as just one loyal Buddhist subject. What really takes center stage are the emotions that his story evokes.

Buddhist histories and the Theravāda Buddhists' historicizing impulse have garnered much scholarly attention.[58] George Turnour's translation of the *Mahāvaṃsa* in 1837 caused excitement among the early Indologists because the chronologies of kings in this text were exposed in a Rosetta Stone fashion to help James Prinsep in his translation of Asokan epigraphy.[59] The early Orientalists took express pleasure in the apparent and relative historical veracity of the *Mahāvaṃsa*, with its "ring of truth" and its attention to the presentation of chronologies of kings that most approximated the standard Western formulation of history that the scholars had always hoped to find in the South Asian context. The *Mahāvaṃsa* even provides dates that correspond with known epigraphical references. Early academic treatments of this text as real, authoritative, and trustworthy history, unlike the overly whimsical and blatantly devotional *purāṇas* of mainland India, subsequently informed the way they were translated, read, and used as documentary texts. In hindsight, we see that the early scholars' interests, priorities, and biases determined how these scholars evaluated their source material, and we see the translation of the term *vaṃsa* as "history" reifying those same interests, priorities, and biases.

We have seen how the depiction of these texts as "histories" happened in the scholarly, external environment of the texts. Do these arguments have internal corollaries? How do the Pāli *Dīpavaṃsa* and *Mahāvaṃsa* frame themselves historically? Walters argues that they construct and participate in a sequence of "dispensations" of the Buddha that challenge any standard historical conception of time and at the same time pay particular attention to chronologies, events, and dates, even dating specifically each of the Buddha's three "prehistorical" visits to the island: " 'History'—thought about the past in the then-present—proceeded in pre-colonial Sri Lanka within an episteme (to borrow M. Foucault's useful term) consisting of a temporal scheme and anthropology quite foreign to modern sensibilities, one that leads me to consider the Vaṃsas as 'successions' of the Buddha's presence rather than as mere 'chronicles' of events."[60] This argument is very useful in destabilizing the dominant method of reading and using these texts because I do see the *vaṃsas* as narratives working to bring the Buddha (and his relics) into proximity with each successive future community.

Here I draw a distinction between the religious work of Buddhist histories and the rather overdetermined semantic field of the terms *history* and *historiography* in contemporary scholarship. By "religious work," I refer to the explicitly contemplative and transforming effects that the act of reading or hearing the text is supposed to engender. There simply is no systematic concept of history at work for the compilers of the *Dīpavaṃsa* and the *Mahāvaṃsa*, and so it would be anachronistic at best to attribute these texts to a historical mode of writing. This does not mean that the *saṅgha* was unconcerned with historical matters.

What, then, is an acceptable understanding of "history" by which we might be amenable to calling the *vaṃsas* "Buddhist histories?" Jan Nattier provocatively suggests that "for most of the Buddhists for most of the time, the question of history—of where we are in the cosmos and of how much time remains in the world as we know it—has been of central, not peripheral, importance."[61] History in the *vaṃsas* is a temporally structured framework that orients the narrative. Relative proximity in the chronology is thus more important than the actual dates of events, and the religious implications or specifically Buddhist elements and interpretations of events expressed bear more weight than the chronologies themselves.

The "religiosity" expressed in the *Mahāvaṃsa* is thus perceived in the way the temporal frame works on the reader. The operative chronology carrying the narrative of the text is synchronized with the biography of the Buddha and with the reign of the Buddhist monarch Asoka. This synchronization can be interpreted as a powerful rhetorical device employed for a specific effect—namely, the construction of a connection between the textual community of the *Mahāvaṃsa*'s compiler and the legitimating, charismatic presence of the Buddha in the past. B. G. Gokhale considers the Theravāda understanding and use of what can be called history, but he, too, connected what is meant by history to what is perceived to be theology. He cites the Buddha as having among his many achievements an aversion to "low talk" (*tiracchānakathā*), which includes "tales of kings and their proconsuls, wars and heroes, cities and countryside, comely maidens and awesome bandits, items commonly regarded as the stuff out of which history is constructed." Gokhale argues that in spite of this presumed aversion to all things historical, the growing "need for hagiological literature" in early Theravāda practice catalyzed the Buddhist return to history from the Buddha's seemingly antihistoricist stance. He also claims that the "growth of the hagiological spirit is intimately related to the development of Buddhism as a religion."[62] At the time Gokhale made these claims, over fifty years ago, the debate about whether Buddhism is more properly characterized as a philosophy or a religion was raging, but we can nonetheless see some relevance to our understanding of the *Mahāvaṃsa*, in particular the accounts of the Buddha's three visits to the island, as working in religious ways. But the predominant method of reading of the *Mahāvaṃsa* is driven by overattentiveness to the political chronologies it contains.[63]

Malalasekera echoes many scholars' assessment when he notes that the Pāli *vaṃsas*' "chronology is admirably accurate . . . and they possess an honesty of intention and an accuracy of chronological record" absent in the Indian texts such as the *purāṇas*. But he also says they "manifest the same credulity and superstition, the same exaggeration in description, the same adulation of kings and princes, as is met with in the annals and religious history of [other] nations," which, for his reading, does not detract from their historical value.[64] For Malalasekera, the whimsical aspect of the *vaṃsas*—that is, the rampant miracle stories and presence of the *nāgas*—does little to diminish the texts' historicity, and much like the exaggerations in other (e.g., European) chronicles, these elements can be ignored in the process of reading for history. His perspective is but one angle of the seemingly universal position among the early scholars that (in Geiger's terms) the "kernel" or "germ" of true history may be culled from the texts, while the more legendary, miraculous, and fantastic material can be downplayed.[65] Yet the mythical aspects are present throughout the text, not just in the first stratum, and so there is no easy division between what is primarily provocative narrative and what is historically sound. Instead of ignoring the "exaggerations," my project here has been to consider the work that the presence and, in fact, the dominance of such mythical elements does to the text's hearer-reader.

Just as the presence of mythical elements challenges a conventional historical reading of the *vaṃsas* and points to poetic and religious concerns, so might the choice of narrative subject (and poetic elements) reveal something about their time of production. It is commonly accepted that the *Mahāvaṃsa* and *Dīpavaṃsa* were written in times of duress. If one reads carefully and considers the narrative of the tumultuous time in which the *Dīpavaṃsa* was composed, the argument is not that the Mahāvihāra is *the* legitimate Buddhist sect but rather merely the first in a line of successive *vihāras*, with the Abhayagiri and other sects described as splinter groups from the main branch that is the Mahāvihāra.[66] As Rahula understands the history, "originally" all *bhikkhus* from all over the island "owed ecclesiastical allegiance" to the Mahāvihāra.[67] Rahula comes to his conclusion by consulting a Mahāvihāran text, one that envisions all rival schools as mere branches of the one authoritative, great Mahāvihāra. In spite of this, Rahula provocatively muses about the designation "Mahāvihāra," "What was meant by the term Mahāvihāra? Was it only a place geographically defined or an institution?"[68]

In this brief comment, we see just how little has been definitively resolved about the history of the textual communities of the *Dīpavaṃsa* and *Mahāvaṃsa*. It may be that "Mahāvihāra" was an umbrella name meant to designate a general Buddhist monastic complex, not a distinct institution or a particular sectarian orientation. It may be that the rival institutions were less disparate than we assume they were, at least when times were good and resources plentiful[69]—that it was in times of duress, with concomitant competition for limited resources, that contention arose. Indeed, many have suggested that it is periods of contention that present the catalyst for literary production in general.[70]

POETICS UNDER PRESSURE

If we follow the timeline of the Mahāvihāra presented in the *Mahāvaṃsa*, the first real schism occurred during the reign of Vaṭṭagāmaṇī in the first century B.C.E.,[71] when the Abhayagiri separated itself from the Mahāvihāra, presumably over practical rather than doctrinal differences. It was also during his reign (29–17 B.C.E.) that the Pāli Tipiṭaka was purportedly committed to written form.[72] Collins notes, "The Pāli canon, like most other religious Canons, was produced in a context of dispute, here sectarian monastic rivalries. King Vaṭṭagāmaṇī supported the rivals of the Mahāviharan monks, those of the recently founded Abhayagiri monastery."[73] E. W. Adikaram argues that the shifting political currents were responsible for the impetus to write down the canon rather than the period of famine or general political strife that is usually considered the cause for the surge in textual production. He suggests that the Tipiṭaka was written by the Mahāvihāra monks in Matale and thus removed from the contested site of the capital Anurādhapura at the time when the Abhayagiri was founded through the support of King Vaṭṭagāmaṇī.[74]

Could it be that the *Dīpavaṃsa* was written at a time when there were immediate concerns for survival and the authenticity and legitimacy of the Mahāvihāra were being challenged? The *Dīpavaṃsa* would then have been a plea for recognition and maybe even continued support, but not a claim for outright superiority vis-à-vis the other monastic institutions or the king himself.

Walters considers the *Dīpavaṃsa* nothing short of a "plea for survival."[75] The *Dīpavaṃsa* is certainly motivated on some level by its compiler's (or compilers') operative ideology, and for that reason alone it cannot be considered a course for purely historical reflection. The only evidence we have for the strain on the textual community comes from within the text itself, although there is external, epigraphical evidence to corroborate its claims that "[s]upport for the ecumenical Abhayagiri monks had reached a fevered pitch at the end of the third century, under Mahāsena (274–301)."[76] The *Dīpavaṃsa* was likely written in the fourth century C.E., just on the heels of the rise in the Abhayagiri's popularity. In a footnote, Walters considers the various epigraphical testimonies to the cosmopolitan and prolific support of the Abhayagiri, citing donation inscriptions from the first and second centuries.[77] As Collins notes, a monastic institution mired in "a context of dispute" becomes a likely site for textual productivity, and duress is a significant catalyst for textual production.[78] He thus echoes Adikaram's observations not of the *vaṃsa* production proper but of two other periods of Pāli literary activity: "It is worthy of notice that the two most important events, namely, the writing down of the Pāli texts at Āloka-vihāra and the translation of the Commentaries into Pāli, both took place during the reigns of kings who were not favorably disposed towards the Mahāvihāra and who actively helped the opposing camp, the Abhayagirivihāra."[79]

CHOOSING PĀLI

Why did these times of duress provoke this particular kind of literary productivity—namely, textual production in the translocal language Pāli over the vernacular Sinhalese? Why would the response to challenging circumstances provoke such translocal aspirations? Perhaps it was all part of the broader agenda of an upstart *vihāra* to recenter the Buddhist world, and making claims about the centrality of Laṅkā in the translocal language of Pāli was a tactic to better convince readers-hearers "out there" of the center "here." Yet these assertions seem audacious. Wouldn't the claims have been more believable coming from a community in a period of growth and prosperity, not from a beleaguered minority voice? The use of Pāli for the composition of these texts may have been to gain greater sway in global Buddhist concerns, but another motivation lies closer to home within the textual community itself. By composing the texts in Pāli, the producers made a statement about the authenticity of their religious vision and of the claims made manifest in the proem and explained through metaphor and *nāga*. Pāli, after all, was claimed to be the *mūla-bhāsa*, or the "root language," the Māgadhan dialect spoken by the Buddha himself. The coming of the Buddha, his relics, Vijaya, and the narratives of the kings of Laṅkā all take on a different hue when heard in the Pāli, the language connected with the canonical *sutta*s and thus with the Buddha's enduring voice. The intended effect of reading the *vaṃsa*s was an emotionally transformative one, and perhaps composing them in Pāli to make the hearer work hard (and most likely to work through an interpreter, one of the key features of Brian Stock's "textual community," for the right interpretation) made the effect even sweeter an attainment.

During the reign of Vohārika Tissa (269–291), the controversial Vaitulyavāda sect (following Mahāyāna elements) was suppressed, and there was also a "purification" of the *saṅgha*. But perhaps most curious for our reading of the two Mahāvihāran literary productions in question is that the reign of Mahāsena saw an accelerated rise of interest in and outright royal support of certain Mahāyāna ideas in circulation at the time. According to the later section of the *Mahāvaṃsa* and the *Vaṃsatthappakāsinī*, Mahāsena oversaw the destruction of some of the Mahāvihāra buildings, and, in a move concretely symbolic of the shifting royal favoritism, instructed that bricks and building materials from the desecrated Mahāvihāra structures be used to enlarge the rival Abhayagiri complex. It was during this same king's reign that a third contender monastic institution, the Jetavana, was built, and the Mahāvihāra itself was deserted.

For the later communities reading and interpreting this "historical" narrative, the designation "Mahāvihāra" signifies much. It cannot be coincidental that the narrative chronicles of both the *Dīpavaṃsa* and the first section of the *Mahāvaṃsa* end with the reign of the Lambakaṇṇa king Mahāsena (334–361). Although the *Dīpavaṃsa* and *Mahāvaṃsa* represent this king's rule as a politically stable period (the *Mahāvaṃsa* even suggests that he was a good king on balance), later texts and epigraphical sources suggest that religious tension among competing institutions was also at a high during his reign. The Abhayagiri seceded from the Mahāvihāra during the reign of Vaṭṭagāmaṇī Abhaya (de Silva gives the date as around 103 B.C.E.[80]), and it appears that there were frequent confrontations and arguments between the two institutions on monastic as well as doctrinal issues. From the *vaṃsa*s themselves, it seems that by this time the Mahāvihāra had by no means secured the position of authoritative hegemony it would come to occupy centuries later. Collins reiterates the common assessment that "during the first millennium the Mahāvihāra was a minority tradition alongside the Abhayagiri and Jetavana monastic fraternities."[81] Thus, the "documentary" content within the *vaṃsa*s reveals a competitive environment among three "minorities" struggling for resources, support, and legitimacy as well as the possibility that the *vaṃsa* production was a tool for one fraternity's claims of authority.

This interpretation becomes yet more evident when we read between the lines, turning our attention away from the documentary "evidence" suggested in the text and toward the underlying narrative. The patterns of alternating patronage and withdrawal of royal support may have been a narrative ploy intended to heighten the audience's sensitivity and response. The *Mahāvaṃsa* attributes much agency to the Coḷa Saṅghamitta, a resentful South Indian monk with allegiance to the Abhayagiri monastery. King Goṭhābhaya (249–262) had continued the policy of Vohārika Tissa (209–231) to suppress the Madhyamaka-influenced Mahāyāna movement known as the Vetullavāda (Sanskrit *vaitulyavāda*), which had become favored by the Abhayagiri institution. Goṭhābhaya deported sixty monks of the Abhayagirivihāra to India; Saṅghamitta was the disciple of one of these displaced (and likely indignant) Sri Lankan monks. We can assume that Saṅghamitta was groomed in a particular way and that he brought his animosity toward the Mahāvihāra with him to Sri Lanka.[82] Saṅghamitta then curried favor with Goṭhābhaya's successor, Jeṭṭhatissa I (263–273), and became the steward for Mahāsena, the intended next in line. Mahāsena's feelings of intolerance for the Mahāvihāra, influenced by his adviser Saṅghamitta, spurred his campaign of destruction of the Mahāvihāra. Its buildings were razed, its monks forced into exile, and its valued possessions pillaged and claimed by the Abhayagiri (*Mahāvaṃsa* XXXVI.11–25, XXXVII).[83] Assuming the *Dīpavaṃsa* was in fact written at the time the events of its narrative cease—that is, during the reign of Mahāsena—then it was certainly written under a particular kind of duress: uncertainty about the king's future patronage and active persecution, including exile to India. Thus, it appears that the *Dīpavaṃsa* may have been composed as an assertive claim to legitimacy in the face of favored contenders. As we have seen, however, it was not written de novo; the *Dīpavaṃsa* drew its content from the native Sinhala *aṭṭhakathā* literature.[84] If the *Dīpavaṃsa* represents earlier, originally Sinhalese source material in its claims to legitimacy, it is a conscious rhetorical strategy.

MINORITY MATTERS

If we are to accept the claims of the texts and their relative chronologies and representation of the relationship of events and the patronage of kings, the *Dīpavaṃsa* appears to have been composed during this time of crisis for the Mahāvihāra, and it is a poem with a pragmatic aim: the reconstitution and rise of the Mahāvihāra, the community of "good people." Even if we do not believe the historical factuality of those claims, the persecution and exile of monks nevertheless makes for a good, emotionally gripping story for a monastic audience.

The nine years the Mahāvihāra monks were in exile should have obliterated their lineage; they had no support from the king, no residence for the monks, and no sense of stability in which to attend to the religious office of the *saṅgha*. Continuity, the theme par excellence, was seemingly interrupted. The later section of the *Mahāvaṃsa* attempts to recast these years, explaining that monks were in actuality left behind (in hiding) to protect the Mahāvihāran monastery grounds and artifacts for the continuity of the community. Walters offers an enticing and plausible reason why the lineage did not fade into oblivion in the nine years of exile. He suggests that "if we read the [*Mahāvaṃsa*] account of Mahāsena's reign as saying that only the Mahāvihāran monks were expelled from the monastery—if the monks had indeed been destitute (and denied access to their libraries) for nine years—then we could explain why the task of pleading for mercy should have fallen upon the remaining nuns."[85]

Malalasekera cites Hugh Nevill's unpublished manuscript catalog at length because Nevill presents a compelling argument that the nuns' community may have been responsible for the production of the *Dīpavaṃsa*: "It [the *Dīpavaṃsa*] can scarcely be a record of the Theravāda fraternity of the Mahāvihāra, because in the very reign in which it was put forward by royal patronage (Dhātusena's) Mahānāma set about to supersede it by his *Mahā-vaṃsa*. It certainly is not a record of the *Dhammaruci* sect of the Abhayagiri community, because it passes over the history of that wealthy, royal foundation with a well-calculated but short notice that could offend no one. But it dilates on a third society, the community of Theravādin nuns." Nevill provocatively asserts that the extensive list of the nuns in *Dīpavaṃsa* XVIII should rightly have been preceded by a corresponding list of monks but that composition and circulation in a nuns' institution would explain why the monks' section would have been omitted. He also suggests that the compilation of the *Mahāvaṃsa* was necessary because Mahānāma was "jealous of the nuns,"[86] a less than satisfactory reason for which there is no evidence, drawing attention to the completely conjectural nature of his observations.

This issue of authorship may also explain the reason for the coarseness of the Pāli in the *Dīpavaṃsa*. Nevill names the possible compiler of the *Dīpavaṃsa* based on the nuns' lineage presented in *Dīpavaṃsa* XVIII, claiming that two historian nuns from India, Sivalā and Mahāruhā, revised the compiled traditions and stories from Princess Mahilā and "very probably formed [them] into the unpolished almost aboriginal Pāli we now possess, to which additions were made by Nāgamittā, and later by Sanhā and Samuddā."[87] Nevill's conclusion that the nuns' community was responsible for the *Dīpavaṃsa* leaves open the possibility that the two *vaṃsas* may have been more contemporaneous than we would think on the basis of stylistic grounds and that the *Mahāvaṃsa* represents another monastic community's reaction to the *Dīpavaṃsa* at the time the *Dīpavaṃsa* was produced.

The main problem with this theory, again, is a lack of corroborating evidence aside from the artful reading of the *Dīpavaṃsa*. Especially problematic is Nevill's attribution of the editions of the *Dīpavaṃsa* to individually named nuns even though there is no evidence to support such a claim. The text certainly pays much attention to the position of nuns, which should grab any reader's attention. But could this, too, have been a rhetorical device utilized by the compiler? The careful attention paid to the nuns' lineage is nowhere evident in the *Mahāvaṃsa*, where even the story of the nun Saṅghamittā seems presented in a reduced form compared to its appearance in the *Dīpavaṃsa*.

The *Dīpavaṃsa* and *Mahāvaṃsa* do share a common conclusion: the death of King Mahāsena. Geiger suggests that the *Dīpavaṃsa* ends with Mahāsena more or less by accident: "It also happens that the fact that [the *Dīpavaṃsa*] finished with Mahāsena was not founded on any definite plan, but depended rather on an unfortunate occurrence. If the Mahāvihāra had not been destroyed at that time and depopulated, then the list of kings would without a doubt have been continued further. According to my idea the '*Mahāvaṃsa* of the ancients' was an independent chronicle, which the monks of the Mahāvihāra carried on to Mahāsena, and certainly would have continued still further had they not been disturbed in their peaceable work in some violent manner."[88] But Walters makes a persuasive argument that the *Dīpavaṃsa*'s temporal end and explicit polemical stance were in fact calculated and intentional. He suggests that the *Dīpavaṃsa* "evaluates Mahāsena's action, implicitly suggesting that it violates the truths of both calculable and incalculable history, and concludes its narrative with him because that is what the entire presentation was leading up to: a demonstration that the Mahāvihāra is worth continuing because it embodies these truths."[89] Here Walters addresses the chronology as serving the narrative. There is a rhetorical need for a Mahāsena for the text to argue against, which serves as the culmination of the text itself. The *Mahāvaṃsa* can then be understood to have shaped the narrative to result in something. The text is not so much documenting the past as it is constructing an argument.

The *Dīpavaṃsa* might have been a conscientious attempt to reorder the various disciplines (especially in the list of those asserting primacy in *Dīpavaṃsa* V.51–21). Malalasekera somewhat defends the artless *Dīpavaṃsa* on these grounds:

> Often different versions are given of the same story, showing that they were derived from different sources and also, possibly, because of a desire to keep the various traditions as they had been, more or less authorized, with due reverence for their antiquity, and to hand them on unaltered to later generations. The *Dīpavaṃsa* was not the work of a single author, but of several generations, a succession of rhapsodies, added to by succeeding authors, as the Introduction tells us, "twisted into a garland of history from generation to generation, like flowers of various kinds." It was, perhaps, originally meant for oral recitation, and so arranged that several of the more important subjects came up before the listener again and again, gradually impressing the full facts on his memory. If that were so, what appears inartistic and clumsy in the written work would appear highly natural when it was handed down orally.[90]

The *Dīpavaṃsa* could have been created by nuns, might represent the written version of orally performed stories, and might be deficient in the criteria of good literature ("here too long, there too short") due to its primary intention to preserve variant authoritative stories. Regardless, it was most likely written in contentious times and thus represents a "plea for survival" in the midst of competition and an uncertain future. Walters concludes that this palpable "plea for survival" may also indicate the "newcomer" status of the *Dīpavaṃsa* compilers: "This reworking of the history of Buddhist orders and their textual canons, which dismisses the claims of the Mahāsāṃghikas and Sarvāstivādins by appropriating Aśoka for the Theravādin cause, hoped to secure a place for the Theravāda at the Mahāvihāra, a Buddhist disciplinary order that was probably a newcomer on the global Buddhist scene."[91] Perhaps the *Dīpavaṃsa* was not a reassertion or a defense of the Mahāvihāra as legitimate heir of the Buddha's *sāsana* but in fact an argument for the Mahāvihāra's nascence in the midst of several competing traditions.

We can piece together some information based on the firsthand witnessing by the Chinese monk Faxian, who visited Sri Lanka in the early years of the fifth century, and nearly all scholars utilize his documentation. But can we be certain of the accuracy or unbiased nature of this monk's impressions? He was, after all, not a disinterested observer, but a temporary resident of the Abhayagiri. Our suspicion aside, he gives the impression that by the time of his fifth-century visit there were three distinct institutions: "According to Fa Hien, at the time he visited Ceylon in the 5th century, there were 5,000 monks at the Abhayagiri, 3,000 at the Mahāvihāra and 2,000 at Mihintalee. Further he says that there were about 60,000 monks who got their food from their common stores, and that the king, besides, prepared elsewhere in the city a common supply of food for five or six thousand more."[92] If this were the case, it is very interesting to consider the reasoning behind Buddhaghosa's choice of the Mahāvihāra for his commentarial work. Buddhaghosa's teacher supposedly sent him to Sri Lanka because of the deplorable state of the commentarial literature in mainland India. Buddhaghosa would have gone to the institution closest in alliance to his home *vihāra*. The Abhayagiri at this time, according to the *Mahāvaṃsa*, was leaning toward the Mahāyāna.

In its conclusion, the *Vaṃsatthappakāsiṇī*[93] asserts an individual author of the *Mahāvaṃsa*, Mahānāma, who is likely the fifth-century *thera* (monk) composer from the Mahāvihāra monastery in Anurādhapura. This is the only reference to the compiler's purported name; it is given nowhere in the *Mahāvaṃsa* itself. Geiger notes: "It [the *Vaṃsatthappakāsiṇī*] says of him [Mahānāma] that he lived in the monk's cell built by the general Dīghasanda. Dīghasanda was, according to [*Māhavaṃsa*] 15, 230, a leader of the army of Devānaṃpiyatissa, and the cell founded by him, which bore after him the name Dīghasandasenāpatipariveṇa, belonged to the Mahāvihāra."[94] The provenance of the *Māhavaṃsa* is thus set in the context of the Mahāvihāra, but that provenance is not attributed until perhaps five or six centuries after the *Māhavaṃsa*'s composition. It is because of this named author that the date of the text is assumed to be fifth century; the running historical narrative (that is, the first narrative that ends with the reign of Mahāsena) leaves off at an earlier date. This endpoint is the same in the *Dīpavaṃsa*, which lends credibility to the theory that the *Mahāvaṃsa* is either a direct reorganization and retelling of the *Dīpavaṃsa* as we know it or that both texts are working from the same urtext and are envisioning themselves to be better, more sophisticated renditions of the same narrative. In either case, there is an undeniable relationship between the *Dīpavaṃsa* and the *Mahāvaṃsa* even if we cannot sufficiently or precisely date either text's composition.

SHARED SOURCES

The most likely relationship between the *Dīpavaṃsa* and *Mahāvaṃsa* is one of shared sources and perhaps a shared textual community, albeit one that extends over time. The *Mahāvaṃsa* may have been composed with reference to the same source material, or *aṭṭhakathā*, that had been the source for the narrative content of the *Dīpavaṃsa*, but in the introduction to his seminal edition and translation of the *Mahāvaṃsa*, Geiger suggests an even more direct relationship between the two texts: "I am now inclined to consider the relation between Mah. and Dīp. as a closer one than in my first work. That the author of the former knew the latter and used it I have naturally never disputed. But I should now wish, in agreement with Fleet, to go much further and regard the Mah. as a conscious and intentional rearrangement of the Dīp., as a sort of commentary to this latter. I also think now that the quotation of the '*Mahāvaṃsa* of the ancients' in the proemium of our Mah. refers precisely to the Dīp."[95] Geiger oscillated in his stance on the possible degree of relationship between the two texts and to the source texts, and many later scholars followed his conclusions. The ambitious proem of the *Mahāvaṃsa* does eviscerate the literary aspirations of the "*Mahāvaṃsa* of the ancients," and when the two texts are read side by side, it is certainly tempting to assume this phrase refers to the earlier *Dīpavaṃsa.*

Along this line contrary to Geiger, Collins, in his own reading of the later commentary *Vaṃsatthappakāsinī*, sees the reference to the "*Mahāvaṃsa* of the ancients" as pointing not to the *Dīpavaṃsa* but to early Sinhalese accounts.[96] This has come to be the more commonly accepted conclusion among scholars. With the information we have, we cannot make a conclusive argument that this phrase in the *Mahāvaṃsa* is not actually referring to the *Dīpavaṃsa*. Even if they are not directly related, reading the proem of the *Mahāvaṃsa* as indicative of a certain view against older source materials, including the likes of the *Dīpavaṃsa* and perhaps, as Geiger wishfully concluded, even the *Dīpavaṃsa* itself, is helpful to highlight the intentionally literary turn made by the *Mahāvaṃsa*.

RECONSTRUCTING HISTORY THROUGH THE *VAṂSAS*

There is undeniably plenty of historical information provided within these two texts, particularly in what has become the accepted chronology of events that is the subject of the narrative of the *Dīpavaṃsa* and the *Mahāvaṃsa*. Scholars write about the community of the early Pāli *vaṃsa* production by leaning on prior interpreters of the later extension of the *Mahāvaṃsa*, the very source of the information about the Mahāvihāra from the fourth and fifth century on (the time of production of the *Dīpavaṃsa* and *Mahāvaṃsa*, respectively). Most scholars agree to a fifth-century date for the *Mahāvaṃsa*, but some, such as G. C. Mendis, consider that "it was probably composed about the sixth century A.D."[97] This discrepancy in dating follows other chronological anomalies in the text itself. In a footnote, Gombrich explains: "Like Rahula, I am keeping to the chronology established by Geiger (1912). According to Mendis (1947), Duṭṭhagāmaṇī's rule should be dated 161–137 BCE and all Sinhala dates from then on til [*sic*] the end of the fourth century be moved back 60 years. The problem is that somewhere between Devānaṃpiya Tissa and the late eleventh century the *Mahāvaṃsa* put in 60 regnal years too many. Geiger thinks it is in the fifth century, at the very beginning of the *Cūlavaṃsa*; Mendis argues that it is between Devānaṃpiya Tissa and Duṭṭhagāmaṇī. I find Mendis' arguments plausible but not conclusive."[98]

In other words, we are unsure of the dates that have been fixed for the composition of the *Mahāvaṃsa*. With the date of the text itself unsettled, how sure can we be of the other information we glean from the text? Can we even be certain of what precisely was meant by the designation "Mahāvihāra" at this early juncture? The bolstering force of the *saṅgha* reforms (purification) by the twelfth-century king Parākramabāhu I has forevermore colored our understanding of the Mahāvihāra community. He unified the three main, competing sects, the Mahāvihāra, Abhayagiri, and Jetavana, under the sole leadership of the Mahāvihāra, which spurred the exportation of the unified Theravāda to other countries and thus secured a relatively unchallenged position of orthodoxy for the Mahāvihāra once and for all. Of course, what we know about Parākramabāhu's royal activity comes from the literary sources, such as the extension of the *Mahāvaṃsa*.

The narrative practices employed within the text—including and perhaps even privileging the mythological elements so readily dismissed by modern historical methods as flights of fancy or, at best, elements that contain merely a germ of the truth—actually prefigure the modern study and interpretation of the text as a work of history by downplaying the centrality of the mythical mores of the text and overinterpreting what are already overdetermined characters (such as the *yakkhas* and *nāgas*). Far more than the chronological structure, these literary elements—first the reading instructions given in the proem, then the subtle employment of metaphor and other poetic devices, and, finally and most importantly, the saturated landscape populated by the *nāgas*—are employed for a lasting effect on the primed audience.

The chronology is the temporal framework, the structural apparatus for organizing and presenting the text's inspirational stories. The representation of time transforms through the narrative: from the Eliadean *illud tempus*, a deeply mythologized aspect of the Buddha's time and the time periods of the former buddhas' visits to the island that are nonetheless represented as particular events in time, to the then-present, a representation of a remembered king's reign. Moving from the mythopoeic to the present within the same narrative construct helps to collapse the immeasurable temporal divide between the Buddha and the audience. Culling historical kernels from the narrative, searching for the germ of historical truth, thus ironically undermines the text's temporal project and obfuscates the narrative arc.

By arguing that the narrative is not to be read as linearly historical, I do not tread entirely new methodological grounds. My approach to the "history" that we glean from our sources is informed by Stephen Berkwitz's warnings regarding the facts or context behind the text: "Attempts to arrive at the historical context—as if a single 'context' ever exists—of Buddhist histories results in a problem directly related to the fictive reconstruction of historical narratives. The particular context upon which an interpretation can be based is, like the plot of histories, something that is as much invented as found. Any historical context that is presumed to exist behind and prior to a given text constitutes an abstract image of the 'real past,' a past that is itself created and synthesized by the historian out of readings from other texts."[99] In other words, what is read as historical "data" within the *Mahāvaṃsa* is itself a part of an inventive, imaginative literary project. The corroborating "evidence" gleaned from other texts, such as the *Vaṃsatthappakāsinī* and the *Mahāvaṃsa* extensions (*Cūlavaṃsa*), is also a part of an ongoing literary project and can hardly provide an objective assessment of the historical context of the *Mahāvaṃsa*. In his consideration of the late-thirteenth-century *Sinhala Thūpavaṃsa*, Berkwitz points to the need to break the hold of the so-called purely historical interpretation of Buddhist history in favor of framing and strategically reading these texts as literature: "The choice to frame Buddhist history as a form of religious narrative used to accomplish religiously defined and sanctioned goals instead of a sequence of real, external events from the past recasts our study of historical texts in Sri Lankan Buddhism. Textuality and language replace historical fidelity as the objects of inquiry in Buddhist historiography."[100] Although his argument refers specifically to the vernacular Buddhist histories of the late medieval period and to the *Sinhala Thūpavaṃsa* in particular, I believe this method may be profitably applied to the reading of the *Dīpavaṃsa* and the *Mahāvaṃsa* as well.[101] The *Mahāvaṃsa* itself defies temporal fixity even in the midst of its finely tuned attention to chronologies and dates. The patterns, icons, and emotional qualities it invokes defy temporal bounds and speak persuasively and practically to Theravāda Buddhist communities in the past, present, and future. Reading the *Mahāvaṃsa* as a religiously conceived and utilized text, one that begins with the Buddha himself, rather than as a history of the acts of kings allows us to begin to see how persuasive the text is and how it does not merely document history but works on its audience to provoke a response. By "religiously conceived," I mean that the compiler or compilers of the *Mahāvaṃsa* worked within a monastic context to inscribe the *vaṃsa* or lineage of his or their monastic institution while simultaneously shaping his or their text to inspire a powerful sense of location, community, and faith in the audience. We see how the *Mahāvaṃsa* builds an argument about its own efficacy and transformative powers vis-à-vis the primed community of reception. Lest we forget the text's express purpose, the line that concludes each chapter of the *Mahāvaṃsa*—"Sujanappasādasaṃvegatthāya kate mahāvaṃse" (Made for the anxious thrill and serene satisfaction of good people)—reminds us, even in the midst of the chronology, that this text is a religious one, as I discuss further in the conclusion.

HISTORY AS A LITERARY DEVICE

We might say that one of the proems' literary effects is to prepare a certain kind of reader of Buddhist histories. In this way, the "spurious" historicity (that is, gauged by empiricist historical criteria) presented in the account of the Buddha's visits no longer detracts from the story itself; ultimately, it is irrelevant whether the Buddha actually made a visit to the island immediately upon his enlightenment. In the world of the story, he does make such a visit, and in the world of the story the island of Laṅkā is transformed by it. As Berkwitz suggests for later medieval texts, "Aiming not for a literal representation of the past but, rather, for a literary one, the Theravāda relic *vaṃsas* suggest to us that historical narratives were once used to structure the emotional and ethical dispositions of a medieval Buddhist audience."[102] For the reader, the way to engage in transformation is by suspending disbelief, literally making a leap of faith from a documentary to a worklike reading in order to position himself or herself as the receptor of a text that has such transformative abilities. Through the act of reading, the reader tacitly accepts the role of the "good person" for whom the text was intended.

The historically situated concerns of the *Dīpavaṃsa* and *Mahāvaṃsa* textual communities may have shaped the way their respective stories unfold in terms of both structure and rhetorical details. Following the story too closely, assuming that the texts are documenting what exists around them rather than participating in a constructive, literary maneuver, obfuscates the work that each text is doing to construct its community. Walters attempts to marry the dominant narrative of writing in a time of political upheaval with the more specialized literary tactics at work in the *Mahāvaṃsa* as compared to those at work in the *Dīpavaṃsa*. He characterizes the salient reasons for the composition of the *Dīpavaṃsa* as an argument for legitimacy in a time of contention:

> The monks and nuns of the Mahāvihāra produced the [*Dīpavaṃsa*], the first Pāli text of Sri Lanka, as a challenge to the privileged position enjoyed by the residents of the Abhayagirivihāra in the fourth century. More than that, by claiming to be the descendants of an originary Buddhist order uncorrupted with later Great Vehicle practices, it also posed a challenge to the "idealist" Buddhists who were coming into prominence in the Gupta-Vākāṭaka imperial formation in response to the "realist" Buddhists who had prevailed when imperial rulers recognized theirs as superior to other ways of life. The complex author of the [*Dīpavaṃsa*] composed that text as part of its fight for survival (in the wake of Mahāsena's disastrous reign).[103]

Walters then contends that the central project of the *Mahāvaṃsa* was to reach beyond the limited concerns of inter-*vihāra* rivalries and defense against the "Great Vehicle" influences that were beginning to infiltrate the thoughts and practices of various *vihāras*. The *Mahāvaṃsa*, he argues, raises the Mahāvihāra and its monkish interests to a prominent position throughout its predominantly royal narrative: "Rather than merely claiming a place for Sri Lankan kings and Mahāvihāran monks within a larger imperial formation, [the *Mahāvaṃsa*] claimed pride of place for them within the world it began to imagine. For nearly four centuries after Dhātusena, however, no king was in a position to do anything more than dream about a world in which a Sri Lankan king and the Theravāda order he supported would exercise such power." In other words, Walters sees the *Mahāvaṃsa* as having "transformed [the *Dīpavaṃsa*'s] strategy" in an unambiguously political sense.[104] I see a parallel transformation at work in a literary sense.

◈ ◈ ◈

Just as the authors or compilers of the *Dīpavaṃsa* and *Mahāvaṃsa* represented stories within the framework of a historical trajectory, so we organize data culled from these texts according to our own most salient frameworks of interpretation. Seneviratne reminds us that "history, therefore, can no longer be fact—not because facts are only the first step in creative interpretation—but because the kind of facts it seeks, namely facts about the past, are inherently unestablishable, and, therefore, those facts with which we endow the past are imaginings based on a present enclosed in its own processes of creating attitude, perspective and value."[105] This statement is as true for our contemporary reading of "historical" texts as it was for the compilers of the *Dīpavaṃsa* and *Mahāvaṃsa*. Seneviratne continues to place himself and his fellow contributors on a scale of historical interpretations, one that I believe extends into history beyond the reflective act of twentieth-century scholarship looking at ancient texts, wherein texts are constantly renegotiating and rearticulating, forging arguments with and against each other, and isolating particularly salient stories. Awareness of both texts' literary aims changes the type of reading we perform on them. It is within the *vaṃsas* that we see the "world wishes" articulating and constructing rather than documenting the worlds in which the texts were composed. Seneviratne continues, thinking about current events in Sri Lanka and how we can see "the present as shaping the past": "Newly centralized and unified polities invent or interpret myths to justify their exclusive rights to habitation in a given locality and to subordinate or exclude those defined as others. Accounts of the past are embellished and interpreted through the perspective of present-day ethnic and other group identities, aspirations, values, interests and so forth."[106]

Turning to the sense of urgency conveyed in the *Mahāvaṃsa*, I am reminded of the volume of recent scholarship on the "*Mahāvaṃsa* mentality," the postcolonial phenomenon of employing the rhetoric and vision of the *Mahāvaṃsa* to bolster nationalistic, hegemonically Sinhalese Buddhist ideas about what Sri Lanka is. Briefly, this "*Mahāvaṃsa* mentality" is susceptible to deconstruction on the basis of its anachronistic conception of statehood.[107] Too often scholars are seduced by the efficacy and interpretability of the chronological structure of the *Mahāvaṃsa*. Indeed, there are recognizable patterns of dissolution and reformation, power struggles and oppositions happening in the text.[108] Consider, for example, what Bardwell Smith has to say about postcolonial Sinhalese Buddhist identity in his essay "Sinhalese Buddhism and the Dilemmas of Reinterpretation" and how it might be fruitful to apply the same deductive logic to the scenario articulated in the proems: "The manner in which a community in times of profound crisis reaches into the past to discover its identity and redefine itself in relationship to this past, even to perceive distinction and uniqueness over against it, has considerable psychological and social importance."[109]

I am inclined to add "ethical importance" here, both for the individual reader-hearer and for the community of interpreters. In the case of our Pāli *vaṃsas*, the same technology of calling forth the past to help define the present is performed in two distinct ways. First, both *vaṃsas* begin with a foray into the deep and legitimating past, the Buddha himself, even though chronologically the Buddha would have lived centuries prior to either text's composition. Second, the *Mahāvaṃsa*'s proem distances itself from what it calls "the *Mahāvaṃsa* of the ancients," commonly understood to be either the *Dīpavaṃsa* itself or the urtext (*aṭṭhakathā*) from which both the *Dīpavaṃsa* and the *Mahāvaṃsa* cull their material.

Paying attention to the circumstances—social, institutional, political, and religious—in which the two earliest extant Sri Lankan *vaṃsas* were produced is obviously an important way to understand the literary devices we have encountered in these texts. But we must be wary that just as our own situatedness affects the way we structure our understanding of the historical time period whence these texts sprang, their fourth- and fifth-century situation also informs the way they have been conceived.

Both *vaṃsas* collect previous information; neither claims to be an original work, and we must remember to read them as products of a literary world in which originality was not the point. But both of them present the past in ways that are influenced by their present. Fresh reading practices help us encounter Buddhist histories on literary terms.[110]

CONCLUSION

THE PĀLI *Mahāvaṃsa* has survived through fifteen hundred years of history to become a seminal text of Sri Lankan Buddhism. It has survived thanks in part to the scribes who were charged along the way with copying it (palm-leaf manuscripts do not hold up indefinitely in the Sri Lankan climate). It survived the early translation performed by George Turnour and the consequent attention it garnered from Western Orientalists. And it survived through numerous other intervening interpretations, finally making its way into the hands of modern interpretive communities and scholars alike. Modern scholars must be grateful to all these scribes and interpreters, without whom the text may not have survived at all. Yet we must not forget the work that these interpretations have exerted on our modern understanding of the text. As I hope to have shown by now, key operative facets of this text—its literary form, function, and aims as well as the emotionally provocative, religious work it can perform on the primed reader—warrant a reorientation of modern scholarship on this monumental text.

The abundance of relatively recent work on the *Mahāvaṃsa*, scholarly and polemical, Western and Sinhalese, initially piqued my interest in this text. As a student, I found myself reading the secondary material more thoroughly than the *Mahāvaṃsa* itself and being swayed by various opinions about the foundational role it has played in forming the consciousness of the modern Sinhalese people. The more I read, the more the *Mahāvaṃsa* receded into the background. I realized that I had lost the text itself in the extensive and persuasive layers of interpretation that enshroud it for the contemporary reader, no matter his or her situation.

Reading translations only compounded this effect of feeling removed from the world of the text. Colorful rhetoric such as Wilhelm Geiger's rendering of the phrase *sāsanujjotanaṭṭhānaṃ* as "a place where [the Buddha's] doctrine should (thereafter) shine in glory," when "glory" is nowhere implied in the Pāli, initially clouded what I understood to be the text's purpose. Reading the *Mahāvaṃsa* in Pāli, I came away with a different impression altogether about the relationship of this text with the rise of Sinhalese nationalist discourse. I began to see the anachronism of attributing to this text the status of foundational charter, let alone the designation "history." The narrative's colorful *nāga* stories drew me deeper into the text, and I wondered why snakes had anything to do with Buddhist history writing. But just as they slipped out of my reach when I privileged historical or political concerns over literary, they engaged my imagination when I read the *Mahāvaṃsa* in the Pāli. I had to ask, What are such evocative literary characters doing in the midst of such a historically minded, culturally defining expression, a relic of the original Mahāvihāran claims to authority and even supremacy?

I began to imagine the utility of reading this text as a work of literature, with all the emotional, aesthetic, and didactic dimensions that such a reading may carry. My hope is that I have been able to illustrate here why a rethinking of the Pāli *Mahāvaṃsa* is not only warranted but also provides an essential corrective in the study of Theravāda Buddhism and Sri Lankan texts.

The *Mahāvaṃsa* itself justifies my approach. As we see in its proem, its agenda is not historical or political but ethical: the text is intended to lead to a particular transformation in the reader-hearer. The *Mahāvaṃsa*'s proem uses language that clearly suggests the text's purpose is to generate first *saṃvega*, anxious thrill, and then the resulting *pasāda*, serene satisfaction. Once primed by the proem, the reader immediately encounters the narrative of the Buddha himself. The *Mahāvaṃsa* thus begins with an impact, calling up an image that was clearly intended to inspire *saddhā* (confidence or faith) and a type of faith-filled reading. The text not only encourages its readers to take on this specific, religious vantage point vis-à-vis the text but also continues to employ various rhetorical techniques throughout, such as the metaphor of the *dhamma* as a light or lamp, that buttress such a reading and ensure that the reader is transformed through the act of reading.

And whom do readers encounter besides the Buddha in this very first chapter of the *Mahāvaṃsa*, in this charged and light-filled atmosphere?

Just as the Buddha encounters the reader and in fact intercedes on his behalf, so the reader is swept into being interested in the *nāgas*. Though scholars are wont to suggest as much, the character of the *nāga* cannot be reduced to any compact, symbolic shorthand for chaos.[1] Nor is it to be understood exclusively as a representation of an indigenous people in the land of Laṅkā, as certain historicist readings, bent on reconstructing the ethnic histories underlying the text, have implied.[2] I suggest, rather, that the *nāga* is an ideal literary character employed in these poetic narratives to provoke desirable emotions and to heighten the reader-hearer's aesthetic response.

The *nāga*'s ontological status sets it apart from the human who confronts it in the text. It is this gap that makes the *nāga* such an effective character to assist in heightening the reader-hearer's emotions as she or he reads the *Mahāvaṃsa*. The *nāgas* act much like humans; they are scared, assuaged, converted, devoted, and anguished when confronted by the Buddha and separated from him or his relics. The audience may empathize with them insofar as their emotional state is concerned. But the *nāgas*' dubious soteriological aptitude leads the audience finally to feel more sympathy than empathy, and this contrast generates in them feelings of gratitude for their human birth and a sense of urgency regarding proper practice. This result makes no literal sense, but it makes great literary sense.[3]

According to the *Mahāvaṃsa*, *nāgas* are soteriologically capable of great faith and transformation. The use of such characters performs a particular kind of work on the reader. Imagining the *nāgas* as distinctly "other" than human rather than as surrogate characters for a human agent or vehicles solely to inspire empathy helps to catalyze for the audience the requisite imaginative processes. In a community where the Buddha himself was never historically present, the reader-hearer must make a significant imaginative leap to cultivate faith and proper practice. This is the purpose of the "other" character, the *nāga*, in the *Mahāvaṃsa*—to catalyze that imaginative leap for the reader and affirm the Buddha's continuing presence.

For the primed reader, the stories of the *nāgas* introduce or underscore the urgency and necessity of these anticipated emotional responses and their concomitant ethical and ritual behaviors—the very actions that engender the community of "good people" purportedly constructed through the reading of this text. In other words, if the *nāgas* can be so affected by the Buddha, riled and thrilled and then pacified and converted, how much more so should this emotional and ethical experience occur for the primed monastic audience? For a member of the monastic community who has already explicitly stated at his *upasampadā* (ordination) that he is not a *nāga*, the *nāgas* in the *Mahāvaṃsa*, faithful and ubiquitous, always proximate and devoted to the Buddha and his relics, would be especially provocative characters to help generate the imaginative, transformative work called for by the text.

It is this monastic community that is responsible for the production and use of the *Mahāvaṃsa*. Scholars typically consider the *Mahāvaṃsa* to have been a conscientious attempt by Mahāvihāran monks to shore up support for their vision of orthodoxy and orthopraxy in an unstable political and religious climate. What is typically overlooked, however, is the way these monks accomplished this assertive project—namely, through a riveting text designed to carry the authority of preordination, or *Heilesgeschichte*, of the Buddha and the coming of his relics to the island of Laṅkā. As Jonathan Walters has noted, the *Mahāvaṃsa* may be considered unique among texts of its era insofar as it represents a deliberate play for historicization by the Mahāvihāra community of monks to secure their particular vision as the Theravāda orthodoxy. Walters reminds us that the *Mahāvaṃsa*, as a Buddhist history, "was not intended to be 'objective' as nineteenth-century historians understood the term; it was intended as a guide in making sense of the present in order to shape the future."[4]

But even this nuanced understanding of the agency and literary consciousness of the *Mahāvaṃsa*'s textual community is colored by the much later medieval commentary on it, the *Vaṃsatthappakāsinī*. Walters calls that commentary a "Mahāvihāran imperial project," written to legitimize the Okkāka dynastic ascendancy and hegemony by recording "the proceedings of a 'committee of inquiry' charged with interpreting the Mahāvihāran *Vaṃsa* (then five hundred years old)."[5] This "commentarial text" was given the title "Ṭīkā" (Commentary) and enabled Turnour and Geiger to read and interpret the *Mahāvaṃsa*, and it may be entirely responsible for creating the Mahāvihāran imperial-project lens that all subsequent readings have utilized.[6] If at the outset we move away from reading the *Mahāvaṃsa* as a political charter or argument by the Mahāvihāra—a reading exacerbated by the entrenched, politicized Mahāvihāran rhetoric of the *Vaṃsatthappakāsinī*—we can begin to access the type of imaginative and aesthetically infused reading the *Mahāvaṃsa* itself advocates.

With this new reading, we see that the *Mahāvaṃsa* does not represent the singular political agenda of an orthodox, nascent, and ambitious Mahāvihāran community. The text's proem has voiced its hopes for the reader-hearer in aesthetic and ethical terms. Poetic elements such as the repetitive metaphor of *dhamma* as "light" or "lamp" work on the textual community not just to edify but to create a circumscribed supporting community of "good people" who are ethically and imaginatively inspired by the text. In the world of the text, these intended effects are brought about using various tactics, one of which is the presence of *nāgas*. The *nāgas* are not used simply as a "narrative hook" or as an accommodation for folk or low lay religious practice but are instead an integral part of the cosmos as understood by the textual community. Both the predominant presence of and the particular use of the *nāga* in the *vaṃsa* narrative renderings of history suggest that the *nāga* is a significant agent in Pāli Buddhist texts, which are compiled "for the anxious thrill and serene satisfaction of good people."

The literary dimension of the *Mahāvaṃsa* has been treated in a cursory way, if at all, in past scholarship. As scholars of religion, we find ourselves building our interpretations on the cumulative readings of the past, including the readings of earlier texts visible in commentarial traditions that have sustained our source texts to the present. But I have argued that the *Mahāvaṃsa* requires a rethinking in its own right and that recent readings and uses (and abuses) of its narrative have obfuscated the text's work.

If, as Kevin Trainor puts it, relic veneration is a "technology of remembrance and representation" of the Buddha, a "cultural strategy for bridging temporal and spatial separation through a complex interaction of material objects, abstract notions, emotional orientations, and ritualized behaviors,"[7] perhaps the *Mahāvaṃsa* is best understood as a relic itself that demands attention, even devotion, from the reader. Really paying attention to the *nāgas* affirms the *Mahāvaṃsa*'s values. The presence and prominence of the *nāgas* in the text is thus to be anticipated and enjoyed; just as the *nāgas* attend the relics described in the text, they are indices of importance for the text itself. The *Mahāvaṃsa* is not exclusively a history but a relic in its own right, which, like a "real" relic, "passes through" the world of the *nāgas* in order to become efficacious. Much like any traditional Buddhist relic, it requires physical proximity for efficacy and an attitude of openness about its intended emotional effect (faith and confidence, or some respectful analogue thereof for the contemporary reader-scholar who is not personally expecting transformation to result from her reading). As a *vaṃsa* that has persisted into our contemporary world, the *Mahāvaṃsa* is certainly a "cultural strategy for bridging temporal and spatial separation" when read in this new light.

NOTES

INTRODUCTION

1. The question of the situated perspective of the one performing the inquiry is prevalent in religious studies today. For an example, see Russell T. McCutcheon, ed., *The Insider/Outsider Problem in the Study of Religion* (London: Cassell, 1999).
2. Hereafter I refer to King Aśoka as "Asoka," as his name appears in Pāli sources.
3. *Sāsana* is a key term and refers to the establishment of the Three Jewels—namely, the Buddha, the *dhamma* (doctrine), and the *saṅgha* (community). In the Theravādin Buddhist understanding of time, there can be only one Buddha at a time. Therefore, so long as the (current) Buddha (Gotama) is remembered, his relics are available for veneration, the *dhamma* is observed and taught, and the *saṅgha* exists as a field of merit, one lives in the *sāsana*. The term *sāsana* is therefore typically translated as "dispensation" and includes all aspects of the Buddhist tradition: the instructional and ritual materials, texts, relics, and so on of the *saṅgha*. Anne Blackburn translates *sāsana* as "Buddhist teachings and institutions" (*Buddhist Learning and Textual Practice in Eighteenth-Century Lankan Monastic Culture* [Princeton: Princeton University Press, 2001], 4).
4. Mahānāma, *The Mahāvaṃsa; or, The Great Chronicle of Ceylon*, trans. Wilhelm Geiger, assisted by Mabel Haynes Bode (London: Frowde for the Pāli Text Society, 1912), x. Note that this classic translation was completed under the patronage of the government of what was then called Ceylon.
5. In the introduction to his critical edition of this text, G. P. Malalasekera assigns the *Vaṃsatthappakāsinī* to the eighth or ninth century (introduction to *Vaṃsatthappakāsinī: Commentary on the* Mahāvaṃsa, 2 vols., ed. G. P. Malalasekera [1935–1936; reprint, London: Pāli Text Society, 1977], 1:cix), in contrast to Wilhelm Geiger's suggestion of sometime between 1000 and 1250 C.E. (*Cūlavaṃsa: Being the More Recent Part of the* Mahāvaṃsa, trans. Wilhelm Geiger and C. Mabel Rickmers (from the German into English) [London: Pāli Text Society, 1929], 267). Walpola Rahula and K. R. Norman agree with Malalasekera (Walpola Rahula, *History of Buddhism in Ceylon: The Anurādhapura Period, 3rd Century BC–10th Century AC*, 2nd ed. [Colombo, Sri Lanka: Gunasena, 1956], xxiv; K. R. Norman, *Pāli-Literature, Including*

the Canonical Literature in Prakrit and Sanskrit of All the Hīnayāna Schools of Buddhism [Wiesbaden, Germany: Otto Harrassowitz, 1983], 139).

6. Jonathan Walters, "Buddhist History: The Sri Lankan Pāli *Vaṃsas* and Their Commentary," in Ronald Inden, Jonathan Walters, and Daud Ali, *Querying the Medieval: Texts and the History of Practices in South Asia* (New York: Oxford University Press, 2000), 99–164.
7. For a similar argument applied to later, vernacular texts, see Steven Berkwitz, *Buddhist History in the Vernacular: The Power of the Past in Late Medieval Sri Lanka* (Leiden: Brill, 2004), and "Emotions and Ethics in Buddhist History," *Religion* 31, no. 2 (2001): 155–173. Also see Charles Hallisey, "Devotion in the Buddhist Literature of Medieval Sri Lanka," Ph.D. diss., University of Chicago, 1988. This "aesthetically sensitive" approach does not preclude a reading of the texts as politically charged and assertive, as shown in chapter 5. The multiple ways the narratives in the *vaṃsas* are used through history points to the genre's useful multivalence.
8. *Mahāvaṃsa* I.3: "Vajjitaṃ tehi dosehi sukkhaggahaṇadhāraṇaṃ /pasādasaṃ vegakaraṃ sutito ca upāgataṃ."
9. *Mahāvaṃsa* I.4: "Pasādajanake ṭhāne tathā saṃvegakārak e / janayantā pasādaṃ ca saṃvegaṃ ca suṇātha taṃ." Geiger translates *ṭhane* not as "ground or condition," as I am inclined, but as "places in the text," with the following result: "[Attend ye to it] while that ye call up serene joy and emotion [in you] at passages that awaken serene joy and emotion" (Mahānāma, *Mahāvaṃsa*, Geiger trans. [1912], 1).
10. See, for instance, *Mahāvaṃsa* I.4 and II.7, among other appearances of this phrase: "Sujanappasādasaṃvegatthāya kate."
11. Martha Nussbaum, *Love's Knowledge: Essays on Philosophy and Literature* (New York: Oxford University Press, 1990), and *Upheavals of Thought: The Intelligence of Emotions* (Cambridge: Cambridge University Press, 2001); Hayden White, *The Content of the Form: Narrative Discourse and Historical Representation* (Baltimore: Johns Hopkins University Press, 1987), and *Tropics of Discourse: Essays in Cultural Criticism* (Baltimore: Johns Hopkins University Press, 1978); Paul Ricoeur, *Oneself as Another*, trans. Kathleen Blamey (Chicago: University of Chicago Press, 1992), and *Time and Narrative*, 3 vols., trans. Kathleen Blamey and David Pellauer (Chicago: University of Chicago Press, 1984–1988); Umberto Eco, *The Role of the Reader: Explorations in the Semiotics of Texts* (Bloomington: Indiana University Press, 1979), and *Six Walks in the Fictional Woods*, Charles Eliot Norton Lectures, 1993 (Cambridge, Mass.: Harvard University Press, 1994).
12. Patterns (of transference of the *dhamma* and of fear followed by satisfaction) and rhetorical structures (metaphors such as the *dhamma* as light; *phalaśruti*, or the fruits of reciting or hearing the text; *slesa* [Sanskrit, *śleṣa*], or double meaning; and puns) introduced in the first chapter of the *Mahāvaṃsa* determine how the rest of the historical narrative is conveyed and received.
13. Kevin Trainor defines "relic veneration" as a "technology of remembrance and representation" of the Buddha, a "cultural strategy for bridging temporal and spatial separation through a complex interaction of material objects, abstract notions, emotional orientations, and ritualized behaviors" (*Relics, Ritual, and Representation in Buddhism: Rematerializing the Sri Lankan Theravāda Tradition* [Cambridge: Cambridge University Press, 1997], 27).
14. See Sheldon Pollock, *The Language of the Gods in the World of Men: Sanskrit, Culture, and Power in Premodern India* (Berkeley: University of California Press, 2006).

15. *Nāgas* are agents both in our world and in the *nāgaloka* (subterranean *nāga* world). *Nāgas* are chthonic inhabitants of and movers on the waters and thus a salient vehicle for the movement of the *dhamma* from India to a new center, Sri Lanka, because they are an accepted part of the pan-Indic cosmos and yet are presented in the Sri Lankan context as autochthonous. They are karmically (bodhilogically) challenged because of their lack of human birth, and yet they are always seen in proximity to the Buddha or his relics.
16. As reviewed in chapter 5, scholars have in the past mined the *vaṃsas* primarily and productively for historical "facts." In a representative dismissal of the power of narrative, Bimala Churn Law identifies the "value" of the *vaṃsas* as follows: "It is, however, important that one should read them with a critical eye as all records of popular and ecclesiastical tradition deserve to be read. Buried in the illumination of myths, miracles, and legends, there are indeed germs which go to make up facts of history, but they can only be gleaned by a very careful elimination of all mythical and unessential details which the pious sentiment of the believer gathered round the nucleus" (*A History of Pāli Literature*, 2 vols. [London: Kegan Paul, Trench, Trübner, 1933], 2:540–541).
17. In other words, scholars' concerns and agendas often predetermine their findings regarding the *Mahāvaṃsa*. When the *Mahāvaṃsa* is read for historical information, that information can be found; when it is read to justify or explain the modern Sinhalese Buddhist sense of mission, it can do so. But what results from such approaches is a shortsighted reading of a complex, multivalent text. By "mythic myopia," I suggest that the text's mythical elements should not be overlooked and should not be explained away as symbolic treatments of historical concerns (for example, the *nāgas* have been identified with aboriginal tribes, an identification that certainly affects the rhetorical force of the mythically imbued sections of the *Mahāvaṃsa* where they play a major role). By focusing on the literary dimensions of the *Mahāvaṃsa*, my reading, including an intentional focus on the mythical aspects, comes closer to the reading outlined in the text's proem and offers a better sense of how the text might have "worked" for its fifth-century textual community.
18. I have chosen to translate *saṃvega* as "anxious thrill" and *pasāda* as "serene satisfaction," although both terms encompass a wide semantic range. In his 1912 translation of the *Mahāvaṃsa*, Geiger translates them as "emotion" and "serene joy," respectively. As indicated later, *saṃvega* (from *saṃ* + *vij*) has a range of meanings, including "agitation," "fear," "anxiety," "thrill," and, according to the Pāli Text Society's *Pāli-English Dictionary*, "religious emotion (caused by contemplation of the miseries of this world)." *Pasāda* (from *pa* + *sad*) incorporates a sense of brightness, clearness, even purity (when referring to colors) as well as joy, satisfaction, happiness, good mind, virtue, and faith; a tertiary meaning extends it to repose, composure, and serenity (T. W. Rhys Davids and William Stede, eds., *Pāli-English Dictionary* [1921–1925; reprint, Oxford: Pāli Text Society, 1995]).
19. See Jonathan Walters, "Mahāsena at the Mahāvihāra: The Interpretation and Politics of History in Medieval Sri Lanka," in *Invoking the Past: The Uses of History in South Asia*, ed. Daud Ali (Oxford: Oxford University Press, 1999), 322–366, and especially Walters, "Buddhist History."
20. See Berkwitz, *Buddhist History in the Vernacular*, and "History and Gratitude in Theravāda Buddhism," *Journal of the American Academy of Religion* 71, no. 3 (2003): 579–604.

21. Trainor, *Relics, Ritual, and Representation in Buddhism*, esp. 82–84, 166–168; see also Kevin Trainor, "*Pasanna/Pasāda* in the Pāli *Vaṃsa* Literature," *Vidyodaya Journal of Social Sciences* 3 (1989): 185–190, and "When Is a Theft Not a Theft? Relic Theft and the Cult of the Buddha's Relics in Sri Lanka," *Numen* 39, no. 1 (1992): 1–26.
22. Andy Rotman, "The Erotics of Practice: Objects and Agency in Buddhist *Avadāna* Literature," *Journal of the American Academy of Religion* 71, no. 3 (2003): 555–578, and *Thus Have I Seen: Visualizing Faith in Early Indian Buddhism* (New York: Oxford University Press, 2008).
23. Maria Heim, "The Aesthetics of Excess," *Journal of the American Academy of Religion* 71, no. 3 (2003): 531–554, and *The Forerunner of All Things: Buddhaghosa on Mind, Intention, and Agency* (New York: Oxford University Press, 2014).
24. Charles Hallisey, "Works and Persons in Sinhala Literary Culture," in *Literary Cultures in History: Reconstructions from South Asia*, ed. Sheldon Pollock (Berkeley: University of California Press, 2003), 689–746; Charles Hallisey, "Devotion in the Buddhist Literature of Medieval Sri Lanka." Ph.D. diss.; and Charles Hallisey and Anne Hansen, "Narrative, Sub-ethics, and the Moral Life: Some Evidence from Theravāda Buddhism," *Journal of Religious Ethics* 24, no. 2 (1996): 305–327.
25. Yigal Bronner, *Extreme Poetry: The South Asian Movement of Simultaneous Narration* (New York: Columbia University Press, 2010). On *kāvya*, see Yigal Bronner, David Shulman, and Gary Tubb, eds., *Innovations and Turning Points: Toward a History of* Kāvya *Literature* (New York: Oxford University Press, 2014).
26. John Strong, *The Relics of the Buddha* (Princeton: Princeton University Press, 2004).
27. Robert DeCaroli, *Haunting the Buddha: Indian Popular Religions and the Formation of Buddhism* (New York: Oxford University Press, 2004).
28. Steven Collins, *Nirvāṇa and Other Buddhist Felicities: Utopias of the Pāli Imaginaire* (Cambridge: Cambridge University Press, 1998); "*Nirvāṇa*, Time, and Narrative," *History of Religions* 31, no. 3 (1992): 215–246; and "On the Very Idea of the Pāli Canon," *Journal of the Pāli Text Society* 15 (1990): 89–126.
29. Blackburn, *Buddhist Learning and Textual Practice.*
30. Anne E. Monius, *Imagining a Place for Buddhism: Literary Culture and Religious Community in Tamil-Speaking South India* (New York: Oxford University Press, 2001).
31. Partly to blame for the absence of this argument is the unwieldiness of the text in the original Pāli; few scholars are inclined to read it, and overreliance on Geiger's 1912 translation (or, worse, on Ananda Guruge's overtly nationalistic rendering published in 1989: Mahānāma, *Mahāvaṃsa: The Great Chronicle of Sri Lanka, Chapters 1-37*, trans. Ananda W. P. Guruge [Colombo, Sri Lanka: Associated Newspapers of Ceylon, 1989]) affects the types of readings one derives from the text. And it is only in a footnote in an appendix that Steven Collins even suggests a retranslation of the key verse in the *Mahāvaṃsa*'s first chapter that might finally destabilize the reading of this text as a charter for Sinhalese supremacy (*Nirvāṇa and Other Buddhist Felicities*, 598–599 n. 17); also see Kristin Scheible, "Priming the Lamp of *Dhamma*: The Buddha's Miracles in the Pāli *Mahavāṃsa*," *Journal of the International Association of Buddhist Studies* 33, nos. 1–2 [2010–2011]: 435–451).
32. There is some interest in the work of proems in Greek and Latin texts, but little in the proems of Sanskrit or Pāli texts.
33. Matthew Kapstein's edited volume *Presence of Light: Divine Radiance and Religious Experience* (Chicago: University of Chicago Press, 2004) brings together scholarship

with a comparative focus. For those sympathetic to Joseph Campbell's interests and methods, his unpublished essays on light have been posthumously edited and published. See Joseph Campbell, *Myths of Light: Eastern Metaphors of the Eternal*, ed. David Kudler (Novato, Calif.: New World Library, 2003).

34. Just think of one's encounter with the Bible, beginning with Genesis 1:3, where God speaks for the first time, and it is to bring forth light, "Let there be light." And for good measure, think of the emphasis on light in John 8:12, where Jesus proclaims, "I am the light of the world. Whoever follows me will never walk in darkness but will have the light of life" (*The New Oxford Annotated Bible*, ed. Michael D. Coogan [New York: Oxford University Press, 2007]).
35. Light in these forms pervades even the titles of great works, such as the tenth century Abhinavagupta's *Tantrāloka* (Light of/on Tantra) or the *Mahāyāna Suvarṇa(pra)bhāsottamāsūtra* (Sutra of Golden Light). Models for quality scholarship on these two texts that pays attention to the literary power of the metaphor of light include Paul E. Muller-Ortega, "Luminous Consciousness: Light in the Tantric Mysticism of Abhinavagupta," in Kapstein, *Presence of Light*, 45–80, and Natalie D. Gummer, "Articulating Potency: A Study of the *Suvarṇa(pra)bhāsottamāsūtra*," Ph.D. diss., Harvard University, 2000.
36. Light saturates the oldest layer of Indic literary production, the Rig Veda; its first verses in praise of the god Agni (himself fire) are filled with light-infused epithets such as "dispeller of the night" and "radiant one" (Rig Veda, book 1, hymn 1).
37. See Luis O. Gomez, *The Land of Bliss: The Paradise of the Buddha of Measureless Light* (Honolulu: University of Hawai'i Press, 1996). The manifestation of light is a result of the Buddha's dharma, a causal relationship that is made apparent in the name of the bodhisattva (prebuddha) who becomes the Buddha Amitābha ("whose light is unlimited"): Dharmakāra (Mine of Dharma; Gomez translates it as "Mine of Virtue").
38. David L. McMahon, *Empty Vision: Ocular Metaphor and Visionary Imagery in Mahāyāna Buddhism* (London: RoutledgeCurzon, 2002), 72.
39. For an excellent study of light, location, and theology, see Diana Eck, *Banaras: City of Light* (New York: Columbia University Press, 1998).
40. Again if we look comparatively to the Bible, the crafty serpent in Genesis 3 sets the fall of humanity in motion.
41. Snakes also inspire creative scholarship. See Jeffrey Kripal, *The Serpent's Gift: Gnostic Reflections on the Study of Religion* (Chicago: University of Chicago Press, 2007).
42. An interesting study of *nāga* worship and of several images can be found in Sadhu Charan Panda, *Nāga Cult in Orissa* (Delhi: B.R. Publishing,1986).
43. Scholars frequently suggest that the subjugation of autochthonous disorder is a vestige in narrative form of sociological patterns of local cultures being subsumed or supplanted by hegemonic ones.
44. As told in the *adi parva* (first section or book 1) of the *Mahābhārata*, the *Bhāgavata Purāṇa*, and the *Viṣṇu Purāṇa*, among others.
45. See the *Bhāgavata Purāṇa*; accessible versions of *nāga* (and light) mythology are found in Cornelia Dimmitt and J. A. B. van Buitenen, *Classical Hindu Mythology: A Reader in the Sanskrit* Puranas (Philadelphia: Temple University Press, 1978), and Heinrich Robert Zimmer, *Myths and Symbols in Indian Art and Civilization* (New York: Pantheon Books, 1946).

46. Kalhaṇa, *Rājataraṅgiṇī*, 3 vols., trans. Aurel Stein (1900; reprint Delhi: Motilal Banarsidas, 1979–1988); Harṣa, *"How the Nāgas Were Pleased"; and "The Shattered Thighs," by Bhāsa*, trans. Andrew Skilton (New York: New York University Press, 2009).
47. *The Lotus Sutra*, trans. Burton Watson (New York: Columbia University Press, 1993). This story is found in chapter 12: "Devadatta."
48. Paul D. L. Avis, *God and the Creative Imagination: Metaphor, Symbol, and Myth in Religion and Theology* (London: Routledge, 1999), 11. As a chaplain to Her Majesty the Queen of England and canon theologian of Exeter Cathedral, Avis is hardly a theological outlier.
49. George Lakoff and Mark Johnson, *Metaphors We Live By* (Chicago: University of Chicago Press, 1980), 1.
50. Dominick LaCapra, *Rethinking Intellectual History: Texts, Contexts, Language* (Ithaca: Cornell University Press, 1983), 30.
51. Blackburn, *Buddhist Learning and Textual Practice*, esp. 10–13; Monius, *Imagining a Place for Buddhism*, esp. 9–10.
52. Brian Stock, "History, Literature, and Medieval Textuality," *Yale French Studies*, no. 70 (1986): 12.

1. INSTRUCTIONS, ADMONITIONS, AND ASPIRATIONS IN VAṂSA PROEMS

1. Steven Collins explicates *pasāda*, which is commonly felt at Buddhist *stūpas*, as "conviction in the religious value of what, or who, evokes the feeling" (*Nirvāṇa and Other Buddhist Felicities: Utopias of the Pāli Imaginaire* [Cambridge: Cambridge University Press, 1998], 593 n. 2. Andy Rotman considers how the mental state of *pasāda* motivates good actions, specifically acts of generosity, defining "good people" (*Thus Have I Seen: Visualizing Faith in Early Indian Buddhism* [New York: Oxford University Press, 2008]).
2. Brian Stock, *The Implications of Literacy* (Princeton: Princeton University Press, 1983).
3. *Mahāvaṃsa* I.2: "porānehi kato."
4. As I assert in chapter 5, I do believe that the *Mahāvaṃsa* (as we have received it) makes reference in a general way to the underlying content of the *Dīpavaṃsa* (as we have received it), although likely not to its precise form, even if both texts were not fixed at the time (as Pāli Text Society critical editions represent fixed texts today). Even though the phrase "*Mahāvaṃsa* of the ancients" within the *Mahāvaṃsa* likely refers to the Sinhalese source materials in the *aṭṭhakathā* (commentarial literature) that predate the compilation of the *Dīpavaṃsa*, the specific "flaws" to which the *Mahāvaṃsa* refers are present and obvious in the *Dīpavaṃsa*. Juxtaposing the two proems thus provides an opportunity to examine the *Mahāvaṃsa*'s literary ambitions.
5. Anne M. Blackburn, *Buddhist Learning and Textual Practice in Eighteenth-Century Lankan Monastic Culture* (Princeton: Princeton University Press, 2001), 9–13.
6. Umberto Eco, *The Limits of Interpretation* (Bloomington: Indiana University Press, 1990), 45.

7. Blackburn, *Buddhist Learning and Textual Practice*, 77.
8. Umberto Eco, *Six Walks in the Fictional Woods*, Charles Eliot Norton Lectures, 1993 (Cambridge, Mass.: Harvard University Press, 1994), 8.
9. This is not to say that readers with agendas will abandon them after reading the proems. A cursory reading of the proems could still result in the overall impression that the Buddha preordained the island of Laṅkā to receive and protect the *dhamma*.
10. Eco, *Six Walks in the Fictional Woods*, 9. For a more comprehensive explanation of model versus empirical readers, see Umberto Eco, *The Role of the Reader: Explorations in the Semiotics of Texts* (Bloomington: Indiana University Press, 1979).
11. This passage from the *Siyabaslakara* is translated in Charles Hallisey, "Works and Persons in Sinhala Literary Culture," in *Literary Cultures in History: Reconstructions from South Asia*, ed. Sheldon Pollock (Berkeley: University of California Press, 2003), 715. G. P. Malalasekera attributes the *Siyabaslakara* to Silāmegha Sena (846–66) (*The Pāli Literature of Ceylon* [1928; reprint, Kandy, Sri Lanka: Buddhist Publication Society, 1994], 167–168).
12. Although J. Brough does not interpret the poetic "work" of this phrase the same way I have here, see his essay "Thus Have I Heard . . . ," *Journal of the Royal Asiatic Society* 13 (1949–1951): 416–426.
13. *Madhuratthavilāsinī* I.6–7, 9–10. The translation is from Buddhadatta Thera, *Madhuratthavilāsinī*, trans. I. B. Horner (London: Pāli Text Society, 1978), 2, parenthetical insertions in the original.
14. Ronald Inden, "Introduction: From Philological to Dialogical Texts," in Ronald Inden, Jonathan Walters, and Daud Ali, *Querying the Medieval: Texts and the History of Practices in South Asia* (New York: Oxford University Press, 2000), 13.
15. Blackburn, *Buddhist Learning and Textual Practice*, 144.
16. Steven Collins, "What Is Literature in Pāli?" in Pollock, *Literary Cultures in History*, 649, 650, 651. Considering the relatively short shelf-life of palm-leaf manuscripts in the warm and moist Sri Lankan climate and therefore the necessity for a continued interest in the copying and perpetuating of texts, it is remarkable we have the Pāli texts *Dīpavaṃsa* and *Mahāvaṃsa* in any form. That we do presumably points to some stability or continuity in their textual community regardless of support from royalty or lack thereof.
17. Ibid., 652.
18. *Cūlavaṃsa: Being the More Recent Part of the* Mahāvaṃsa, trans. Wilhelm Geiger and C. Mabel Rickmers (from German into English) (London: Pāli Text Society, 1929), 260. See also *Cūlavaṃsa*, 2 vols., ed. Wilhelm Geiger (London: Pāli Text Society, 1925–1927).
19. S. G. Perera, *A History of Ceylon*, 2 vols., ed. H. C. Ray (Colombo: Associated Newspapers of Ceylon, 1955–1959), 1:50.
20. Perhaps this difficulty is the reason the *Dīpavaṃsa* has but two published translations. See *Dīpavaṃsa: An Ancient Buddhist Historical Record*, ed. and trans. Hermann Oldenberg (1879; reprint, New Delhi: Asian Educational Services, 1982); and *The Dīpavaṃsa: A Historical Poem of the 4th Century A.D., in Pāli*, ed. and trans. Bimala Churn Law, *Ceylon Historical Journal* 7 (July 1957–April 1958).
21. Wilhelm Geiger, *The* Dīpavaṃsa *and* Mahāvaṃsa *and Their Historical Development in Ceylon*, trans. Ethel Coomaraswamy (Colombo, Sri Lanka: Cottle, 1908), 68–69, 5.
22. Ibid., 11.

23. T. W. Rhys Davids, *Buddhist India* (New York: Putnam's, 1903), 182.
24. Geiger, *The* Dīpavaṃsa *and* Mahāvaṃsa, 12.
25. For a discussion of the memory verses and their function, see ibid., 8–14.
26. Ibid., 14.
27. Geiger states, "We find therefore in the [*Dīpavaṃsa*] the first effort towards the poetical development of material, although it is certainly rather clumsy, whilst many parts of it bear the character of the old Ākhyāna style. It thus builds the bridge which leads from the latter to the *Mahāvaṃsa*, an epic written according to the laws of art" (ibid., 66).
28. Dominick LaCapra, *Rethinking Intellectual History: Texts, Contexts, Language* (Ithaca: Cornell University Press, 1983), 30.
29. Ibid.
30. Collins, *Nirvāṇa and Other Buddhist Felicities*, 41.
31. *Dīpavaṃsa* I.14: "bujjhitvā sabbadhammānaṃ udānaṃ katvā pabhaṃkaro tad'eva pallaṅkavare sattāhaṃ vītināmayi."
32. As we will see in chapter 2, the envisioning of the Buddha as "Light Maker" early on in the text also primes the reader-hearer for the idea of the light of the dharma (*dhammadīpa*).
33. Geiger, *The* Dīpavaṃsa *and* Mahāvaṃsa, 5.
34. "Namo tassa bhagavato arahato sammāsaṃbuddhassa."
35. LaCapra, *Rethinking Intellectual History*, 30.
36. The term *thuti* (see note 37) refers to a type of praise text, hence the inclusion of the insertion "[text]" in my translation.
37. *Dīpavaṃsa* I.1–5:

> Dīpāgamanaṃ buddhassa dhātu ca bodhiyāgamaṃ saṃgahācariyavādañ ca dīpamhi
> sāsanāgamaṃ narindāgamanaṃ vaṃsaṃ kittayissaṃ, suṇātha me.
> Pītipāmojjajananaṃ pasādeyyaṃ manoramaṃ anekākārasampannaṃ cittikatvā suṇātha me.
> Udaggacittā sumanā pahaṭṭhā tuṭṭhamānasā niddosaṃ bhadravacanaṃ sakkaccaṃ
> sampaṭicchatha.
> Suṇātha sabbe paṇidhāya mānasaṃ, vaṃsaṃ pavakkhāmi paramparāgataṃ
> thutippasatthaṃ bahunābhivaṇṇitaṃ etamhi nānākusumaṃ va ganthitaṃ,
> Anūpamaṃ vaṃsavaraggavāsinaṃ apubbaṃ anaññaṃ tatha suppakāsitaṃ ariyāgataṃ
> uttamasabbhi vaṇṇitaṃ suṇātha dīpatthuti sādhusakkataṃ.

38. Stephen Berkwitz notes that the ideal action resulting from a sensibility triggered by emotions is that of giving: "'Virtuous persons' are consistently depicted and fashioned by medieval Sri Lankan Buddhist histories as individuals who are compelled by emotions such as gratitude to engage in ethical reflection and ritualized acts of making offerings to relics shrines. Far from being counterproductive or risky and, therefore, something to be suppressed, certain emotions are rendered in Theravāda histories as crucial to one's moral development" ("History and Gratitude in Theravāda Buddhism," *Journal of the American Academy of Religion* 71, no. 3 [2003]: 584).
39. Blackburn, *Buddhist Learning and Textual Practice*, 13. For Blackburn's adaptation of Brian Stock's phrase *textual community* (used in his book *The Implications of Literacy*) in the Theravādin context, see pages 10–13.

40. Walpola Rahula notes that the development of *gantha-dhura* specialists at the Mahāvihāra was responsible in part for the *vaṃsa* production. "Originally *gantha-dhura* meant only the learning and teaching of the Tripiṭaka," but, Rahula asserts, it later expanded to include other writing, such as "history" (*History of Buddhism in Ceylon: The Anurādhapura Period 3rd Century BC–10th Century AC* [Colombo, Sri Lanka: Gunasena, 1956], 161).
41. Daṇḍin's text *Kāvyādarśa* articulates the literary value of thirty-six particular rhetorical devices and is a very early systematic analysis of literary value.
42. Ranjini Obeyesekere, *Sinhala Writing and the New Critics* (Colombo, Sri Lanka: Gunasena, 1974), 5. Obeyesekere refers to *Siyabaslakara* I.3 and provides the unpublished translation by Charles Hallisey: "Having worshipped them [Sarasvati and the old masters of the science of poetry], I will express some aspects of the science of poetry in Sinhala for two groups of people: those who do not know the older treatises (in Sinhala) at least in their summary form, and those who do not know Sanskrit."
43. Geiger, *The* Dīpavaṃsa *and* Mahāvaṃsa, 64.
44. "Namo tassa bhagavato arahato sammāsaṃbuddhassa."
45. *Mahāvaṃsa* I.1–4:

    Namassitvāna saṃbuddhaṃ susuddhaṃ suddhavaṃsajaṃ Mahāvaṃsaṃ pavakkhāmi nānānūnādhikārikaṃ.

    Porāṇehi kato p'eso ativitthārito kvaci, atīva kvaci saṃkhitto, anekapunaruttako.

    Vajjitaṃ tehi dosehi sukhaggahaṇadhāraṇaṃ pasādasaṃvegakaraṃ sutito ca upāgataṃ.

    Pasādajanake ṭhāne tathā saṃvegakārake janayantā pasādaṃ ca saṃvegaṃ ca suṇātha taṃ.

46. Rahula writes, "The rugged nature of its language and style, its grammatical peculiarities, its many repetitions and the absence of any plan or scheme in its narrative convince the reader that the *Dīpavaṃsa* is not the continuous work of one individual, but a heterogeneous collection of material like ballads of some unskilled versifiers who lived at different periods in different parts of the Island" (*History of Buddhism in Ceylon*, xxi).
47. Geiger writes about the hypothesized urtext, the *Aṭṭhakathā-Mahāvaṃsa*, upon which the subsequent *Dīpavaṃsa* is based: "Of this work the *Dīpavaṃsa* presents the first clumsy redaction in Pāli verses. The *Mahāvaṃsa* is then a new treatment of the same thing, distinguished from the *Dīp*. by greater skill in the employment of the Pāli language, by more artistic composition and by a more liberal use of the material contained in the original work" (*Mahāvaṃsa, or The Great Chronicle of Ceylon*, trans. Wilhelm Geiger, assisted by Mabel Haynes Bode [London: Frowde for Pāli Text Society, 1912], x–xi).
48. "Sujanappasādasaṃvegatthāya kate."
49. *Dīpavaṃsa* I.2: "Pītipāmojjajananaṃ pasādeyyaṃ manoramaṃ anekākāra sampannaṃ cittikatvā suṇātha me."
50. Rahula, *History of Buddhism in Ceylon*, 161–162. Rahula also draws bolstering support from an observation of the rhetorical structure of the lists of kings in the *Dīpavaṃsa*: "The author of the *Dīpavaṃsa*, too, after enumerating the list of names from King Mahāsammata down to Prince Siddhattha, suddenly inserts the verse beginning

with *aniccā vata saṅkhārā*, signifying the impermanence of worldly things, as if he had recited the whole list of names in the Mahāsammata dynasty in order to prove the impermanence of things! This, too, was in conformity with the idea expressed in the Commentaries" (162). See *Dīpavaṃsa* V.49.

51. Rahula, *History of Buddhism in Ceylon*, 164.
52. Andy Rotman, "The Erotics of Practice: Objects and Agency in Buddhist *Avadāna* Literature," *Journal of the American Academy of Religion* 71, no. 3 (2003): 557. Also see Andy Rotman, *Thus Have I Seen: Visualizing Faith in Early Indian Buddhism* (New York: Oxford University Press, 2008). Kevin Trainor also discusses the motive to act based on the feelings of *pasāda* aroused by seeing the relics of the Buddha perform miracles (*Relics Ritual, and Representation in Buddhism: Rematerializing the Sri Lankan Theravāda Tradition* [Cambridge: Cambridge University Press, 1997], 167–171).
53. Steven Collins, "*Nirvāṇa*, Time, and Narrative," *History of Religions* 31, no. 3 (1992): 242–243. Also see Steven Collins, "Oral Aspects of Pāli Literature," *Indo-Iranian Journal* 35 (1992): 121–135, and William Graham, *Beyond the Written Word* (Cambridge: Cambridge University Press, 1987).
54. Émile Benveniste, *Problems in General Linguistics*, trans. Mary Elizabeth Meek (Coral Gables, Fla.: University of Miami Press, 1971), 208, quoted in Hayden White, *The Content of the Form: Narrative Discourse and Historical Representation* (Baltimore: Johns Hopkins University Press, 1987), 3.

2. RELOCATING THE LIGHT

1. Hayden White, *The Content of the Form: Narrative Discourse and Historical Representation* (Baltimore: Johns Hopkins University Press, 1987), 6.
2. As we will encounter in chapter 5, Jonathan Walter's assessment that the *Dīpavaṃsa* represents a "plea for survival" culminates the hypothesizing by generations of scholars about the social, historical, and political milieu of the *Dīpavaṃsa*'s textual community ("Buddhist History: The Sri Lankan Pāli *Vaṃsas* and Their Commentary," in Ronald Inden, Jonathan Walters, and Daud Ali, *Querying the Medieval: Texts and the History of Practices in South Asia* [New York: Oxford University Press, 2000], 111).
3. Anne M. Blackburn, *Buddhist Learning and Textual Practice in Eighteenth-Century Lankan Monastic Culture* (Princeton: Princeton University Press, 2001), 158.
4. Steven Collins, *Nirvāṇa and Other Buddhist Felicities: Utopias of the Pāli Imaginaire* (Cambridge: Cambridge University Press, 1998), 593 n. 2.
5. To be "religiously moved" in this context is no mere abstraction. I agree with Stephen Berkwitz's assessment of the pragmatic consequences of the heightening of one's emotional states by the text. Stemming from his work on the *Sinhala Thūpavaṃsa*, he develops an argument where he is "not merely suggesting that historical narratives 'evoked' or 'elicited' feelings of gratitude from within the 'hearts' of medieval Buddhist devotees" but instead arguing that "gratitude is a cultural disposition *instilled* by historical narratives and then *embodied* in a moral subjectivity that is understood to condition devotional acts of making offerings (*pūjā*) to the Buddha's relics" ("History and Gratitude in Theravāda Buddhism," *Journal of the American Academy of Religion* 71, no. 3 [2003]: 582, emphasis in original).

6. Maria Heim, "The Aesthetics of Excess," *Journal of the American Academy of Religion* 71, no. 3 (2003): 546. Heim also notes that it "is a tool for the Tathāgata to stir up religious motivation in those mired in complacency and comfort" (547).
7. On serial similes, see Charles Hallisey, "Nibbānasutta: An Allegedly Non-canonical *Sutta* on *Nibbāna* as a Great City," *Journal of the Pāli Text Society* 18 (1993): 97–130.
8. As quoted in Blackburn, *Buddhist Learning and Textual Practice*, 159.
9. Ibid., 162.
10. Charles Hallisey, "Tuṇḍilovāda: An Allegedly Non-canonical *Sutta*," *Journal of the Pāli Text Society* 15 (1990): 163, quoted in Blackburn, *Buddhist Learning and Textual Practice*, 162.
11. In chapter 3, I revisit these questions and examine how the character of the *nāga* facilitates the transference of meaning from text to interpreter. In the current chapter, I examine how light is used as a "code" for the elucidation of meaning, which has led me to see a clear connection between the meaning of the text and the character of the *nāga*.
12. Susan R. Suleiman, "Introduction: Varieties of Audience-Oriented Criticism," in *The Reader in the Text*, ed. Susan R. Suleiman and Inge Crosman (Princeton: Princeton University Press, 1980), 12.
13. "Sujanappasādasaṃvegatthāya kate Mahāvaṃse" (This *Mahāvaṃsa* made for the religious emotion [fear] and serene satisfaction of good people).
14. White, *Content of the Form*, ix.
15. Blackburn, *Buddhist Learning and Textual Practice*, 163. Here Blackburn refers to the use of the metaphor of the three sense doors in *Sārārthadīpanī*.
16. Poetry is a perfect genre to represent the pattern suggested here. We should consider what Michael Riffaterre has said about the function of poetic texts as conveyors of structured significance: "The chief characteristic of a poetic text, as opposed to the purely cognitive use of language, is that while the text seems to progress from image to image, from episode to episode, it is in fact repeating the same information. The text progresses syntactically and lexically, and it keeps adding meanings, but each step forward is actually a repetition of one significance. Each of these steps is only a transcodage of that significance from one means of expression to another. . . . The significance is found in the structure given by the text. Every subsequent transcodage is a variant of this structure" ("Interpretation and Descriptive Poetry," *New Literary History* 4 [1973]: 238).
17. This recentering of the Buddhist world may have been part of a larger project to destabilize the centrality of northern India in the fifth and sixth centuries. On this recentering project, see Anne Monius's examination of the sixth-century Tamil Maṇimekalai in *Imagining a Place for Buddhism: Literary Culture and Religious Community in Tamil-Speaking South India* (New York: Oxford University Press, 2001), especially pages 100–115. Buddhaghosa considered all of Jambudīpa to be Majjhimadesa (Middle Lands), not just the northern India sites familiarly associated with the Buddha's biography: "Tambapaṇṇidīpe anurādhapuraṃ majjhimadeso nāma." "Majjhimadesa" is then extended to include even the city of Anurādhapura on Tambapaṇṇi (Sri Lanka) (as in Buddhaghosa's commentary on the *Aṇguttara Nikāya*, quoted in Monius, *Imagining a Place for Buddhism*, 106; see also Buddhaghosa, *Manorathapūraṇī: Commentary on the* Aṇguttara Nikāya, 5 vols., ed. Edmund Hardy and Max Walleser [London: Oxford University Press for Pāli Text Society, 1924–1956]).

18. I discuss this correction of mythological myopia elsewhere. See Kristin Scheible, "Priming the Lamp of *Dhamma*: The Buddha's Miracles in the Pāli *Mahavāṃsa*," *Journal of the International Association of Buddhist Studies* 33, nos. 1–2 (2010–2011): 435–451.
19. Richard F. Gombrich, *Theravāda Buddhism: A Social History from Ancient Benares to Modern Colombo* (London: Routledge, 1988), 141.
20. Pierre Maranda, "The Dialectic of Metaphor," in Suleiman and Crosman, *The Reader in the Text*, 185, quoting Pierre Maranda, *Mythology: Selected Readings* (New York: Penguin, 1972), 15–16.
21. In this light, it is helpful to consider the semantic field of the term *vaṃsa*, which encompasses a range of temporal and spatial meanings such as the nodes on bamboo, the lineage (of teachers or of kings), and history in its most documentary sense. Any way you choose to translate *vaṃsa*, the dominant image is of something that grows outward from a single origin, and in this case the origin is the Buddha himself.
22. *Dīpavaṃsa* I.14: "bujjhitvā sabbadhammānaṃ udānaṃ katvā pabhaṃkaro tad'eva pallaṇkavare sattāhaṃ vītināmayi."
23. It is because of this obvious physical transformation that the Buddha's first disciples, former partners in ascetic practices who had shunned him as he followed the middle way, recognized and were attracted to the Buddha in the Deer Park at Sarnath. The light thus attracts followers, specifically the followers who are spiritually progressed enough to be profitably affected. In this case, it sets the scene for the first dissemination of the *dhamma* in the *Dhammacakkappavattana Sutta* (the first sermon, the "turning of the wheel of *dhamma*"). Also, the Buddha is commonly described as being radiant and golden.
24. "We will use such expressions as life-wish, royal wish, imperial wish, world wish, life-account, world account, and world vision in place of such conceptually overloaded terms as myth, ideology, and worldview to denote the effects of certain activities that people carried out in the course of their lives, activities that were crucial to the ways of life they pursued. The transformation of heterogeneous life- and world wishes into more coherent and stable world accounts and, in some cases, visions, was crucial to the practices of disciplinary orders" (Ronald Inden, "Introduction: From Philological to Dialogical Texts," in Inden, Walters, and Ali, *Querying the Medieval*, 23). Although I appreciate Inden's emphasis on agency and malleability, I am not fully convinced of the utility of so many new words. I am intrigued by "world wish," however, a concept that implies the hopeful and intentional revision of the world, perhaps amid negotiation, rather than the more static, ossified, and singular concept "worldview."
25. Richard F. Gombrich, *How Buddhism Began: The Conditioned Genesis of the Early Teachings* (London: Athlone Press, 1996), 71–72.
26. Jonathan Walters, "*Suttas* as History: Four Approaches to the *Sermon on the Noble Quest* (Aryapariyesanasutta)," *History of Religions* 38, no. 3 (1999): 259.
27. *Dīpavaṃsa* I.17: "Laṅkādīpaṃ varuttamaṃ"; I.19: "Laṅkādīpavaraṃ"; I.22: "Laṅkādīpavare."
28. *Dīpavaṃsa* I.20–21:

    Laṅkādīpe imam kālaṃ yakkhabhūtā ca rakkhasā
    sabbe buddhapaṭikuṭṭhā sakkā uddharituṃ balaṃ

    nīharitvā yakkhagaṇe pisāce avaruddhake/ khemaṃ katvāna taṃ dīpaṃ vasāpessāmi mānusse

29. Herman Oldenberg's translation renders the beings "too low for (adopting the doctrine of) the Buddhas" (*The Dīpavaṃsa: An Ancient Buddhist Historical Record*, ed. and trans. Hermann Oldenberg [1879; reprint, New Delhi: Asian Educational Services, 1982], 119).
30. *Dīpavaṃsa* I.24: "parinibbāyi suriyo."
31. The insertion of historically verifiable elements—here posited as future happenings—does work to elicit confidence in the reader-hearer. At the time of the *vaṃsas*' compilations, these future, prophesized events were in fact in the past. The effect of such insertions on the reader-hearer is confidence—he or she is reassured that events have unfolded according to the Buddha's intended plan.
32. Walters, "Buddhist History," 115, 116, 118.
33. Umberto Eco, *Six Walks in the Fictional Woods*, Charles Eliot Norton Lectures, 1993 (Cambridge, Mass.: Harvard University Press, 1994), 87.
34. *Dīpavaṃsa* I.36–37:

agyāgāre ahināgaṃ damesi purisuttaṃo
disvā acchariyaṃ sabbe nimantiṃsu tathāgataṃ

hemantañ cātumāsamhi idha vihara Gotama
mayaṃ taṃ niccabhattena sadā upaṭṭhahāmase

35. *Dīpavaṃsa* I.54: "Ṭhito naro iddhi vikubbamāno yakkho va mahiddhi mahānubhāvo khaṇiyaṃ ghanā meghasahassadhārā pavassati sītalavātaduddini." It seems significant that the *yakkhas* mistake the Buddha as one of their own. The *yakkhas* are unworthy of even entering the path toward Buddhahood, according to this vignette.
36. The word for "body" here is *kāye*, and it carries the meaning of a collective body (as in an assembly) as well as of a physical body. The double meaning might here be intentional because the heat is viscerally perceived.
37. *Dīpavaṃsa* I.58–59:

Ṭhite majjhantike kāle gimhānaṃ suriyo yathā
evaṃ yakkhānaṃ ātāpo kāye ṭhapita dāruṇaṃ

Yathā kappaparivaṭṭe catusuriyātapo
evaṃ nisīdane satthu tejo hoti tatuttari

38. *Dīpavaṃsa* I.66: "Buddho ca kho isinisabho sukhāvaho disvāna yakkhe dukkhite bhayaṭṭite anukampako kāruṇiko mahesi vicintayi attasukhaṃ amānuse."
39. *Dīpavaṃsa* I.74: "Etehi aññehi guṇeh' upeto manussavāso anekabhaddako dīpesu dīpissati sāsan' āgate supuṇṇacando va nabbhe uposathe."
40. It is beyond the scope of this project to consider here the interrelationship of literary devices and actual practices, but in relation to the Uposatha the *Muluposatha Sutta* (AN 3.70) should be consulted. In it, each of the Three Jewels—the Buddha, *dhamma*, and *saṅgha*—is in turn highlighted as the means, accessed through recollection, to transform a defiled mind into a cleansed one, primed for the arising of joy. This transformation structurally echoes the transformation from dark to light or from unprimed to primed reader that is at the heart of my argument. For example: "There is the case where the disciple of the noble ones recollects the Tathāgata, thus: 'Indeed, the Blessed One is worthy and rightly self-awakened, consummate in

knowledge & conduct, well-gone, an expert with regard to the world, unexcelled as a trainer for those people fit to be tamed, the Teacher of divine & human beings, awakened, blessed.' As he is recollecting the Tathāgata, his mind is calmed, and joy arises; the defilements of his mind are abandoned, just as when the head is cleansed through the proper technique. And how is the head cleansed through the proper technique? Through the use of cosmetic paste & clay & the appropriate human effort. This is how the head is cleansed through the proper technique. In the same way, the defiled mind is cleansed through the proper technique. And how is the defiled mind cleansed through the proper technique? There is the case where the disciple of the noble ones recollects the Tathāgata. . . . As he is recollecting the Tathāgata, his mind is cleansed, and joy arises; the defilements of his mind are abandoned. He is thus called a disciple of the noble ones undertaking the Brahma-Uposatha. He lives with Brahma [the Buddha]. It is owing to Brahma that his mind is calmed, that joy arises, and that whatever defilements there are in his mind are abandoned. This is how the mind is cleansed through the proper technique" (*Muluposatha Sutta: The Roots of the Uposatha (AN 3.70)*, trans. Thanissaro Bhikkhu, Access to Insight, December 10, 2011, http://www.accesstoinsight.org/tipitaka/an/an03/an03.070.than.html).

41. *Dīpavaṃsa* II.2: "Tasmiñ Jetavane buddho dhammarājā pabhaṃkaro sabbalokam avekkhanto Tambapaṇṇivar' addasa."
42. *Dīpavaṃsa* II.5–6: "Sabbe mahiddhikā nāgā sabbe ghoravisā ahū sabbeva kibbisā caṇḍā madamānā avassitā // khippakāpi mahātejā paduṭṭhā kakkhalā kharā ujjhānasaññī sukopā uragā vilaratthikā."
43. *Dīpavaṃsa* II.23: "Aññamaññaṃ na passanti tasitā nāgā bhayaṭṭitā jitam pi na passanti kuto saṃgāma kārituṃ."
44. *Dīpavaṃsa* II.26–27: "Āloko 'va mahā āsi abbhuto lomahaṃsano sabbe passanti sambuddhaṃ nabhe candaṃ va nimmalaṃ // chahi vaṇṇehi upeto jalanto nabhakantare dasa disā virocanto ṭhito nāge abhāsatha."
45. *Dīpavaṃsa* II.32: "Saṃvejesi tadā nāge nirayadukkhena cakkhumā manussayoniṃ dibbañ ca nibbānañ ca pakittayi."
46. *Koṭi* usually refers to space (as in the extreme reaches) or time (a division of time with reference to past or future in the context of *saṃsāra*). It can also refer to numbers, perhaps 100,000 (see T. W. Rhys Davids and William Stede, eds., *Pāli-English Dictionary* [1921–1925; reprint, Oxford: Pāli Text Society, 1995], 227).
47. If we were to read this passage creatively, looking for clues about the contemporary political and economic aims of the community responsible for the text's creation, perhaps we might see the throne in the possession of these two kings as symbolic of contested royal patronage in general. The fact that the throne is thus turned over to the very head of the *saṅgha*, the Buddha himself, may be interpreted as a model for how the *saṅgha* should be supported. Also, the gift of the throne buttresses my assertion in the next chapter that relics of the Buddha seem to need to pass through the *nāgas* to become activated and efficacious for future generations.
48. *Dīpavaṃsa* II.39: "Patiṭṭhapiṃsu pallañkaṃ nāgā dīpānam antare, nisīdi tattha pallañke dhammarājā pabhaṃkaro." It is possible that *dīpa* in this context simply means "place" because the two places are presumably the mountain and ocean areas where the two groups of *nāgas* are from.
49. *Dīpavaṃsa* II.57: "samāpatti samāpajji mettaṃ sabadisaṃ phari."

50. See *Dīpavaṃsa* XVII.3–25, XVIII.18, and *Mahāvaṃsa* XV.8, 24. The park was given to the *saṅgha* by King Devānampiyatissa; it contained the Mahāvihāra and later (by the time of the composition of our texts) the rival communities, the Abhayagirivihāra and the Jetavanārāma.
51. Eco, *Six Walks in the Fictional Woods*, 49.
52. Perhaps beginning at an earlier point makes transparent a new tack of legitimacy. In the face of Mahāyāna influences seeping into Sri Lanka and resulting in the formation of rival *vihāras* (monastic complexes), here the Mahāvihāra posits a lineage of buddhas—multiple buddhas but here in a succession, a *vaṃsa*, an authoritative, single lineage. It is not so much invention as a conventional expansion of the *Buddhavaṃsa* (which dates to the second or first century B.C.E. and hails from India rather than Sri Lanka).
53. "Lokaṃ dukkhā pamocetuṃ," which Wilhelm Geiger translates as "that he might release the world from evil" (Mahānāma, *The Mahāvaṃsa, or The Great Chronicle of Ceylon*, trans. Wilhelm Geiger, assisted by Mabel Haynes Bode [London: Frowde for Pāli Text Society, 1912], 1). Translating *dukkha* as "evil," however, imparts connotations that I believe undermine the gist of the text, which is that the island will be a refuge for humans in the future, an ideal location to develop themselves spiritually and ethically along the path toward buddhahood. *Dukkha* is not evil per se; it is just a condition of existence, and it is from this condition that the Buddha's path can liberate one. What is important to take away from this verse is that the *bodhisatta* was inspired by coming in contact with Dīpaṅkara, the current Buddha of his day, and that coming into the presence of an enlightened being provokes one to become a certain kind of ethical agent in this world.
54. See John S. Strong, *The Buddha: A Short Biography* (Oxford: Oneworld, 2001).
55. Sumedha's story is frequently told in Theravādin texts. An early rendition rich with light metaphors, the Dure Nidāna of the *Jātakaṭṭhakathā Nidāna-kathā*, can be found in *The Story of Gotama Buddha: The Nidāna-kathā of the Jātakaṭṭhakathā*, trans. N. A. Jayawickrama (Oxford: Pāli Text Society, 1990), 1–36.
56. The draw of the Buddha here is like the "entrapment" we considered in chapter 1. Here we see an inescapable appeal pulling worthy ones toward him; there we considered the effect of texts reaching out through the reader-hearers' emotional responses to trap them into giving.
57. The story "Vakkali Sutta" in the "Samyutta Nikāya" section of the Sutta Pitaka: "Yo kho dhammaṃ passati, so maṃ passati // Yo maṃ passati, so dhammaṃ passati."
58. *Mahāvaṃsa* I.20: "Sāsanujjotanaṭṭhānaṃ Laṅkā ñātā jinena hi / yakkhapuṇṇāya Laṅkāya yakkhā nibbāsiyā ti ca." Geiger problematically translates *sāsanujjotanaṭṭhānaṃ* as "a place where his doctrine should (thereafter) shine in glory" (Mahānāma, *The Mahāvaṃsa*, Geiger 1912 trans., 3), when "glory" is not implied in the Pāli.
59. Jonathan Walters translates *sāsana* variously as " 'instructions,' 'dispensation,' 'religion' " ("Buddhist History," 105).
60. *Mahāvaṃsa* I.43: "Evaṃ dīpaṃ imaṃ katvā manussāraham issaro."
61. *Mahāvaṃsa* I.58–59: "Saṃgāmamajjhe ākāse nisinno tattha nāyako tamaṃ tamonudo tesaṃ nāgānaṃ bhiṃsanaṃ akā // Assāsento bhayaṭṭe te ālokaṃ pavidhaṃsayi te disvā sugataṃ tuṭṭhā pāde vandiṃsu satthuno."

62. In chapter 4, I consider the function of *nāgas* as hoarders and protectors of the Buddha's relics and how this function may explain the Buddha's conversion rather than outright expulsion of this particular class of being. Being liminal agents, edge-dwellers, and world transgressors, the *nāgas* help to spread the doctrine.
63. Relating to this story cycle, for an analysis of "expected miracles" and the work that such miracles do for a reader, see Scheible, "Priming the Lamp of *Dhamma*."
64. *Mahāvaṃsa* I.84: "Evaṃ Laṅkāya nātho hitam amitamatī āyatiṃ pekkhamāno tasmiṃ kālamhi Laṅkāsurabhujagagaṇādīnam atthaṃ ca passam āgā tikkhattum etaṃ ativipuladayo lokadīpo sudīpaṃ dīpo tenāyam āsi sujanabahumato dhammadīpāvabhāsīti." Translated in Collins, *Nirvāṇa and Other Buddhist Felicities*, app. 2, 598, parenthetical insertions in Collins's translation.
65. Collins, *Nirvāṇa and Other Buddhist Felicities*, 598–99 n. 17.
66. Ananda Guruge's translation reflects this sentiment: "came to be resplendent as the righteous Dhamma" (Mahānāma, *Mahāvaṃsa: The Great Chronicle of Sri Lanka, Chapters 1-37*, trans. Ananda W. P. Guruge [Colombo, Sri Lanka: Associated Newspapers of Ceylon, 1989], 496).
67. Collins, *Nirvāṇa and Other Buddhist Felicities*, 599 n. 17.
68. Walters, "Buddhist History," 147 n. 134. Collins's explanation here is a corrective to his earlier view: "It has long been recognised that the ideology of these *vaṃsa* texts is that of the *dhammadīpa*, the island which the Buddha prophesied would be the historical vehicle of his saving truth" ("On the Very Idea of the Pāli Canon," *Journal of the Pāli Text Society* 15 [1990]: 100).
69. The image of light is so prevalent in Pāli texts, whether employed as a metaphor or used descriptively in the various epithets for the Buddha or considered a miraculous by-product, a visible marker of the supernatural, that I cannot list all references here.
70. Walpola Rahula, *History of Buddhism in Ceylon: The Anurādhapura Period 3rd Century BC-10th Century AC*, 2nd ed. (Colombo, Sri Lanka: Gunasena, 1956), 156 n. 1.
71. On *śleṣa*, see Charles Hallisey, "Works and Persons in Sinhala Literary Culture," in *Literary Cultures in History: Reconstructions from South Asia*, ed. Sheldon Pollock (Berkeley: University of California Press, 2003). Also, for an excellent analysis of *śleṣa*—double meaning, homophones, homonyms, and the like—in Sanskrit poetics, see Yigal Bronner, *Extreme Poetry: The South Asian Movement of Simultaneous Narration* (New York: Columbia University Press, 2010).
72. The image of a lamp with a wick needing to be primed would have been a ubiquitous one for the fifth-century community of production. Wilhelm Geiger gleans information about lamp use from the *Mahāvaṃsa* and *Cūlavaṃsa*: "Among the smaller household articles first of all lamps (*dīpa*) must be mentioned. The wicks were made of strips of stuff and the oil with which the lamps were filled, was sometimes a fragrant one (73.76), as the *madhuka*-oil pressed from the seeds of the tree *Bassia laitfolia*, or sesamum-oil (34.55–56), or camphor-oil (85.41; 89.43). The terrace of Duṭṭhagāmaṇī's palace was lit with fragrant oil lamps (25.101). The 'Brazen Palace' in Anurādhapura caught fire from a lamp and was destroyed during the reign of that ruler's successor (33.6)" (*Culture of Ceylon in Mediaeval Times*, ed. Heinz Bechert [Wiesbaden, Germany: Harrassowitz, 1960], 47). He also notes how widely lamps were used in festivals, where temples and streets would be illuminated. Granted, all of this information is relayed through the text itself and cannot be verified by external sources.

73. Walters, "Buddhist History," 125–141. Collins points to an odd verse indicative of the ideological impetus behind the composition of this commentary on the *Mahāvaṃsa*: "It is true that the commentary, Mhv-t 118–9, glosses *dīpa* in both *loka-dīpa* and *dhamma-dīpa* not only as *pajjota-karaṇa*, maker of light, but also, ignoring the word-play, as *patitthā-* (*bhuta*), foundation, basis. In the first case it gives no further exegesis; in the second Laṅkā is said to be a 'basis' for Buddhists (*sāsanikajana*) and for the Buddha himself, through his relics. Pāli commentaries, like other Southern Asian exegeses of poetry (*kāvya*), eschew historical accuracy and see as much meaning as possible in the texts they are explicating; this is a version of the ubiquitous practice of giving historically inaccurate but creative 'etymologies'" (*Nirvāṇa and Other Buddhist Felicities*, 599 n. 17).
74. *Vaṃsatthappakāsinī* I:1, translated in Walters, "Buddhist History," 126, parenthetical insertions in the original.

3. *NĀGAS*, TRANSFIGURED FIGURES INSIDE THE TEXT, RUMINATIVE TRIGGERS OUTSIDE

1. Robert DeCaroli, *Haunting the Buddha: Indian Popular Religions and the Formation of Buddhism* (New York: Oxford University Press, 2004), 35.
2. Values modeled include generally having a right attitude as well as the particular *pāramīs* (perfections) required for the cultivation of buddhahood, such as *dāna* (generosity) and *sīla* (morality).
3. Charles Hallisey and Anne Hansen, "Narrative, Sub-ethics, and the Moral Life: Some Evidence from Theravāda Buddhism," *Journal of Religious Ethics* 24, no. 2 (1996): 313.
4. Joseph Walser, "Nāgārjuna and the *Ratnāvalī*: New Ways to Date an Old Philosopher," *Journal of the International Association of Buddhist Studies* 25, nos. 1–2 (2002): 233–234.
5. Ibid., 234.
6. Ibid.
7. Ibid.
8. Claude Lévi-Strauss, *Totemism*, trans. Rodney Needham (London: Merlin Press, 1964), 89.
9. I refer here to the phrase coined by Hayden White in *Tropics of Discourse: Essays in Cultural Criticism* (Baltimore: Johns Hopkins University Press, 1978).
10. Although I refer later to other instances in Pāli texts where *nāgas* factor in the delivery of the narrative, this chapter is by no means a survey of all *nāga* references in Pāli literature, which would be an extensive project of its own. For a general, if outdated and incomplete, survey of the *nāga* in Indian literature, material culture, and religious practice, see Jean Philippe Vogel, *Indian Serpent-Lore; or, The Nāgas in Hindu Legend and Art* (London: Probsthain, 1926). For focused attention on images of *nāgas*, see Robert DeCaroli, "Shedding Skins: Naga Imagery and Layers of Meaning in South Asian Buddhist Contexts," in *Buddhist Stupas in South Asia*, ed. Jason Hawkes and Akira Shimada (New Delhi: Oxford University Press, 2009), 94–113.
11. Jonathan Walters, "Buddhist History: The Sri Lankan Pāli *Vaṃsas* and Their Commentary," in Ronald Inden, Jonathan Walters, and Daud Ali, *Querying the Medieval: Texts and the History of Practices in South Asia* (New York: Oxford University Press, 2000), 150.

12. Ibid.
13. As E. B. Cowell notes in his preface to an edited translation of the *Jātakas*, "The Sutta and Vinaya Piṭakas are generally accepted as at least older than the Council at Vesāli (380 B.C.?); and thus the *Jātaka* legends must have been always recognised in Buddhist literature" (*The Jātaka, or Stories of the Buddha's Former Births*, 7 vols., ed. E. B. Cowell [1895–1913; reprint, London: Pali Text Society, 1963], 1:vi).
14. Achariya Dhammapāla, *Paramatthadīpanī, Being the Commentary on the* Cariyā-Piṭaka, ed. D. L. Barua (London: Pāli Text Society, 1939). Oskar von Hinüber notes that Dhammapāla was likely a South Indian, though he could have been from Sri Lanka, and that he did not use Mahāvihāran recensions of the *Apadāna* or, important to consider here, the *Cariyāpiṭaka* (*A Handbook of Pāli Literature* [Berlin: Walter de Gruyter, 1996], 137).
15. *The Jātaka, Together with Its Commentary*, 7 vols., ed. Viggo Fausbøll (1877–1897; reprint, London: Pāli Text Society, 1963).
16. The *nāgaloka* is a place for those *nāgas* who have accrued great merit and a fortunate rebirth. For example, when the mother of Bhūridatta, Samuddajā, first encounters the *nāgaloka*, with all of its jeweled pavilions and tanks and gardens, she asks her attendant, "This city is magnificently adorned, it is not like our city; whose is it?" "O lady," esponds the attendant, "it belongs to your lord,—it is not those of scanty merits who win such glory as this,—you have obtained it by reason of your great merits" (*The Jātaka*, Cowell ed., 6:86).
17. There is even an actual, explicit birth story, thus highlighting Bhūridatta's slippery ontology, yet another reason to choose this story among the three possible contenders.
18. Samuddajā (Ocean Born) has this name because she was born on the shore; even her name stresses the liminality of this character. She is also half-*nāga*, half-human, which then makes Bhūridatta one-quarter human. I wonder if this fraction of humanity is what avails the *dhamma* to him?
19. *The Jātaka*, Cowell ed., 6:87.
20. The appropriate place for ascetic practices is the human realm, where the choices one makes are most weighted. We know from *Vinaya* I:68, the story where a *nāga* infiltrates the *saṅgha* to be close to the Buddha but is discovered when he reverts to his *nāga* status while he sleeps, that *nāgas* are indeed capable of taking on human form in the human realm. But Bhūridatta chooses the form of a snake.
21. *The Jātaka*, Cowell ed., 3:170, 88.
22. Here we see the same fluidity among supernatural entities as we saw in chapter I of the *Mahāvaṃsa*, where the *yakkhas* initially mistake the Buddha for a *yakkha*. A being might be any sort of being; difference is not immediately apparent.
23. There may be apparently dishonest actions, such as taking a form other than one's own, but telling a lie pushes the moral limit.
24. Jewels placed on riverbanks tend to have some sort of homing device and frequently vanish and return to the *nāgaloka*. This "homing" mechanism sets up an interesting reason for the *nāgas*' sanctioned hoarding of Buddha relics. The connections with treasures or jewels and the Buddha's relics are explored in chapter 4.
25. *The Jātaka*, Cowell ed., 6:98. I believe the captivity being referred to is in fact Bhūridatta's *nāga* birth and not his subjugation under the snake charmer; the double entendre is rich.

26. Bhūridatta's mother is in fact human, duped into believing she inhabits a beautiful earthly kingdom (the *nāgarāja* tricks her by commanding all the *nāgas* of the *nāgaloka* to assume human form). Bhūridatta thus has some human in him, although the *nāga* dominates and determines his soteriological aptitude in that birth.
27. *The Jātaka*, Cowell ed., 6:102.
28. This discourse recalls the reading of the *Mahāvaṃsa*'s emphasis on light and dark as a renegotiation or even co-optation of Vedic imagery for nascent Buddhist practical purposes. See chapter 2.
29. John C. Holt, *The Religious World of Kīrti Srī* (London: Oxford University Press, 1996), 19. Also see Bardwell L. Smith, "The Ideal Social Order as Portrayed in the Chronicles of Ceylon," in *Religion and Legitimation of Power in Sri Lanka*, ed. Bardwell L. Smith (Chambersburg, Pa.: Anima Books, 1978), 48. Steven Collins says that the history of the *vaṃsas* is, "to be sure, 'Sacred History,' *Heilsgeschichte*, but it expresses and preserves an explicit sense of mundane historical continuity, both within the countries we now call Sri Lanka, Burma, Thailand, Cambodia and Laos, and in connecting these areas with the Buddha and Buddhism in India" (*Nirvāṇa and Other Buddhist Felicities: Utopias of the Pāli Imaginaire* [Cambridge: Cambridge University Press, 1998], 255).
30. In *Haunting the Buddha*, Robert DeCaroli translates *bhūta devatā* as "spirit-deities," lumping the various nonhuman, semidivine agents together in the term *spirit*, a loaded term to say the least. *Bhūta* (as past passive participle, "become" or "been") is a common term for ghosts and spirits. I appreciate DeCaroli's broader project about auxiliary beings' proximity to the Buddha, especially articulated in his closing thoughts, but I think his terminology undermines the central, foundational importance of the cluster of symbols, the constellation of myths, and the abundance of practices that he designates "spirit religions" but that are in fact part and parcel of Buddhism. The appearance of (and arguably the prominence or centrality of) "spirit-deities" suggests to me that the distinction was never as abrupt or definite as is painted in modern scholarship or in "Protestant Buddhism." Defending the term *popular spirit religions*, DeCaroli explains: "This term refers to the myriad popular religious practices in India which center on the propitiation and veneration of various local and minor deities. The term seems fitting because these beings hold a liminal position between the realms of ghosts (*preta, bhūta*) and the gods (*deva*) and frequently seem to share the nature of both. I do realize that combining several categories of supernatural beings under one title also poses certain problems. Given the fluidity and frequency with which the primary sources use these categories interchangeably and the uniformity in the Buddhist response to all these types of beings, however, it is helpful to use this collective term within the confines of the present discussion. Conversely, if I were to limit the discussion to just cases of one type (*yakṣa, nāga*, or *devatā)* I would only be able to explore a fraction of the available evidence detailing the monastic response to preexistent, non-Brahmanical, nonsoteriological forms of religious expression that center on the appeasement of a deity or deities who possess explicitly limited power" (*Haunting the Buddha*, 190 n. 17). Setting aside altogether what DeCaroli might mean by "nonsoteriological," I think *nāgas* function in a different way. Whether pre-Buddhist elements incorporated into the Buddhist fold or designed by Buddhists,

nāgas are not minor deities to propitiate. The first chapter of the *Mahāvaṃsa* illustrates that it is not propitiation of the *nāgas* that occurs, but actual conversion. They are crucial characters in the cosmological and literary landscape who reveal what is important, including the Buddha's relics, how to worship them, and how to feel gratitude for the opportunity to worship.

31. Acariya Dhammapāla explicitly classifies the *Bhūridatta Jātaka* as a text on the *Sīlapāramitā*—together with other stories gleaned from the *Jātaka-Nidānakathā*, *Cariya-Piṭaka* (and commentary), and *Atthasālinī* (see the editor's preface in Dhammapāla, *Paramatthadīpanī*, vii–ix). In the final part of this chapter, on ethics, I turn to this classification of the *Bhūridatta Jātaka* as teaching about the "perfection of morality."
32. Buddhaghosa, *Visuddhimagga*, trans. Bhikkhu Ñanamoli, 5th ed. (Kandy, Sri Lanka: Buddhist Publication Society, 1991), XIII.93, italics in this translation.
33. Perhaps it stretches Fernand Braudel's term *longue durée* too much to apply it to the Buddhist understanding and experience of *saṃsāra*, yet the possibility of animal births through time must impact one's sense of selfhood in the human present and must affect one's reading of animal stories on some level.
34. Christopher Key Chapple, "Animals and Environment in the Buddhist Birth Stories," in *Buddhism and Ecology*, ed. Mary Evelyn Tucker and Duncan Ryuken Williams (Cambridge, Mass.: Harvard University Press, 1997), 133.
35. Ibid., 143.
36. Philip Kapleau, *Of the Same Root*, Parabola, vol. 8, no. 2 (New York: Society for the Study of Myth and Tradition, 1983), 76.
37. DeCaroli, *Haunting the Buddha*, 11.
38. Heinrich Zimmer, *Myths and Symbols in Indian Art and Civilization* (New York: Pantheon, 1946). For examples of those who trace their lineages to great *nāgarājas* (*nāga* kings), from Udayana to the Pallavas to the Khmer of Cambodia, see Vogel, *Indian Serpent-Lore*, 34–37. DeCaroli remarks that "images of the Buddha seated on the *nāga* Muchalinda, although almost non-existent in the north of India, are common on first- to third-century Andhran monuments. This shift in iconography may be due to the regional importance given to *nāgas* in the south and serve as a recognition of their important role as ancestral figures. Given the importance of spirit-deities to Buddhist expansion, it should not be surprising that the occurrence of spirit-deities on Buddhist monuments would be directly related to the popularity of those spirit-deities within the region" (*Haunting the Buddha*, 93).
39. *The Story of Gotama Buddha: The Nidāna-kathā of the Jātakaṭṭhakathā*, trans. N. A. Jayawickrama (Oxford: Pāli Text Society, 1990), 107.
40. Ibid.
41. *The Jātaka*, Cowell ed., 6:86.
42. Note that a *nāga* who has assumed human form also assumes natural human behaviors, such as nursing, which a fully reptilian snake would not do.
43. *The Jātaka*, Cowell ed., 6:87.
44. Ibid., 6:88.
45. Ibid., 6:93.
46. Ibid., 6:97.
47. Hallisey and Hansen. "Narrative, Sub-ethics, and the Moral Life," 313.

48. This is the argument by which Asoka retrieved the relics from the *nāgas*. Although the worship of the *doṇa* (measure) of relics by the *nāgas* was exemplary and far more elaborate than what the humans could do, it made more sense for the relics to return to the human world, where they could be worshipped by people, who are able to reach enlightenment. See Xuanzang [Hiuen Tsiang], *Si-Yu-Ki: Buddhist Records of the Western World*, 2 vols., trans. Samuel Beal (London: Kegan Paul, Trench and Trübner, 1884) 2:26–31; compare Vogel, *Indian Serpent-Lore*, 127. We will also see this argument developed in the next chapter, which tells the story of Soṇuttara retrieving the relics from the *nāgaloka* on the basis that the *nāgas* cannot proceed on the path of enlightenment in spite of their devotional appreciation of the relics.
49. The well-known story of the guardianship of the Mahāyāna *Prajñāpāramitā* (Perfection of Wisdom) *sūtras*, in which the *nāgas* invited the philosopher Nāgārjuna to discover the cache, is explained thus: "It is said by some that when the Buddha began teaching his doctrine, he soon realized that men were not prepared to accept it in its fullness. They shrank from the extreme implications of his vision of the universal Void (*śūnyata*). Therefore, he committed the deeper interpretation of reality to an audience of *nāgas*, who were to hold it in trust until mankind should be made ready to understand. . . . Not until some seven centuries had past was the great sage Nāgārjuna, 'Arjuna of the Nāgas,' initiated by the serpent kings into the truth that all is void (*śūnya*)" (recounted in Zimmer, *Myths and Symbols in Indian Art and Civilization*, 68).
50. *The Jātaka*, Cowell ed., 6:97.
51. Ibid.
52. Hallisey and Hansen, "Narrative, Sub-ethics, and the Moral Life," 314, parenthetical citations omitted.
53. Ibid., 312, parenthetical citation omitted.
54. Ibid., 313.
55. Vinaya Piṭaka, I.63.
56. With this story in mind, it is worth considering the placement of the *Vinaya* within the entire canon because we see *nāgas* at the very outset: "The arrangement of texts in the Theravāda canon underlines the importance of Buddhist law, for it is contained in the first part of the Tipiṭaka, the 'basket of the discipline' ('Vinaya-piṭaka') followed by the 'basket of the teaching' (Sutta-piṭaka)" (Oskar von Hinüber, "Buddhist Law According to the Theravāda-Vinaya: A Survey of Theory and Practice," *Journal of the International Association of Buddhist Studies* 18, no. 1 [1995]: 8).
57. It is thus ironic that novice monks are called "*nāgas*," perhaps reflecting their namesakes' liminal status but good intentions. Perhaps this moniker also addresses the novices' slippery nature—not all of them stay for full ordination—or their place or low status at the start of the soteriological path.
58. DeCaroli, *Haunting the Buddha*, 50.
59. Collins, *Nirvāṇa and Other Buddhist Felicities*, 254–281; see especially Collins's discussion of Paul Ricoeur's idea, found in *Time and Narrative* (3 vols., trans. Kathleen Blamey and David Pellauer [Chicago: Chicago University Press, 1984–1988]), of "the structure of temporality as an ultimate referent" in both fictional and historical narratives (256–257).

4. *NĀGAS* AND RELICS

1. For example, corporeal relics, bits of bones, and impure bodies repulsed the Nigaṇṭhas (Jains, followers of the teacher Nigaṇṭha Nātaputta, a contemporary of the Buddha), although Phyllis Granoff has argued that in the *Dāṭhavaṃsa* reference to the Nigaṇṭhas is not to a particular sect but to "any non-Buddhist who is hostile to the Buddhist faith" ("The Ambiguity of Miracles: Buddhist Understandings of Supernatural Power," *East and West* 46 [1996]: 82). In Pāli texts, Mahāvīra is referred to as "Nigaṇṭha Nātaputta." The third chapter of this later (thirteenth- or fourteenth-century) *Dāṭhāvaṃsa* tells of the trials the tooth relic of the Buddha is subjected to in order to appease the dubious Nigaṇṭhas' challenge to its authenticity. The relic is burned by a fire (but it rises unharmed on a lotus pedestal), pounded on an anvil (but it responds by sinking halfway into the anvil and emitting rays of colored light), and finally tossed into an impure cesspool filled with corpses (but the power of the relic turns the pool into a sea filled with blooming lotuses). Some of the Nigaṇṭhas then validate the power of the relic but interpret it to be the tooth of Janāddana, or Viṣṇu, from one of his worldly incarnations. I recount the story here to point out the interesting comparative nature of my topic and to show that relics in Buddhism represent a significant shift in the Indic religious landscape. For the story of the tooth relic, see *The Dāṭhāvaṃsa (A History of the Tooth-Relic of the Buddha)*, ed. and trans. Bimala Churn Law (Lahore: Motilal Banarsidass, 1925), and John S. Strong, *The Relics of the Buddha* (Princeton: Princeton University Press, 2004), 12–18.
2. Throughout Buddhist narratives, *nāgas* function to draw attention to what is most important. For example, in many sources the *nāgas* Nanda and Upananda bathe the baby Siddhattha Gotama; *nāgas* support the Buddha's jeweled throne at Śrāvastī as he performs the miracle of the Double (see the *Lalitavistara*); and after his cremation, they transport the *doṇa* (portion) of his relics that had washed out to sea in a flood to their *nāgaloka* for safekeeping (see the *Mahāparinibbāṇa-sutta*, also recalled in the *vaṃsas*). As told in the *Buddhavaṃsa* and *Jātaka Nidāna-kathā* accounts of Gotama's biography, when he reaches enlightenment, it is the *nāgarāja* Kāla (Kālika) who first recognizes and announces the momentous event as the Buddha's rice bowl floats upstream on the river Nerañjana and sinks, hitting all the bowls of the former Buddhas and rousing that *nāgarāja* from his slumber. The *nāgarāja* functions here as a translator of the sign (the clink) to the rest of the universe. Significantly, time is portrayed as being of little consequence to the long-lived *nāgarāja*, and he perceives the passage of vast swaths of time as the difference between "yesterday and today." See *The Story of Gotama Buddha: The Nidāna-kathā of the Jātakaṭṭhakathā*, trans. N. A. Jayawickrama (Oxford: Pāli Text Society, 1990): "And sinking at a whirlpool [the bowl] went to the abode of the *nāga* king Kāla, and making a clanging noise striking against the bowls used by the three previous Buddhas placed itself as the bottommost among them. The *nāga* king Kāla heard that sound and began to sing songs of praise in many hundred verses, saying 'A Buddha was born yesterday, and again another today.' For to him all this interval during which the great earth rose filling the sky to the extent of a *yojana* and three *gāvutas* was like yesterday and today" (93).
3. As suggested in chapter 3, the *Jātaka* stories, as a significant inclusion in the Pāli canon and an "open" interpretive site, may be more related to the *vaṃsas* than previously considered.

4. *Mahāparinibbāṇa-sutta, Dīgha Nikāya* 16.6.28 reads:

> Eight portions of relics there were of him,
> The All-Seeing One. Of these, seven remained
> In Jambudīpa with honour. The eighth
> In Rāmagāma's kept by nāga kings.
> One tooth the Thirty Gods have kept,
> Kalinga's kings have one, the nāgas too.
> They shed their glory o'er the fruitful earth.
> Thus the Seer's honoured by the honoured.
> Gods and nāgas, kings, the noblest men
> Clasp their hands in homage, for hard it is
> To find another such for countless aeons.
>
> (*DĪGHA NIKĀYA*, TRANS. MAURICE WALSHE [BOSTON: WISDOM, 1995], 277)

According to the commentary (*Sumangalavilāsinī* 2:615), this concluding verse explaining that one of eight portions of the Buddha's relics is being preserved in the *nāgaloka* was a later addition by the *theras* (monks) of Sri Lanka. It is especially interesting to note the *nāga*'s presence among the most honored beings (gods, kings, and noblest men) and not ensconced in a list of *bhūta devatā*. In his translation, Maurice Walsh omits the line explaining that another tooth of the Buddha was kept "in Gandhāra city" (John Strong, personal communication, 6/8/2016).

5. The *nāga* here also mediates symbolically between the righteous royal and the Buddha; in all of the examples given, the *nāga* stands in between the rulers and their experience of the relics. See, also, John Strong's discussion of this episode as it appears in the *Aśokāvadāna* in *The Legend of King Aśoka* (Princeton: Princeton University Press, 1983), 122–125.
6. Monier Monier-Williams, *Sanskrit-English Dictionary* (1899; reprint, New Delhi: Munshiram Manoharlal, 1976), 910, and T. W. Rhys Davids and William Stede, eds., *Pāli-English Dictionary* (1921–1925; reprint, Oxford: Pāli Text Society, 1995), 590. Also see Steven Collins, "On the Very Idea of a Pāli Canon," *Journal of the Pāli Text Society* 15 (1990): 100, and *Nirvāṇa and Other Buddhist Felicities: Utopias of the Pāli Imaginaire* (Cambridge: Cambridge University Press, 1998), 254–258, as well as Kevin Trainor, *Relics, Ritual, and Representation in Buddhism: Rematerializing the Sri Lankan Theravāda Tradition* (Cambridge: Cambridge University Press, 1997), 72–75.
7. In other words, the *Mahāvaṃsa* both chronicles or documents narratives of power and exerts power (in a worklike way) on the reader-hearer. See chapter 1 for a discussion of Dominick LaCapra's helpful terms *documentary* and *worklike*.
8. Greenwald states that the purpose of her study is to "explore how historiography both mediates and justifies the contradiction inherent in a Buddhist king who would go so far as to place a relic of the Buddha in his battle lance and call for a company of 500 monks to escort his troops to war" ("The Relic on the Spear: Historiography and the Saga of Duṭṭhagāmaṇī," in *Religion and Legitimation of Power in Sri Lanka*, ed. Bardwell L. Smith [Chambersburg, Pa.: Anima Books, 1978], 13).
9. *Mahāvaṃsa* XXV.109–111: "Saggamaggantarāyo ca nātthi te tena kammunā, diyaḍḍhamanujā vettha ghātitā manujādhipa, saraṇesu ṭhito eko, pañcasīle pi cāparo, micchādiṭṭhī ca dussīlā sesā pasusamā matā. Jotayissasi ceva tvaṃ bahudhā buddhasāsanaṃ, manovilekhaṃ tasmā tvaṃ vinodaya narissara" (From

this act of yours there is no obstacle to the way to heaven. In this world the Lord of Men has killed only one and a half human beings. One was steadfast in the Refuges, and the other in the Five Precepts; the remainder, like beasts, had bad character and wrong views. But in many ways you will cause the *buddhasāsana* to shine, therefore, Lord of Men, remove the perplexity from your mind).

10. *Mahāvaṃsa* XVII.3: "dhātusu diṭṭhesu diṭṭho hoti jino." This recalls the Buddha's didactic but reproachful formula "he who sees the dhamma, sees me; he who sees me, sees the dhamma," uttered to Vakkali, a monk exceedingly desirous of the Buddha's image (*Saṃyutta Nikāya* 3:120). The Vakkali *sutta* emphasizes the deleterious effect of too much emotion, the power of the affective domain.
11. There are a few notable exceptions: Kevin Trainor considers the *nāga* in the section "The Theft of Presence" in his book *Relics, Ritual, and Representation in Buddhism*, 125–135, and in his article "When Is a Theft Not a Theft? Relic Theft and the Cult of the Buddha's Relics in Sri Lanka," *Numen* 39, no. 1 (1992): 1–26. Also see Strong, *Relics of the Buddha*, esp. 168–169.
12. This is not to say that the *nāgas* are models for human relationships with the relics. By "model agent," I am suggesting the exemplary agency displayed through the character of the *nāga* regarding relics and relic veneration. The *nāgas* are anything but apathetic or passive in their connection to the Buddha; they are active agents in constructing an enduring relationship with the absent teacher. In this way, they are "model agents," and their narratives illustrate the active nature of the thought and practice behind relic veneration.
13. There is an interesting parallel between the traditions narrating the pedigree and hagiography of Christian relics and the *vaṃsas* I focus on. Patrick J. Geary points out, "Thefts were, however, more than random acts or good stories appearing from time to time across Europe. They were perpetrated (or more frequently, alleged) at particular moments of crisis by members of religious or secular communities as means of crisis intervention. Further, not only were thefts similar to each other in the types of crises that gave them birth, but in many cases contemporary descriptions of them betray their authors' awareness that in describing thefts they were writing in a particular hagiographic tradition, that of *furta sacra*, which had its own limitations, *topoi*, and forms" (*Furta Sacra: Thefts of Relics in the Central Middle Ages* [1978; reprint, Princeton: Princeton University Press, 1990], xiii).
14. John Strong observes the same phenomenon and extends the *nāga* layover to the period of provisional ordination experienced by novices in the *saṅgha*. He writes, "The *nāga* state is thus something that needs to be abandoned, but it is also something that needs to be passed through on the way to its abandonment. The same may perhaps be said of relics, for which enshrinement in a *stūpa* may be a kind of ordination. No relic can become enshrined without undergoing a 'rite of passage,' symbolized here by 'passing through' or at least being in the possession of *nāgas*" (*Relics of the Buddha*, 168). Could it be said that the *nāgas*, as characters in the *Mahāvaṃsa*, function in an imagination-provoking way as "novice humans"? (Thanks to Anne Monius for this observation; personal communication, 2006). As we saw in the previous chapter, by taking a *nāga* birth (as told in *Bhūridatta Jātaka*), the bodhisatta was cultivating the perfection of *sīla* (morality), one of ten requisite *pāramitā* (perfections). Could the experience of a *nāga* birth be somehow requisite on the path toward a fulfilled existence as a human Buddhist, aspiring for *nibbāṇa*?

15. Stanley Tambiah writes, "So he [Ānanda] concludes that only a great wisdom tree that has been 'associated' with a Buddha is fit to be a *cetiya* [sanctuary or sanctified place], whether the Buddha is still living or is extinguished" (*The Buddhist Saints of the Forest and the Cult of Amulets* [Cambridge: Cambridge University Press, 1984], 202). Also see the *Kalingabodhi Jātaka* story retold in the next section.
16. In the three pre-*parinibbāṇa* (final extinguishing) visits the Buddha makes to the island of Sri Lanka (as told in the fourteenth-century work *Dhātuvaṃsa*), he brings along the *nāgarāja* Sumana from his own hometown in India and Sumana's *nāga* retinue to be his personal assistants. The Buddha then leaves them in Sri Lanka to identify and stand guard over the sacred spots he visited until shrines and relics can be established there in the future. For a discussion of this story, see Trainor, *Relics, Ritual, and Representation in Buddhism*, 146–147.
17. See the *Theravāda Vinaya* I.3–4 and *The Story of Gotama Buddha*, Jayawickrama trans.
18. The term *cetiya* (Sanskrit, *caitya*) refers to a sanctuary or sanctified place. It also became a designation for *stūpas*, or memorial monuments, throughout Southeast Asia.
19. This story has a correlation in the Mahāyāna traditions about the Buddha's spiritual relics, the *Prajñāpāramitā* (Perfection of Wisdom) texts. The story has it that the relics were kept by the *nāgas* in the *nāgaloka* to await a human sufficiently capable for their interpretation and introduction to the human world. This human turned out to be Nāgārjuna.
20. As we have seen, the tradition is explicit that *nāgas*, in their corrupt birth station, are incapable of reaching enlightenment. This inability does not, however, diminish the their intense desire to be near the Buddha or his relics. As we saw in chapter 3, the *nāgas* even take human form in order to join the *saṅgha*, although their inclusion is prohibited in the *Vinaya*.
21. The same general story appears in the later *Dhātuvaṃsa*, but there the novice is named Siva; see the discussion of this story in Trainor, *Relics, Ritual, and Representation in Buddhism*, 131–134, and in Strong, *Relics of the Buddha*, 81.
22. A human birth is regarded as extremely fortunate; as a human, one has the opportunity to make the difficult ethical choices that contribute to one's cultivation, whereas other births may not be soteriologically conducive. For example, the *Sangīti Sutta* (D III.261) claims that human and god births are deemed good, whereas birth in the hells as *peta* (hungry ghosts), *asura*, or animals is undesirable.
23. Trainor writes: "Buddhist relics, as material objects around which particular ritualized activities are centered, draw their meaning and authority from their alleged connection with powerful religious figures from the past. The practice of relic veneration therefore functions as a 'technology of remembrance and representation,' i.e., as a cultural strategy for bridging temporal and spatial separation through a complex interaction of material objects, abstract notions, emotional orientations, and ritualized behaviors. The cult of the Buddha's relics has to do, in some basic sense, with the problem of remembering and representing the Buddha, who is believed by his followers to have utterly passed away from history over 2,500 years ago" (*Relics, Ritual, and Representation in Buddhism*, 27).
24. Charles Hallisey has used a resonant concept from Pierre Nora, *lieux de memoire* (memory sites), as a helpful way to think about *stūpas* and *cetiyas* ("Relics as Memory Sites in the Buddhist Literature of Medieval Sri Lanka," papercirculated

for the American Academy of Religion seminar on Buddhist relic veneration, various locations, 1994–1997, copy in author's files). The *lieux de memoire* are an especially helpful technology developed out of necessity in the absence of *milieux de memoire* (contexts of memory); in the Buddhist case, the former would be the relic-enshrining *stūpas*, whereas the latter would be the presence of the Buddha himself. See Pierre Nora, *Realms of Memory: The Construction of the French Past* (New York: Columbia University Press, 1998).

25. See *Anāgatavaṃsa*, ed. J. Minayeff, *Journal of the Pāli Text Society* 2 (1886): 33–53, and its translation in *Buddhism in Translations*, ed. Henry Clarke Warren (1896; reprint, New York: Atheneum, 1976), 481–486. Even though the *Anāgatavaṃsa* likely dates centuries after the *Mahāvaṃsa* (the date is uncertain, but it is a late Pāli text), the idea of the relics disappearing at the end of a Buddha era was known and discussed in the fifth century.
26. *Kalingabodhi Jātaka* (number 479), in *The Jātaka, or The Stories of the Buddha's Former Births*, vol. 4, ed. W. H. D. Rouse (Cambridge: Cambridge University Press, 1901), 142–148.
27. Jonathan Walters asserts that the *vaṃsas* are "'successions' of the Buddha's presence" rather than "mere chronicles of events" ("Buddhist History: The Sri Lankan Pāli *Vaṃsas* and Their Commentary," in Ronald Inden, Jonathan Walters, and Daud Ali, *Querying the Medieval: Texts and the History of Practices in South Asia* [New York: Oxford University Press, 2000], 99. The *Jātakas* are also literarily successions of the Buddha's presence, albeit in his pre-Buddha form as the bodhisatta, perfecting himself through various births.
28. The term *uddesika* later comes to mean "images," particularly of the Buddha, but also, in later Thai understandings, of secondary or reflective *pāribhogika* relics (relics of use) such as cuttings or seedlings from the original bodhi tree. Trainor notes that this tripartite classification is well developed by the fifth-century commentarial period. He draws attention to "evidence of an earlier twofold classification" in the *Milindapañha* 341, (trans. 2.188) (*Relics, Ritual, and Representation*, 89).
29. *Kalingabodhi Jātaka* (number 479), in *The Jātaka*, Rouse ed., 4:142.
30. "Vandami cetiyam sabbam sabbatthanesu patitthtam / Sarīrika dhatu maha bodhim Buddharupam sakalam sada" (Richard Gombrich, *Buddhist Precept and Practice*, 2nd ed. [Delhi: Motilal Banarsidass, 1991], 124, which gives Gombrich's own text as well the Pāli verses and Gombrich's English translation).
31. The later *Pāli Dhātuvaṃsa* considers Sumana a *nāga*, not a *deva*, who lived in a lotus pond near the Buddha, where he was "filled with mental joy from beholding the great splendor of the Buddha's physical form [tāthāgatassa rūpasobhaggappattaṃ attabhāvaṃ oloketvā]" (quoted in Trainor, *Relics, Ritual, and Representation in Buddhism*, 146).
32. Again, this narrative may suggest that the *Mahāvaṃsa* was arguing for the veneration of relics in a context that may have been less than favorable to such practices. Although this suggestion is entirely speculative, we may benefit from considering what Laurie Patton has concluded in *Myth as Argument: The* Bṛhaddevatā *as Canonical Commentary* (Berlin: Walter de Gruyter, 1996).
33. *Mahāvaṃsa* XII.2: "paccantesu." This reminds me of the *Saṅgīti Sutta* classification of inauspicious birth sites, which explicitly designates birth in a border country (without access to the Buddha, *dhamma*, and *saṅgha*) as inauspicious.

34. It is noteworthy that Asoka laments the tree's departure with a verse recalling the transfer of light imagery from *Mahāvaṃsa* I in the halo around the bodhi tree: "Emitting a net like rays [of light], the great bodhi tree of the Ten-powered One departs!" (*Mahāvaṃsa* XIX.15: "muñcamāno mahābodhirukkho, dasabalassa so jālaṃ sarasaraṃsiṃ va gacchati vata re iti").
35. *Mahāvaṃsa* XIX.19: "devatāhi anekāhi pūjānekā pavattitā, gahetuṃ ca mahābodhiṃ nāgākaṃsu vikkubbanaṃ" (Various offerings were proffered by various divine beings, and the *nāgas* performed a miracle to seize the Mahābodhi).
36. This story is recounted in *Mahāvaṃsa* XIX.17–23. Jean Philippe Vogel notes, "In the corresponding passage of the *Dipavaṃsa*, xvi, 8–29, the Nāgas are mentioned among the classes of beings which worship the Bodhi-tree on its way to Ceylon, but we read of no attempt on their part to seize it" (*Indian Serpent-Lore; or, The Nāgas in Hindu Legend and Art* [London: Probsthain, 1926], 24 n. 2). Actually, in the *Dīpavaṃsa* account, the *nāgas* do in fact seize it—the text explains that the boat is stalled and whisked away to the *nāgaloka*. Vogel misread.
37. *Mahāvaṃsa* XIX.21–23:

> Te tāsitā mahātheriṃ yācitvāna mahoragā nayitvāna mahābodhiṃ bhujaṃgabhavanaṃ tato
>
> sattāhaṃ nāgarajjena pūjāhi vividhāhi ca pūjayitvāna ānetvā nāvāya ṭhapayiṃsu te
>
> Tadahe va mahābodhi Jambukolaṃ idhāgamā.

38. On the process of Buddha image consecration, see Donald Swearer, "Hypostasizing the Buddha: Buddha Image Consecration in Northern Thailand," *History of Religions* 34, no. 3 (1995): 263–280, and *Becoming the Buddha: The Ritual of Image Consecration in Thailand* (Princeton: Princeton University Press, 2004).
39. The relic's eventual recovery is a sort of "expected miracle," to use art historian Robert Brown's useful phrase ("Expected Miracles: The Unsurprisingly Miraculous Nature of Buddhist Images and Relics," in *Images, Miracles, and Authority in Asian Religious Traditions*, ed. Richard H. Davis [Boulder: Westview Press, 1998], 23–36). On the epistemology relying on expected miracles, see Kristin Scheible, "Priming the Lamp of *Dhamma*: The Buddha's Miracles in the Pāli *Mahavāṃsa*," *Journal of the International Association of Buddhist Studies* 33, nos. 1–2 (2010–2011): 435–451.
40. Buddhaghosa's commentary on the *Mahāparinibbāṇa-sutta*, however, refuses to address the final verses dealing with the Buddha's prediction that this final one-eighth portion of his relics will be enshrined in Laṅkā, probably because it was assumed at the time the commentary was produced that this material was an accretion. In *Sumaṅgala-vilāsinī* 2.615, he writes that the closing verses of the *Mahāparinibbāṇa-sutta* were "spoken by the Elders of Tambapaṇṇi" and thus not original *Buddha-vacanā* (word of the Buddha).
41. An interesting comparison can be made here to Nāgārjuna's retrieval of the *Prajñāpāramitā* texts—dharma relics (*dharmadhātu*)—which the *nāgas* held until humans were sufficiently capable of understanding them.
42. What I refer to here as a "conventional reading of the Soṇuttara story as a model for the nascent state-*saṅgha* relationship" dominates in Gananath Obeyesekere, Frank Reynolds, and Bardwell L. Smith, *The Two Wheels of Dhamma: Essays on the Theravāda Tradition in India and Ceylon*, ed. Bardwell L. Smith (Chambersburg, Pa.: American Academy of Religion, 1972); the essays in Smith, *Religion and Legitimation*

of Power in Sri Lanka; and Trainor, "When Is a Theft Not a Theft?" This reading maintains that there is a mutual reliance between the king and the *saṅgha* that is exemplified in the stories of the acquisition of relics. For example, the *dhammarāja* (*dhamma* king) himself, Asoka, is the one who initiates the process of the transfer of the *sāsana* to Laṅkā when he sends Mahinda there (*Mahāvaṃsa* XIII), and it is he who bestows the first set of relics on the island (*Mahāvaṃsa* XVII), and, of course, it is King Duṭṭhagāmaṇī who builds the Mahāthūpa for the *saṅgha* while the *saṅgha* procures the relics for its enlivenment (*Mahāvaṃsa* XXXI).

43. Geary, *Furta Sacra*.
44. Relics, at least of the *sarīrika* (corporeal) variety, are available only at times when the Buddha is no longer living but has passed into *parinibbāṇa*. As we have seen, however, the next Buddha will not arise until after all the vestiges of the previous Buddha (his *sāsana*: the relics, teachings, and *saṅgha*) have disappeared. Relics thus exist in a time of both lamentation and the development of technologies to represent the absent Buddha as well as in a time of anticipation of the imminent coming of the next Buddha.
45. If there is any remaining doubt about the snakelike ontology of the *nāga*, the image of Vāsuladatta sheds it: "Having created thousands of various hoods, he, the great powered [*nāga*], lay down [puffing] smoke and fire. Having created thousands of various snakes [*ahī*] like himself, he made them all lie about in a circle" ("Anekāni sahassāni māpetvāna phaṇāni ca dhūmāyati pajjalati sayitvā so mahiddhiko // Anekāni sahassāni attanā sadise ahī māpayitvā sayāpesi samantā parivārite" [*Mahāvaṃsa* XXXI.54–55]).
46. *Mahāvaṃsa* XXXI.56: "Bahū nāga ca devā ca osariṃsu tahiṃ tadā, yuddhaṃ ubhinnaṃ nāgānaṃ passissāma mayaṃ iti."
47. *Mahāvaṃsa* XXXI.62: "Mahāsakkāraṭhānamhā appasakkāraṭhānakaṃ."
48. In his discussion of the later *Sinhala Thūpavaṃsa*, Steven Berkwitz notes that "the *Sinhala Thūpavaṃsa*'s presentation of this event appears focused on highlighting the moral dilemma related to acquiring those relics. The issue over who deserves to have relics to venerate is purposefully drawn out in order to exercise the moral reasoning of an audience" ("The Ethics of Buddhist History: A Study of the Pāli and Sinhala Thūpavaṃsas," Ph.D. diss., University of California, Santa Barbara, 1999, 163).
49. It is very interesting to note how this scene is radically embellished by later Mahāvihāran interpreters. In the *Sinhala Thūpavaṃsa*, the *nāgas* ask, "Is it only for humans that this suffering of *saṃsāra* is acute? Is it only for humans that *nirvāṇa* is sweet? Is it only for humans that the Dear Lord, who is the Buddha, fulfilled the perfections and became a Buddha?" (quoted in Steven Berkwitz, *Buddhist History in the Vernacular: The Power of the Past in Late Medieval Sri Lanka* [Leiden: Brill, 2004], 170–171).
50. See Trainor, "When Is Theft Not a Theft?" 8–10.
51. *Mahāvaṃsa* V.73: "Tato rājā pasanno so diguṇena dine dine bhikkhū saṭṭhisahassāni anupubbena vaḍḍhayi" (Thereafter, with happy faith the king doubled each day the *bhikkhus* [who were to receive alms] until they were 60,000).
52. *Mahāvaṃsa* V.91–92: "Dvattiṃsalakkhaṇūpetaṃ asītivyañjanujjalaṃ vyāmappa bhāparikkhittaṃ ketumālābhisobhitaṃ / nimmāyi nāgarājā so buddharūpaṃ manoramaṃ."
53. *Mahāvaṃsa* V.92–93: "Taṃ disvātipasādassa vimhayassa ca pūrito / etena nimmitaṃ rūpaṃ īdisaṃ kīdisaṃ nu kho tathāgatassa rūpaṃ ti āsi pītunnatunnato."

54. *Mahāvaṃsa* V.93: "āsi pītunnatunnato."
55. *Mahāvaṃsa* V.94: "Akkhipūjaṃ ti saṃññātaṃ taṃ sattāhaṃ nirantaraṃ mahāmahaṃ mahārājā kārāpesi mahiddhiko." Wilhelm Geiger translates *akkhipūja* as "feast of the eyes" in Mahānāma, *The Mahāvaṃsa, or The Great Chronicle of Ceylon*, trans. Wilhelm Geiger, assisted by Mabel Haynes Bode (London: Frowde for Pāli Text Society, 1912), 34.
56. Mahānāma, *Mahāvaṃsa: The Great Chronicle of Sri Lanka, Chapters 1-37*, trans. Ananda W. P. Guruge (Colombo, Sri Lanka: Associated Newspapers of Ceylon, 1989), 496.
57. This notion of pegging down relics to a location recalls the Burmese practice of driving a stake into the ground to symbolically pin down the head of the great serpent in the correct position before the construction of a *stūpa*. For an examination of the significance of the transportability of the relics, see Strong, *Relics of the Buddha*.

5. HISTORICIZING (IN) THE PĀLI *DĪPAVAṂSA* AND *MAHĀVAṂSA*

1. An extensive discussion of the boundaries and ramifications of the genres of history and literature is well beyond the scope of this project. This topic has provided fodder for numerous intellectual historians. Relating precisely to the Buddhist historical imagination exemplified in the Pāli (and in this case Sinhalese) *vaṃsas*, an overview can be found in Stephen Berkwitz, *Buddhist History in the Vernacular: The Power of the Past in Late Medieval Sri Lanka* (Leiden: Brill, 2004), 135–181.
2. Hayden White, *Tropics of Discourse: Essays in Cultural Criticism* (Baltimore: Johns Hopkins University Press, 1978), 86–89, especially White's discussion of the use of metaphor, metonymy, synecdoche, and irony in the representation of history as elements that underscore its fictive qualities. Also see his introduction to his book *Metahistory: The Historical Imagination in Nineteenth-Century Europe* (Baltimore: Johns Hopkins University Press, 1973).
3. Dominick LaCapra, *Rethinking Intellectual History: Texts, Contexts, Language* (Ithaca: Cornell University Press, 1983), 30.
4. Paul Ricoeur, *Time and Narrative*, 3 vols., trans. Kathleen Blamey and David Pellauer (Chicago: University of Chicago Press, 1984–1988), esp. vol. 3.
5. Anne E. Monius, *Imagining a Place for Buddhism: Literary Culture and Religious Community in Tamil-Speaking South India* (New York: Oxford University Press, 2001), 159.
6. Gregory Schopen, *Bones, Stones, and Buddhist Monks: Collected Papers on the Archaeology, Epigraphy, and Texts of Monastic Buddhism in India* (Honolulu: University of Hawai'i Press, 1997), 2–12, 114–115.
7. For the inscriptions, see *Epigraphia Zeylanica*, 8 vols. to date (Colombo, Sri Lanka: Department of Government Printing, 1904– (in progress); *Inscriptions of Ceylon*, ed. and trans. Senarat Paranavitana, Archaeological Survey of Ceylon (Colombo, Sri Lanka: Ceylon Department of Archaeology, 1970); Lakshman S. Perera, *The Institutions of Ancient Ceylon from Inscriptions*, vol. 1 (Kandy, Sri Lanka: International Centre for Ethnic Studies, 2001); Robin A. E. Coningham, "Monks, Caves, and Kings: A Reassessment of the Nature of Early Buddhism in Sri Lanka," *World Archaeology* 27, no. 2 (1995): 222–242.

8. Paul Ricoeur, *Freud and Philosophy: An Essay on Interpretation* (New Haven: Yale University Press, 1970), 32–35. Ricoeur advises one to apply the "hermeneutics of suspicion" in one's interpretation of a text to penetrate the text's surface concerns to reveal the ideology that actually motivates the text.
9. Rather than being condemned to relativism and the unproductive interpretations that result from such a sabotaging method of reading, I acknowledge that multiple readings are possible with any text and that readings are influenced by the reader's concerns and dispositions. This does not, however, mean that all readings are equal. Literary theorists can argue about it. I merely suggest here that if you approach the *vaṃsas* intent on finding historiography, you will see what looks like historiography at work in the text. But that reading is framed by your context, and several other readings are possible from other contexts or from other dimensions of the text. On this point, see Umberto Eco, *The Open Work*, trans. Anna Cancogni (Cambridge, Mass.: Harvard University Press, 1989).
10. G. P. Malalasekera gives the dates 664–673 B.C.E. for Dāṭhopatissa, identifying him as the king called "Bhāgiṇeyya-Dāṭhopatissa" in the *Vaṃsatthappakāsinī* (introduction to *Vaṃsatthappakāsinī: Commentary on the* Mahāvaṃsa, 2 vols., ed. G. P. Malalasekera [1935–1936; reprint, London: Pāli Text Society, 1977], 1:cv). Note that Malalasekera also refers to this text as the "MṬ," or *Mahāvaṃsa Ṭīkā*, an applied designation that is never used within the *Vaṃsatthapakkāsiī* itself, which sometimes refers to itself as the *Padya-(Pajja-) padoruvaṃsa-vaṇṇanā*, or the "Commentary on the *Padya-(Pajja-) padoruvaṃsa-vaṇṇanā*" (the *Mahāvaṃsa*) (ibid., cvii).
11. Wilhelm Geiger, *The* Dīpavaṃsa *and* Mahāvaṃsa *and Their Historical Development in Ceylon*, trans. Ethel M. Coomaraswamy (Colombo, Sri Lanka: Cottle, 1908), 82.
12. Malalasekera, introduction to *Vaṃsatthappakāsinī*, 1:cix. Malalasekera repeats the claim that soon after Buddhaghosa finished compiling material in Pāli from original Sinhalese sources, these sources went into disuse, and the *Mahāvaṃsa* "bore to the Sinhalese chronicles exactly the same sort of relation as Buddhaghosa's works did to the scriptural *Aṭṭhakathā*" (1:cix). The *Vaṃsatthappakāsinī* must therefore have been compiled prior to the loss of the source material.
13. Steven Collins agrees with the compilers of the *Critical Pali Dictionary* that Geiger's arguments for this nomenclature are "unpersuasive" and that the title *Cūlavaṃsa* should be dropped in favor of the "indigenous practice of referring to the whole work as the *Mahāvaṃsa* or Great Chronicle" ("What Is Literature in Pali?" in *Literary Cultures in History: Reconstructions from South Asia*, ed. Sheldon Pollock [Berkeley: University of California Press, 2003], 652–653 n. 5). Geiger is primarily responsible for this nomenclature. See Mahānāma, *Mahāvaṃsa*, ed. Wilhelm Geiger (London: Pāli Text Society, 1908); Mahānāma, *The Mahāvaṃsa, or The Great Chronicle of Ceylon*, trans. Wilhelm Geiger, assisted by Mabel Haynes Bode (London: Frowde for Pāli Text Society, 1912); *Cūlavaṃsa*, 2 vols., ed. Wilhelm Geiger (London: Pāli Text Society, 1925–1927); and *Cūlavaṃsa: Being the More Recent Part of the* Mahāvaṃsa, trans. Wilhelm Geiger (into German) and C. Mabel Rickmers (from the German into English) (London: Pāli Text Society, 1929). The text itself does not claim the title *Cūlavaṃsa* (Lesser *Vaṃsa*) and instead envisions itself as a continuous whole, even if authors or compilers several centuries removed from each other are responsible for penning the two sections. It has become common practice to refer to these two sections as separate texts, and I have in fact been

concerned only with the earlier segment. In *Buddhist Learning and Textual Practice in Eighteenth-Century Lankan Monastic Culture* (Princeton: Princeton University Press, 2001), Anne Blackburn successfully thwarted Geiger's accepted convention when, following the eighteenth-century monastic convention in the text she discusses, the *Sārārthadīpanī*, she refused to separate the two sections, calling the entire text *Mahāvaṃsa*. Of course, this approach reflects the very argument of the later text itself, that it is in fact a legitimate continuation of the earlier text, and the concerns of the textual community that is her focus. The split in the narrative comes at the conclusion of King Mahāsena's reign, which concludes the earlier *Mahāvaṃsa*, and the reign of King Sirimeghavaṇṇa (reign beginning around 362), which begins the later *Mahāvaṃsa* (which Geiger titled *Cūlavaṃsa*). This king restored the primacy of the Mahāvihāra, according to the text, and thus made right what his father had destroyed.

14. Parākramabāhu was both a reformer of Buddhist practices and culture as well as a successful unifier of the land—he brought together three kingdoms to unify the island of Sri Lanka under one vision.
15. For how a given reading of history says more about contemporaneous concerns than about the "facts" of the past, see Michel de Certeau, *The Writing of History* (New York: Columbia University Press, 1988).
16. R. G. Collingwood, *The Idea of History* (London: Oxford University Press, 1956), 156. Ronald Inden also responds to and extends several of Collingwood's ideas of history, most notably his concepts of "complex agency" and "scale of texts": "[Collingwood's] discussion of agency in connection with historical knowledge seems to offer a way both of criticizing current intellectual practices and of formulating an attractive alternative to the individualist and structuralist, as well as the antistructuralist, approaches in cultural history" ("Introduction: From Philological to Dialogical Texts," in Ronald Inden, Jonathan Walters, and Daud Ali, *Querying the Medieval: Texts and the History of Practices in South Asia* [New York: Oxford University Press, 2000, 11).
17. Brian Stock, "History, Literature, and Medieval Textuality," *Yale French Studies*, no. 70 (1986): 16.
18. Jonathan Walters, "*Suttas* as History: Four Approaches to the *Sermon on the Noble Quest* (Ariyapariyesana Sutta)," *History of Religions* 38, no. 3 (1999): 282.
19. Hayden White, *The Content of the Form: Narrative Discourse and Historical Representation* (Baltimore: Johns Hopkins University Press, 1987), 209.
20. With such a long history of colonialization (from the Portuguese in 1505 through the Dutch in the seventeenth century and the British occupation beginning in 1796 and continuing to 1948), it is understandable that the *Mahāvaṃsa* was regarded as a viable resource for autonomous, authentic identity construction. See Steven Kemper, *The Presence of the Past: Chronicles, Politics, and Culture in Sinhala Life* (Ithaca: Cornell University Press, 1991). Also consider the way D. S. Senayake framed independence in terms of Sinhala identity in 1939 when he said that the Sinhala "are one blood and one nation. We are a chosen people. Buddha said that his religion would last for 5,500 [*sic*] years. That means that we, as the custodians of that religion, shall last as long" (quoted in Tessa J. Bartholomeusz, *In Defense of Dharma: Just-War Ideology in Buddhist Sri Lanka* [London: RoutledgeCurzon, 2002], 142, "[*sic*]" added by Bartholomeusz).

21. For example, as examined in chapter 2, in *Mahāvaṃsa* I.20 Geiger translated a particularly influential verse to state that the *dhamma* would thereafter "shine in glory" in Lanka (see note 59, chapter 2). There is no word for "glory" in the verse—the word used in the compound *sāsanujjotanaṭṭhānaṃ* simply means "shine." My impression is that scholars who would not intentionally perpetuate in their own critical work any misreadings conducive of a nationalist interpretation have nevertheless done so. For example, Berkwitz refers to this verse in a documentary way, stating that perceptions of Laṅkā "as the place where his [the Buddha's] Dharma should thereafter shine in glory are often highlighted as the ancient roots of Sinhala Buddhist nationalism" (*Buddhist History in the Vernacular*, 35).
22. Heinz Bechert, "The Beginnings of Buddhist Historiography: *Mahāvaṃsa* and Political Thinking," in *Religion and Legitimation of Power in Sri Lanka*, ed. Bardwell L. Smith (Chambersburg, Pa.: Anima Books, 1978), 7–8.
23. That the king was identified as a *cakkavattin* (*cakravartin* in Sanskrit; usually translated as "world-conquering monarch," although "wheel turner" is more accurate) challenges the idea that there could be a specifically "state" ideology. As Benedict Anderson sees it, "Kingship organizes everything around a high centre. Its legitimacy derives from divinity, not from populations, who, after all, are subjects, not citizens. In the modern conception, state sovereignty is fully, flatly, and evenly operative over each square centimetre of a legally demarcated territory. But in the older imagining, where states were defined by centres, borders were porous and indistinct, and sovereignties faded imperceptibly into one another" (*Imagined Communities: Reflections on the Origin and Spread of Nationalism* [1983; reprint, London: Verso, 1991], 19). According to the *Mahāvaṃsa*, the king at the time of Mahinda's mission to Sri Lanka, Devānaṃpiya Tissa, underwent a second coronation with accoutrements from Asoka, including a crown. Prior to that, kings had only a staff to designate their sovereignty. The extra accoutrements might indicate an ambitious move by Devānaṃpiya Tissa to exceed the boundaries of his local Anurādhapura kingship, although their presence is most frequently understood as Asoka's move to include Sri Lanka in his realm.
24. Richard Gombrich, *Theravāda Buddhism: A Social History from Ancient Benares to Modern Colombo* (London: Routledge, 1988), 142.
25. Ibid., 141.
26. Bardwell L. Smith, "The Ideal Social Order as Portrayed in the Chronicles of Ceylon," in *Religion and Legitimation of Power in Sri Lanka*, ed. Bardwell L. Smith (Chambersburg, Pa.: Anima Books, 1978), 48.
27. The term *Heilsgeschichte* is most properly translated as "salvation history," which works for "Christian theology." *Salvation*, however, is not the most salient term in the Theravāda understanding of soteriology.
28. The first line of the proem of the *Mahāvaṃsa* does employ the term *suddha* (pure): "Namassitvāna saṃbuddhaṃ susuddhaṃ suddhvaṃsajaṃ" (Having paid honor to the pure buddha of the pure lineage). But here it refers to the Buddha and not to anything terrestrially Lankan. The idea of the Buddha's predestination of Laṅkā is from *Mahāvaṃsa* I.20: "Sāsanujjotanaṭṭhānaṃ Laṅkā ñātā jinena hi/ yakkhapuṇṇāya Laṅkāya yakkhā nibbāsiyā ti ca" (For Lankā was known by the Conqueror as a place where the *sāsana* would shine, and that from Laṅkā full of *yakkhas*, the *yakkhas* must be removed). But the Buddha here is pictured as

omniscient and making an observation, not prescribing or determining the land's future sacrality.

29. David Little, *The Invention of Enmity* (Washington, D.C.: United States Institute of Peace Press, 1993), 26.
30. Alice Greenwald, "The Relic on the Spear: Historiography and the Saga of Duṭṭhagāmaṇī," in Smith, *Religion and Legitimation of Power in Sri Lanka*, 14.
31. Stock, *The Implications of Literacy*, 522.
32. By "religious" here, I refer to both the personally powerful, ethically transformative aims as well as the circumscription of a particular community of faith and the beliefs that hold such a group together.
33. *Mahāvaṃsa* XXXII.81–83:

    Duṭṭhagāmaṇirājā so rājanāmāraho mahā
    Metteyyassa bhagavato hessati aggasāvako

    Rañño pitā pitā tassa, mātā mātā bhavissati
    Saddhātisso kaniṭṭho tu dutiyo hessati sāvako

    Sālirājakumāro yo tassa rañño suto tu, so
    Metteyyassa bhagavato putto yeva bhavissati.

34. H. L. Seneviratne, "Identity and the Conflation of Past and Present," in *Identity, Consciousness, and the Past: Forging of Caste and Community in India and Sri Lanka*, ed. H. L. Seneviratne (Delhi: Oxford University Press, 1997), 6.
35. Bartholomeusz, *In Defense of Dharma*, 21.
36. White, *Content of the Form*, 5.
37. Although it is beyond the purview of the present examination, a comparative study of the early *vaṃsas* and the Sanskrit *Mahāpurāṇas*, especially with a focus on their literary elements, would be helpful.
38. Steven Collins, "On the Very Idea of a Pāli Canon," *Journal of the Pāli Text Society* 15 (1990): 100.
39. Buddhaghosa, *Samanta-Pāsādikā*, ed. J. Takakusu (London: Pāli Text Society, 1924), I.62, 70, 71, 74, 75. Jonathan Walters notes that this reference to the *Dīpavaṃsa* as *purāṇa* has the effect of "implicitly comparing it with the Theist Purāṇas, originary accounts which also had accounts of royal lineages as one of their topics." He also notes that "it is possible that when Buddhaghosa cites 'the ancients' (*porāṇā*) he means not the *Dpv* [*Dīpavaṃsa*] itself but the source of *Dpv*, that is, the *Sīhalaṭṭhakathā-Mahāvaṃsa* (and/or the men who wrote it), in which case these *Dpv* verses are also quotations from that ancient source" ("Buddhist History: The Sri Lankan Pāli *Vaṃsas* and Their Commentary," in Inden, Walters, and Ali, *Querying the Medieval*, 119).
40. Berkwitz, *Buddhist History in the Vernacular*, 3.
41. Carolyn Dewald, "Does History Matter? Meaning-Making and the First Two Greek Historians," in *Historical Knowledge in Biblical Antiquity*, ed. Jacob Neusner, Bruce D. Chilton, and William S. Green (Blandford Forum, U.K.: Deo, 2007), 34–35.
42. Considering the wide variety of literariness of Pāli *vaṃsas*, Collins writes, "The earliest, the *Dīpavaṃsa* (Chronicle of the Island)—i.e., Sri Lanka—is a clumsy verse composition with grammatical and other errors, made probably in the third or fourth century C.E." ("What Is Literature in Pāli?" 652).

43. Walpola Rahula, *History of Buddhism in Ceylon: The Anurādhapura Period, 3rd Century BC–10th Century AC*, 2nd ed. (Colombo, Sri Lanka: Gunasena, 1956), xxi.
44. *Vaṃsatthappakāsinī* 36.7, 36.9, 42.1, 47.31, 48.1, 48.3; see Malalasekera's introduction to *Vaṃsatthappakāsinī*, 1:lvi–lvii.
45. The example given by Malalasekera is from *Vaṃsatthappakāsinī* 36.5: "Mahāvaṃsan ti laddhanāmaṃ Mahāvihāravāsīnaṃ vācanāmaggaṃ Porāṇaṭṭhakathaṃ" (introduction to *Vaṃsatthappakāsinī*, 1:lviii).
46. Ibid., 1:lvii. For the references to Oldenberg and Geiger, see *Dīpavaṃsa: An Ancient Buddhist Historical Record*, ed. and trans. Hermann Oldenberg (1879; reprint, London: New Delhi: Asian Educational Services, 1982), 4, and Mahānāma, *The Mahāvaṃsa*, Geiger 1908 ed., 64.
47. For a catalog of a large body of sources for the *Dīpavaṃsa* and *Mahāvaṃsa* (including *Uttaravihāra-aṭṭhakathā*, *Vinayaṭṭhakathā*, *Dīpavaṃsaṭṭhkathā*, *Sīmākathā*, *Cetiyavaṃsaṭṭhakathā*, *Mahābodhivaṃsakathā*, *Sumedhakathā*, *Sahassavatthu-aṭṭhakathā*, and several *vaṇṇanā* [commentaries]), none of which is extant but is evident through later references and quotations, see Malalasekera, introduction to *Vaṃsatthappakāsinī*, 1:lxv–lxxii.
48. *Dīpavaṃsa*, Oldenberg ed., 3.
49. Malalasekera, introduction to *Vaṃsatthappakāsinī*, 1:lxii–lxiv, where Malalasekera sums up Geiger's and Adikaram's arguments.
50. Ibid., 1:lxxiv, citing *Vaṃsatthappakāsinī* 46–51.
51. Max Weber, *The Theory of Social and Economic Organization*, trans. A. R. Anderson and Talcot Parsons (London: Hodge, 1947), 363–373.
52. Latter-day *suttas* are routinely cast in the authoritative and legitimizing voice of the Buddha. Mahāyāna *suttas* frequently used Śakyamuni as the narrator or as the character in a narrative who introduces another Buddha (for example, Śakyamuni introduces and extols the many virtues of Amitābha in the *Sukhāvativyūha sutra*). See Luis O. Gomez, *The Land of Bliss: The Paradise of the Buddha of Measureless Light* (Honolulu: University of Hawai'i Press, 1996).
53. K. M. de Silva, *A History of Sri Lanka* (Berkeley: University of California Press, 1981), 9.
54. Collins, "On the Very Idea of a Pāli Canon," 99–100.
55. G. P. Malalasekera, *The Pāli Literature of Ceylon* (1928; reprint, Kandy, Sri Lanka: Buddhist Publication Society, 1994), 128.
56. Although the account of the Buddhist councils is also represented early in each text, expressly connecting the monastic community in Laṅkā to translocal, foundational Buddhist concerns, I am here interested only in the story cycles that revolve around the island of Laṅkā itself. The stories of events on the island of Laṅkā proper are all fixed to a timeline that defies the timelessness of the Eliadean *illud tempore*; events correspond with events from mainland India, even if they happen in Laṅkā.
57. This is not to say that Duṭṭhagāmaṇī is only a good hero. Certainly in the text's future-thinking mode, the extensive attention lavished on this hero, significantly a king and even more significantly a king who is understood to become Metteyya's (the future Buddha's) right-hand man in the future, is an important statement about the role and obligations of royalty. Here I suggest that Duṭṭhagāmaṇī's royal function is secondary to the role he will have in a different sort of lineage of the future, one where he will be directly proximate to the Buddha and thus an ideal

exemplar of the devout Buddhist practitioner, and that this special role is due to the ethical and behavioral choices he made in his past role as king.

58. See Berkwitz, *Buddhist History in the Vernacular*, chapter 2, for a full literature review of recent and past scholarship.
59. Mahānāma, *The First Twenty Chapters of the Mahāwanso and a Prefatory Essay on Pali Buddhistical Literature*, trans. George Turnour (Cotta, Sri Lanka: Cotta Church Mission Press, 1837). See Walters, "Buddhist History," 157.
60. Walters, "Buddhist History," 99. Also consider Steven Collins's understanding of the relationship between time and concerns for *nirvāṇa*, where the *Mahāvaṃsa* can be interpreted as a way to bring the Buddha's *nibbāna*-conducive proximity into different time periods (*Nirvāṇa and Other Buddhist Felicities: Utopias of the Pāli Imaginaire* [Cambridge: Cambridge University Press, 1998]).
61. Jan Nattier, *Once Upon a Future Time: Studies in a Buddhist Prophecy of Decline* (Berkeley: Asian Humanities Press, 1991), 8–9.
62. B. G. Gokhale, "The Theravāda-Buddhist View of History," *Journal of the American Oriental Society* 85, no. 3 (1965): 355.
63. Collins cites several canonical references (together with corresponding commentaries) to "suttantā kavikatā kāveyyā" and notes the early Buddhist tradition's aversion to unnecessary poetics: "The sterner side of the Teaching easily disapproves of literary frivolity. The Buddha laments the future decline of his Teaching, contrasting sermons given by himself with those to be given in the future by his disciples, which will be merely 'literature made by kavis' " ("What Is Literature in Pāli?" 670).
64. Malalasekera, *The Pāli Literature of Ceylon*, 146.
65. Wilhelm Geiger, introduction to *The Mahāvaṃsa, or The Great Chronicle of Ceylon*, li, lvii.
66. See *Dīpavaṃsa* V.51–52:

    Sattarasa bhinnavādā eko vādo abhinnako
    sabbev'aṭṭhārasa honti 'bhinnavādena te saha
    nigrodho va mahārukkho theravādānam uttamo anūnam anadhikañ c'eva kevalaṃ jinasāsanaṃ
    kaṇṭakā viya rukkhamhi nibbattā vādasesakā

    "Of all the eighteen there is one unbroken sect, and seventeen dissenting sects. The best is [the sect of] the Theravāda, like a great Banyan tree with nothing added or nothing lacking, the complete *sāsana* of the Conqueror. The seventeen dissenting sects (*bhinnavādā*) are altogether like thorns growing forth from this same sect."
67. Rahula, *History of Buddhism in Ceylon*, 303. Also see G. C. Mendis, *The Pāli Chronicles of Sri Lanka* (Colombo, Sri Lanka: Karunaratne & Sons, 1996).
68. Rahula, *History of Buddhism in Ceylon*, 303–304.
69. Ibid., 303. Rahula notes that even in contemporary usage a monk's name refers to the location of reception of the *upasampadā* (higher ordination), even if that monk lives elsewhere.
70. That a threatened existence is related to a community's literary productivity has been pursued vis-à-vis the writing down of the Pāli canon, which is commonly thought to have occurred in the first century B.C.E. after famine threatened the stability and continuity of the monastic lineage responsible for its oral preservation. This idea, however, is counter to Jean-Jacques Rousseau's argument

in *Discourse on the Sciences and the Arts* (trans. and ed. Donald A. Cress [1750; reprint, Indianapolis, Ind.: Hackett, 1987]) that it is leisure that breeds literary and artistic achievement. Berkwitz challenges the common assumption that in the premodern Lankan context the *vaṃsas* were produced in stressful times: "And while it is possible to argue that monastic competition between the Mahāvihāra fraternity of monks and its rivals in the Abhayagiri and Jetavana fraternities contributed to the writing of the Mahāvaṃsa in the sixth century, the flourish of history writing after King Parākramabāhu's forced unification of the Saṅgha in the twelfth century suggests that the existence of the sole-surviving Mahāvihāra fraternity probably did not need further justification" (*Buddhist History in the Vernacular*, 150).

71. There is quite a discrepancy in dates given in scholarship on the royal history of Sri Lanka. Most scholars, such as Rahula, give Vaṭṭagāmaṇī's dates as 29–17 B.C.E. (*History of Buddhism in Ceylon*, 305). R. A. L. H. Gunawardana gives Vaṭṭagāmaṇī's reign as 89–77 B.C.E. (*Robe and Plough: Monasticism and Economic Interest in Early Medieval Sri Lanka* [Tucson: University of Arizona Press, 1979], 7), dates that obviously conflict with those given for Duṭṭhagāmaṇī, 101–77. The sixty-year discrepancy is due to the different calculations made by scholars interpreting the *Mahāvaṃsa*.
72. Gunaratne Panabokke, *History of the Buddhist Saṅgha in India and Sri Lanka* (Sri Lanka: Postgraduate Institute of Pāli and Buddhist Studies, 1993), 106–107.
73. Collins, "On the Very Idea of a Pāli Canon," 96.
74. E. W. Adikaram, *Early History of Buddhism in Ceylon* (Migoda, Sri Lanka: Puswella, 1946), 79.
75. Walters, "Buddhist History," 111.
76. Ibid., 112.
77. Ibid. Walters directs attention to *Inscriptions of Ceylon*, 2.1:46, and *Epigraphia Zeylanica*, 7:99–106, and notes, "No unambiguous evidence for royal donations to the Mahāvihāra exists from this period. However, a donation to the Mahāvihāra dated to the reign of Bhātika Tissa II [c. 143–67] was made by one of his ministers [see *Inscriptions of Ceylon*, 2.1:116–17]" ("Buddhist History," 112, n. 17).
78. Collins, "On the Very Idea of the Pāli Canon," 96. Also see Gunawardana, *Robe and Plough*, 7–37.
79. Adikaram, *Early History of Buddhism in Ceylon*, 94.
80. De Silva, *A History of Sri Lanka*, 47.
81. Collins, "What Is Literature in Pāli?" 651.
82. For an excellent overview, see Jonathan Walters, "Mahāsena at the Mahāvihāra: The Interpretation and Politics of History in Medieval Sri Lanka," in *Invoking the Past: The Uses of History in South Asia*, ed. Daud Ali (Oxford: Oxford University Press, 1999), 322–366.
83. Also see Walter's excellent examination of the *Dīpavaṃsa* account in which he suggests that its composition was close enough in time to the mentioned events that the monks would have remembered them all. He suggests the *Dīpavaṃsa* moniker "Dummitta" (Bad Friend) substituted for "Saṅghamitta" (Friend of the *Saṅgha*) implies that the *Dīpavaṃsa* compiler monk(s) "still remembered" the grievous acts against them. He concludes that "this text was written as a polemical work within the context of contemporary debate centered upon the events of Mahāsena's reign" ("Buddhist History," 113–114).
84. Rahula exemplifies this conclusion. Because of quotations in Buddhaghosa's *Samantapāsādikā* that say their source is the *Porāṇas*, similar but not the same as the

Dīpavaṃsa, "it can be conjectured that the ancient Sinhalese *Aṭṭhakathā* formed the sources of the [*Dīpavaṃsa*]" (*History of Buddhism in Ceylon*, xxi).

85. Walters, "Buddhist History," 114–115.
86. Hugh Nevill, manuscript catalog, cited in Malalasekera, *The Pāli Literature of Ceylon*, 136.
87. Ibid., 137, italics in original.
88. Geiger, *The* Dīpavaṃsa *and* Mahāvaṃsa, 64.
89. Walters, "Buddhist History," 114.
90. Malalasekera, *The Pāli Literature of Ceylon*, 135.
91. Walters, "Buddhist History," 117.
92. Rahula, *History of Buddhism in Ceylon*, 139.
93. *Mahāwaṇsa-Ṭīkā*, ed. Baṭuwantuḍāwe and Ñāṇissara Bhikshu (Columbo, Sri Lanka: Cottle, 1895), 502, 35.
94. Geiger, *The* Dīpavaṃsa *and* Mahāvaṃsa, 41.
95. Geiger, introduction to Mahānāma, *The Mahāvaṃsa, or, The Great Chronicle of Ceylon*, xi. In his earlier work, *The* Dīpavaṃsa *and* Mahāvaṃsa, Geiger had declared that although the *Dīpavaṃsa* and *Mahāvaṃsa* "were not only in agreement with regard to the matter contained in each, but also with regard to the order in which this matter was arranged," allowing for no doubt that "either the M. has borrowed its material and arrangement from the D., or else both the M. and the D. have borrowed from the same sources," with the latter conclusion being more probable (14).
96. Collins, "What Is Literature in Pāli?" 652.
97. Mendis, *Pāli Chronicles of Sri Lanka*, 93.
98. Gombrich, *Theravāda Buddhism*, 140–141 n.
99. Berkwitz, *Buddhist History in the Vernacular*, 151.
100. Ibid., 27. For a very good survey of the merits and problems of the scholarship on Buddhist histories to date, especially regarding scholars' assessments of their "trustworthiness" as historical documents, see chapter 2, "Buddhist History Now and Then," in Berkwitz, *Buddhist History in the Vernacular*, esp. 40–61. For an excellent review of the nineteenth-century representations of Sri Lankan Buddhism, see Kevin Trainor, *Relics, Ritual, and Representation in Buddhism: Rematerializing the Sri Lankan Theravāda Tradition* (Cambridge: Cambridge University Press, 1997), 5–23. For a review of colonial and national readings of the Pāli *vaṃsas*, see Jonathan Walters, "Appendix: Colonial and National Readings of the Pāli *Vaṃsas*," in Inden, Walters, and Ali, *Querying the Medieval*, 152–164.
101. Regarding how the later *vaṃsas* repeat patterns, Berkwitz seems to distance the vernacular, later medieval *vaṃsa* he analyzes from the *Dīpavaṃsa* and *Mahāvaṃsa*. "Instead of seeing the *Sinhala Thūpavaṃsa* as a text wholly derivative of the *Mahāvaṃsa* and written to legitimate a political ideology reflecting modern interests, this and other 'vernacular' *vaṃsas* that were composed during a period of political turbulence in late medieval Sri Lanka had a different significance altogether. These texts were more likely written as a new polity was emerging from a condition of disunity and weakness than as a mature polity attempting to reassert a so-called 'Buddhist hegemony.' As such, they may well represent attempts of defining and consolidating new communities in what Raymond Williams has called an 'emergent culture,' which is characterized by the creation of new meanings, values, and relationships vis-à-vis older, more dominant systems" (*Buddhist History in the Vernacular*, 34, quoting Raymond Williams, *Marxism and Literature* [Oxford: Oxford University Press, 1977], 123).

102. Stephen Berkwitz, "History and Gratitude in Theravāda Buddhism," *Journal of the American Academy of Religion* 71, no. 3 (2003): 598, citing the distinction between "literal" and "literary" articulated by Luis Gomez in *Land of Bliss*, 51–52.
103. Walters, "Buddhist History," 121–122.
104. Ibid., 122, 120.
105. Seneviratne, "Identity and the Conflation of Past and Present," 5.
106. Ibid.
107. It would behoove us to consider Benedict Anderson's often-cited brainchild "imagined communities" as we interpret the modern use and abuse of the *Mahāvaṃsa*. A full critique of both Sinhalese and Western scholarly use of the *Mahāvaṃsa*, however, is beyond the purview of this work.
108. In *The Presence of the Past*, Steven Kemper has done the best job presenting the various ways the past as conceived by the *Mahāvaṃsa* intrudes on and supports certain positions vis-à-vis Sinhalese identity and hegemony in Sri Lanka.
109. Bardwell L. Smith, "Sinhalese Buddhism and the Dilemmas of Reinterpretation," in Obeyesekere, Reynolds, and Smith, *Two Wheels of Dhamma*, 87. Note that this essay was published after decades of ratcheting political rhetoric in Sri Lanka but about a decade before the beginning of the civil war in 1983.
110. As Berkwitz points out, "Not all 'pasts' are created equally, of course, but all accounts of the past are created" (*Buddhist History in the Vernacular*, 25).

CONCLUSION

1. Bardwell Smith offers a typical rendering of the *nāga* as a symbolic force of chaos in need of subjugation by the Buddha: "These mythic beings are to be seen not literally as beasts, but as symbols of disorder, whose power is sought on the *Dhamma*'s behalf. . . . On two of his legendary three trips to Laṅkā the Buddha encounters these forms of the demonic, reducing disorder to impotency, and ultimately enlists them in service to the *Dhamma*" ("Kingship, the *Saṅgha*, and the Process of Legitimation in Anurādhapura Ceylon: An Interpretive Essay," in *Buddhism in Ceylon and Studies on Religious Syncretism in Buddhist Countries: Report on a Symposium in Göttingen*, ed. Heinz Bechert [Göttingen, Germany: Vandenhoeck & Ruprecht, 1978], 103).
2. The most interesting of this sort of historicist "scholarship" is E. M. C. Amunugama, *The History of Ancient Aryan Tribes in Sri Lanka: Yaksas, Nāgas, Devas, Sakyas* (Colombo, Sri Lanka: J. R. Jayewardene Cultural Centre, 1994).
3. Luis Gomez explains the difference between modern and premodern Buddhist readers and interpreters of texts. He suggests that whereas modern readers' imaginations are inhibited by their "literal mind[s]," the premodern Buddhists (such as those of the *Mahāvaṃsa*'s textual community) would engage a "literary mind," wherein a poetic project arouses the hearers' imagination and subsequent emotional responses (introduction to *The Land of Bliss: The Paradise of the Buddha of Measureless Light* [Honolulu: University of Hawai'i Press, 1996], 52–53).
4. Jonathan Walters, "Mahāsena at the Mahāvihāra: The Interpretation and Politics of History in Medieval Sri Lanka," in *Invoking the Past: The Uses of History in South Asia*, ed. Daud Ali (Oxford: Oxford University Press, 1999), 363.

5. Jonathan Walters, "Buddhist History: The Sri Lankan Pāli *Vaṃsas* and Their Commentary," in Ronald Inden, Jonathan Walters, and Daud Ali, *Querying the Medieval: Texts and the History of Practices in South Asia* (New York: Oxford University Press, 2000), 127.
6. Walters writes: "The court of the Okkākas, in collaboration with the Mahāvihāran monks was, I am convinced, responsible for the composition of an imperial Purāṇa in the form of a commentary on the [*Mahāvaṃsa*]: the very commentary that has allowed George Turnour and later scholars to read the history in the Pāli *Vaṃsas*" (ibid., 125). Although Turnour and Geiger referred to this text as the "Ṭīkā" (Commentary), it nowhere claims this title for itself.
7. Kevin Trainor, *Relics, Ritual, and Representation in Buddhism: Rematerializing the Sri Lankan Theravāda Tradition* (Cambridge: Cambridge University Press, 1997), 27.

BIBLIOGRAPHY

PRIMARY SOURCES

Anāgatavaṃsa. Ed. J. Minayeff. *Journal of the Pali Text Society* 2 (1886): 33–53. Translated in *Buddhism in Translations*, ed. Henry Clarke Warren, 481–486. 1896. Reprint. New York: Atheneum, 1976.

Aṅguttara Nikāya. Parts 1–2. Ed. Richard Morris. Oxford: Pāli Text Society, 1995–1999.

Buddhadatta Thera. *Madhuratthavilāsinī*. Trans. I .B. Horner. London: Pāli Text Society, 1978.

Buddhaghosa. *Manorathapūraṇī: Commentary on the* Aṇguttara Nikāya. 5 vols. Ed. Edmund Hardy and Max Walleser. London: Oxford University Press for Pāli Text Society, 1924–1956.

——. *Samanta-Pāsādikā*. Ed. J. Takakusu. London: Pāli Text Society, 1924.

——. *Sumaṅgalavilāsinī*. 2nd ed. Ed. T. W. Rhys Davids and J. Estlin Carpenter. London: Luzac for the Pali Text Society, 1968.

——. *Visuddhimagga*. Trans. Bhikkhu Ñanamoli. 5th ed. Kandy, Sri Lanka: Buddhist Publication Society, 1991.

Buddhavamsa; and, Cariyapitaka. Trans. N. A. Jayawickrama. London: Pāli Text Society, 1974.

Buddhavaṃsa: Chronicle of Buddhas and Cariyāpiṭaka: Basket of Conduct. Trans. I. B. Horner. Part 3 of *The Minor Anthologies of the Pali Canon*. London: Pāli Text Society, 1975.

Buddhavaṃsa: The Lineage of the Buddhas. Trans. Bimala Churn Law. London: Pāli Text Society, 1938.

Cariyāpiṭaka. Ed. Bimala Churn Law. Poona, India: Bhandarkar Oriental Research Institute, 1949.

Cūlavaṃsa. 2 vols. Ed. Wilhelm Geiger. London: Pāli Text Society, 1925–1927.

Cūlavaṃsa: Being the More Recent Part of the Mahāvaṃsa. Translated into German by Wilhelm Geiger and from the German into English by C. Mabel Rickmers. London: Pāli Text Society, 1929.

The Dāṭhāvaṃsa (A History of the Tooth-Relic of the Buddha). Edited and trans. Bimala Churn Law. Lahore: Motilal Banarsidass, 1925.

Dhammapāla, Achariya. *Paramatthadīpanī, Being the Commentary on the* Cariyā-Piṭaka. Ed. D. L. Barua. London: Pāli Text Society, 1939.

Dhātuvaṃsa. Ed. Kamburupiṭiya Nandaratana. Colombo, Sri Lanka: Cultural Publications, 1984.

Dīgha Nikāya. Ed. T. W. Rhys Davids and J. Estlin Carpenter. London: Pāli Text Society, 1911.

Dīgha Nikāya. Trans. Maurice Walshe. Boston: Wisdom, 1995.

Dīpavaṃsa: An Ancient Buddhist Historical Record. Edited and trans. Hermann Oldenberg. 1879. Reprint. New Delhi: Asian Educational Services, 1982.

The Dīpavaṃsa: A Historical Poem of the 4th Century A.D., in Pāli. Edited with an introduction and a new English translation by Bimala Churn Law. *Ceylon Historical Journal* 7 (July 1957–April 1958).

Epigraphia Zeylanica. 8 vols. to date. Colombo, Sri Lanka: Department of Government Printing, 1904– (in progress).

Harṣa. *"How the Nāgas were Pleased"; and "The Shattered Thighs," by Bhāsa*. Trans. Andrew Skilton. New York: New York University Press, 2009.

Inscriptions of Ceylon. Edited and trans. S. Paranavitana. Archaeological Survey of Ceylon. Colombo, Sri Lanka: Ceylon Department of Archaeology, 1970.

The Jātaka, or Stories of the Buddha's Former Births. 7 vols. Ed. E. B. Cowell. 1895–1913. Reprint. London: Pāli Text Society, 1963.

The Jātaka, or The Stories of the Buddha's Former Births. Vol. 4. Ed. W. H. D. Rouse. Cambridge: Cambridge University Press, 1901.

The Jātaka, Together with Its Commentary. Ed. Viggo Fausbøll. 7 vols. London: Kegan Paul, Trench, Trubner, 1877–1897.

Kakusandha Thera. *Dhātuvaṃsaya*. Ed. Munidāsa Kumāratuṇga. Colombo, Sri Lanka: Gunasena, 1961.

Kalhaṇa. *Rājataraṅgiṇī*. 3 vols. Trans. Aurel Stein. 1900. Reprint. Delhi: Motilal Banarsidas, 1979–1988.

The Lotus Sutra. Trans. Burton Watson. New York: Columbia University Press, 1993.

Mahānāma. *The First Twenty Chapters of the* Mahawanso *and a Prefatory Essay on Pali Buddhistical Literature*. Trans. George Turnour. Cotta, Sri Lanka: Cotta Church Mission Press, 1837.

——. *The Mahāvaṃsa*. Ed. Wilhelm Geiger. London: Frowde for Pāli Text Society, 1908.

——. *The Mahāvaṃsa, or The Great Chronicle of Ceylon*. Trans. Wilhelm Geiger, assisted by Mabel Haynes Bode. London: Frowde for Pāli Text Society, 1912.

——. *Mahāvaṃsa: The Great Chronicle of Sri Lanka, Chapters 1–37*. Trans. Ananda W. P. Guruge. Colombo, Sri Lanka: Associated Newspapers of Ceylon, 1989.

——. *The Mahāvaṃsa: Pali Text Together with Some Later Additions*. Ed. A. P. Buddhadatta. Colombo, Sri Lanka: Gunasena, 1959.

Mahāwaṇsa-Ṭīkā. Ed. Baṭuwantuḍāwe and Ñāṇissara Bhikshu. Columbo, Sri Lanka: Cottle, 1895.

Muluposatha Sutta: The Roots of the Uposatha (AN 3.70). Trans. Thanissaro Bhikkhu. Access to Insight, December 10, 2011. http://www.accesstoinsight.org/tipitaka/an/an03/an03.070.than.html.

Saṃyutta Nikāya. Ed. M. Leon Feer. Reprint. London: Pāli Text Society, 1970.

The Sheaf of Garlands of the Epochs of the Conqueror. Trans. N. A. Jayawickrama. London: Pāli Text Society, 1968.

The Story of Gotama Buddha: The Nidāna-kathā of the Jātakaṭṭhakathā. Trans. N. A. Jayawickrama. Oxford: Pāli Text Society, 1990.

Sumangalavilāsinī: Buddhaghosa's Commentary on the Dīgha Nikāya. 2nd ed. Ed. William Stede. London: Pāli Text Society, 1971.
Vācissaratthera. *The Chronicle of the Thūpa and the Thūpavaṃsa.* Trans. N. A. Jayawickrama. London: Pāli Text Society, 1971.
Vaṃsatthappakāsinī: Commentary on the Mahāvaṃsa. 2 vols. Ed. G. P. Malalasekera. 1935–1936. Reprint. London: Pāli Text Society, 1977.
Xuanzang [Hiuen Tsiang]. *Si-Yu-Ki: Buddhist Records of the Western World.* 2 vols. Trans. Samuel Beal. London: Kegan Paul, Trench and Trübner, 1884.

SECONDARY SOURCES

Adikaram, E. W. *Early History of Buddhism in Ceylon.* Migoda, Sri Lanka: Puswella, 1946.
Ali, Daud, ed. *Invoking the Past: The Uses of History in South Asia.* London: Oxford University Press, 1999.
Amunugama, E. M. C. *The History of Ancient Aryan Tribes in Sri Lanka: Yaksas, Nāgas, Devas, Sakyas.* Colombo, Sri Lanka: J. R. Jayewardene Cultural Centre, 1994.
Anderson, Benedict. *Imagined Communities: Reflections on the Origin and Spread of Nationalism.* 1983. Reprint. London: Verso, 1991.
Avis, Paul D. L. *God and the Creative Imagination: Metaphor, Symbol, and Myth in Religion and Theology.* London: Routledge, 1999.
Bareau, André. "Les Récits canoniques description funérailles du Buddha ethics leurs anomalies: Nouvel essai d'interprétation." *Bulletin de l'Ecole Française d'Extrême-Orient* 62 (1975):151–189.
Barthes, Roland. "From Work to Text." In *Textual Strategies: Perspectives in Post-structuralist Criticism*, ed. Josue V. Harari, 73–81. Ithaca: Cornell University Press, 1979.
Bartholomeusz, Tessa. *In Defense of Dharma: Just-War Ideology in Buddhist Sri Lanka.* London: RoutledgeCurzon, 2002.
Bechert, Heinz. "The Beginnings of Buddhist Historiography: *Mahāvaṃsa* and Political Thinking." In *Religion and Legitimation of Power in Sri Lanka*, ed. Bardwell L. Smith, 1–12. Chambersburg, Pa.: Anima Books, 1978.
——, ed. *Buddhism and Ceylon and Studies on Religious Syncretism in Buddhist Countries.* Symposium zur Buddhismusforschung no. 1. Göttingen, Germany: Vandenhoeck and Ruprecht, 1978.
——. "The *Nikāyas* of Mediaeval Sri Lanka and the Unification of the *Sangha* by Parākramabahu I." In *Studies on Buddhism in Honour of Professor A. K. Warder*, ed. N. K. Nagle and F. Watanabe, 11–21. Toronto: Centre for South Asian Studies, University of Toronto, 1993.
——. "On the Identification of Buddhist Schools in Early Sri Lanka." In *Indology and Law: Studies in Honour of Professor J. Duncan M. Derrett*, ed. Günther-Dietz Sontheimer and Parameswara Kota Aithal, 60–76. Wiesbaden, Germany: Steiner, 1982.
Benveniste, Émile. *Problems in General Linguistics.* Trans. Mary Elizabeth Meek. Coral Gables, Fla.: University of Miami Press, 1971.
Berkwitz, Stephen C. *Buddhist History in the Vernacular: The Power of the Past in Late Medieval Sri Lanka.* Leiden: Brill, 2004.
——. "Emotions and Ethics in Buddhist History." *Religion* 31, no. 2 (2001): 155–173.

——. "The Ethics of Buddhist History: A Study of the Pāli and Sinhala Thūpavaṃsas." Ph.D. diss., University of California, Santa Barbara, 1999.

——. "History and Gratitude in Theravāda Buddhism." *Journal of the American Academy of Religion* 71, no. 3 (2003): 579–604.

Blackburn, Anne M. *Buddhist Learning and Textual Practice in Eighteenth-Century Lankan Monastic Culture.* Princeton: Princeton University Press, 2001.

Bloss, Lowell. "Ancient Indian Folk Religion as Seen Through the Symbolism of the *Nāga*." Ph.D. diss., University of Chicago, 1971.

Bond, George. *The Buddhist Revival in Sri Lanka: Religious Tradition, Reinterpretation, and Response.* Columbia: University of South Carolina Press, 1988.

Bourdieu, Pierre. *The Field of Cultural Production: Essays on Art and Literature.* Ed. Randal Johnson. Cambridge: Polity, 1993.

——. *Outline of a Theory of Practice.* Trans. Richard Nice. Cambridge: Cambridge University Press, 1977.

Bronner, Yigal. *Extreme Poetry: The South Asian Movement of Simultaneous Narration.* New York: Columbia University Press, 2010.

Bronner, Yigal, David Shulman, and Gary Tubb, eds. *Innovations and Turning Points: Toward a History of* Kāvya *Literature.* New York: Oxford University Press, 2014.

Brough, J. "Thus Have I Heard . . ." *Journal of the Royal Asiatic Society* 13 (1949–1951): 416–426.

Brown, Robert. "Expected Miracles: The Unsurprisingly Miraculous Nature of Buddhist Images and Relics." In *Images, Miracles, and Authority in Asian Religious Traditions*, ed. Richard H. Davis, 23–36. Boulder: Westview Press, 1998.

Campbell, Joseph. *Myths of Light: Eastern Metaphors of the Eternal.* Ed. David Kudler. Novato, Calif.: New World Library, 2003.

Chapple, Christopher Key. "Animals and Environment in the Buddhist Birth Stories." In *Buddhism and Ecology*, ed. Mary Evelyn Tucker and Duncan Ryuken Williams, 131–148. Cambridge, Mass.: Harvard University Press, 1997.

Clifford, Regina T. "The *Dhammadīpa* Tradition of Sri Lanka: Three Models Within the Sinhalese Chronicles." In *Religion and Legitimation of Power in Sri Lanka*, ed. Bardwell L. Smith, 36–47. Chambersburg, Pa.: Anima Books, 1978.

Cohen, Richard. "Naga, Yaksini, Buddha: Local Deities and Local Buddhism in Ajanta." *History of Religions* 37 (1998): 360–400.

Collingwood, R. G. *The Idea of History.* London: Oxford University Press, 1956.

Collins, Steven. *Nirvāṇa and Other Buddhist Felicities: Utopias of the Pāli Imaginaire.* Cambridge: Cambridge University Press, 1998.

——. "*Nirvāṇa*, Time, and Narrative." *History of Religions* 31, no. 3 (1992): 215–246.

——. "On the Very Idea of the Pāli Canon." *Journal of the Pāli Text Society* 15 (1990): 89–126.

——. "Oral Aspects of Pāli Literature." *Indo-Iranian Journal* 35 (1992): 121–135.

——. "What Is Literature in Pāli?" In *Literary Cultures in History: Reconstructions from South Asia*, ed. Sheldon Pollock, 649–688. Berkeley: University of California Press, 2003.

Coningham, Robin A. E. "Monks, Caves, and Kings: A Reassessment of the Nature of Early Buddhism in Sri Lanka." *World Archaeology* 27, no. 2 (1995): 222–242.

Coomaraswamy, Ananda Kentish. *Medieval Sinhalese Art.* New York: Pantheon, 1956.

——. "*Saṃvega*, 'Aesthetic Shock.'" *Harvard Journal of Asiatic Studies* 7 (1942–1943): 174–179.

——. *Yaksas: Essays in the Water Cosmology.* 1928–1931. Reprint. New Delhi: Indira Gandhi National Centre for the Arts; Oxford: Oxford University Press, 1993.

Dagenais, John. *The Ethics of Reading in Manuscript Culture.* Princeton: Princeton University Press, 1994.
Daniels, E. Valentine. *Charred Lullabies: Chapters in an Anthropology of Violence.* Princeton: Princeton University Press, 1996.
Davis, Richard H., ed. *Images, Miracles, and Authority in Asian Religious Traditions.* Oxford: Westview Press, 1998.
——. *Lives of Indian Images.* Princeton: Princeton University Press, 1997.
DeCaroli, Robert. *Haunting the Buddha: Indian Popular Religions and the Formation of Buddhism.* New York: Oxford University Press, 2004.
——. "Shedding Skins: Naga Imagery and Layers of Meaning in South Asian Buddhist Contexts." In *Buddhist Stupas in South Asia*, ed. Jason Hawkes and Akira Shimada, 94–113. New Delhi: Oxford University Press, 2009.
De Certeau, Michel. *The Writing of History.* New York: Columbia University Press, 1988.
Deegalle, Mahinda, ed. *Buddhism, Conflict, and Violence in Modern Sri Lanka.* New York: Routledge, 2006.
De Silva, K. M. *A History of Sri Lanka.* Berkeley: University of California Press, 1981.
Dewald, Carolyn. "Does History Matter? Meaning-Making and the First Two Greek Historians." In *Historical Knowledge in Biblical Antiquity*, ed. Jacob Neusner, Bruce D. Chilton, and William S. Green, 32–52. Blandford Forum, U.K.: Deo, 2007.
Dharmadasa, K. N. O. *Language, Religion, and Ethnic Assertiveness: The Growth of Sinhalese Nationalism in Sri Lanka.* Ann Arbor: University of Michigan Press, 1992.
Dimmitt, Cornelia, and J. A. B. van Buitenen. *Classical Hindu Mythology: A Reader in the Sanskrit* Puranas. Philadelphia: Temple University Press, 1978.
Duroiselle, C. "Upagutta et Māra." *Bulletin de l'Ecole Française d'Extrême-Orient*, 1904, 414–428.
Eck, Diana. *Banaras: City of Light.* New York: Columbia University Press, 1998.
Eco, Umberto. *The Limits of Interpretation.* Bloomington: Indiana University Press, 1990.
——. *The Open Work.* Trans. Anna Cancogni. Cambridge, Mass.: Harvard University Press, 1989.
——. *The Role of the Reader: Explorations in the Semiotics of Texts.* Bloomington: Indiana University Press, 1979.
——. *Six Walks in the Fictional Woods.* Charles Eliot Norton Lectures, 1993. Cambridge, Mass.: Harvard University Press, 1994.
Eco, Umberto, with Richard Rorty, Jonathan Culler, and Christine Brooke-Rose. *Interpretation and Overinterpretation.* Ed. Stephan Collini. Cambridge: Cambridge University Press, 1994.
Eliade, Mircea. *The Myth of the Eternal Return, or, Cosmos and History.* Trans. Willard R. Trask. 1954. Reprint. Princeton: Princeton University Press, 1971.
Epstein, Marc Michael. "Harnessing the Dragon: A Mythos Transformed in Medieval Jewish Literature and Art." In *Myth and Method*, ed. Laurie L. Patton and Wendy Doniger, 352–389. Charlottesville: University Press of Virginia, 1996.
Falk, Nancy. "To Gaze on Sacred Traces." *History of Religions* 16, no. 4 (1977): 281–293.
Fergusson, James. *Tree and Serpent Worship: Or, Illustrations of Mythology and Art in India in the First and Fourth Centuries After Christ. From the Sculptures of the Buddhist Topes at Sanchi and Amaravati.* London: Allen, 1873.
Geary, Patrick. *Furta Sacra: Thefts of Relics in the Central Middle Ages.* 1978. Reprint. Princeton: Princeton University Press, 1990.

Geertz, Clifford. "Religion as a Cultural System." In *Interpretation of Cultures: Selected Essays*, 87–125. New York: Basic Books, 1973.

Geiger, Wilhelm. *Culture of Ceylon in Mediaeval Times*. Ed. Heinz Bechert. Wiesbaden, Germany: Harrassowitz, 1960.

—. *The* Dīpavaṃsa *and* Mahāvaṃsa *and Their Historical Development in Ceylon*. Trans. Ethel M. Coomaraswamy. Colombo, Sri Lanka: Cottle, 1908.

Germano, David, and Kevin Trainor, eds. *Embodying the Dharma: Buddhist Relic Veneration in Asia*. Albany: State University of New York Press, 2004.

Godakumbura, C. E. "The *Dipavamsa* and the *Mahavamsa*." *Ceylon Historical Journal* 25 (1978): 143–152.

—. *Sinhalese Literature*. Colombo, Sri Lanka: Colombo Apothecaries' Company, 1955.

Gokhale, B. G. "The Theravāda-Buddhist View of History." *Journal of the American Oriental Society* 85, no. 3 (1965): 354–360.

Gombrich, Richard F. *Buddhist Precept and Practice*. 2nd ed. Delhi: Motilal Banarsidass, 1991.

—. *How Buddhism Began: The Conditioned Genesis of the Early Teachings*. London: Athlone Press, 1996.

—. *Theravāda Buddhism: A Social History from Ancient Benares to Modern Colombo*. London: Routledge, 1988.

Gombrich, Richard F., and Gananath Obeyesekere. *Buddhism Transformed: Religious Change in Sri Lanka*. Princeton: Princeton University Press, 1988.

Gomez, Luis O. *The Land of Bliss: The Paradise of the Buddha of Measureless Light*. Honolulu: University of Hawai'i Press, 1996.

Graham, William A. *Beyond the Written Word*. Cambridge: Cambridge University Press, 1987.

Granoff, Phyllis. "The Ambiguity of Miracles: Buddhist Understandings of Supernatural Power." *East and West* 46 (1996): 79–96.

Greenwald, Alice. "The Relic on the Spear: Historiography and the Saga of Duṭṭhagāmaṇī." In *Religion and Legitimation of Power in Sri Lanka*, ed. Bardwell L. Smith, 13–35. Chambersburg, Pa.: Anima Books, 1978.

Gummer, Natalie D. "Articulating Potency: A Study of the *Suvarṇa(pra)bhāsottamāsūtra*." Ph.D. diss., Harvard University, 2000.

Gunawardana, R. A. L. H. "The Kinsmen of the Buddha: Myth as Political Charter in the Ancient and Early Medieval Kingdoms of Sri Lanka." *Sri Lanka Journal of the Humanities* 2, no. 1 (1976): 53–62.

—. "The People of the Lion: The Sinhala Identity and Ideology in History and Historiography." In *Sri Lanka: History and the Roots of Conflict*, ed. Jonathan Spencer, 45–87. London: Routledge, 1990.

—. *Robe and Plough: Monasticism and Economic Interest in Early Medieval Sri Lanka*. Tucson: University of Arizona Press, 1979.

Hallisey, Charles. "Devotion in the Buddhist Literature of Medieval Sri Lanka." Ph.D. diss., University of Chicago, 1988.

—. "*Nibbānasutta*: An Allegedly Non-canonical *Sutta* on *Nibbāna* as a Great City." *Journal of the Pāli Text Society* 18 (1993): 97–130.

—. "Relics as Memory Sites in the Buddhist Literature of Medieval Sri Lanka." Paper circulated for the American Academy of Religion seminar on Buddhist relic veneration, various locations, 1994–1997.

——. "Roads Taken and Not Taken in the Study of Theravāda Buddhism." In *Curators of the Buddha: The Study of Buddhism Under Colonialism*, ed. Donald S. Lopez Jr., 31–61. Chicago: University of Chicago Press, 1995.

——. "Tuṇḍilovāda: An Allegedly Non-canonical *Sutta*." *Journal of the Pāli Text Society* 15 (1990): 155–195.

——. "Works and Persons in Sinhala Literary Culture." In *Literary Cultures in History: Reconstructions from South Asia*, ed. Sheldon Pollock, 689–746. Berkeley: University of California Press, 2003.

Hallisey, Charles, and Anne Hansen. "Narrative, Sub-ethics, and the Moral Life: Some Evidence from Theravāda Buddhism." *Journal of Religious Ethics* 24, no. 2 (1996): 305–327.

Harris, Ian. "'A Vast Unsupervised Recycling Plant': Animals and the Buddhist Cosmos." In *A Communion of Subjects: Animals in Religion, Science, and Ethics*, 207–217. New York: Columbia University Press, 2006.

Harrison, Paul. "Commemoration and Identification in *Buddhānusmṛti*." In *In the Mirror of Memory*, ed. Janet Gyatso, 215–238. Albany: State University of New York Press, 1992.

Harvey, Peter. *An Introduction to Buddhist Ethics: Foundations, Values, and Issues.* Cambridge: Cambridge University Press, 2000.

Heim, Maria. "The Aesthetics of Excess." *Journal of the American Academy of Religion* 71, no. 3 (2003): 531–554.

——. *The Forerunner of All Things: Buddhaghosa on Mind, Intention, and Agency.* New York: Oxford University Press, 2014.

Hinüber, Oskar von. "Buddhist Law According to the Theravāda-Vinaya: A Survey of Theory and Practice." *Journal of the International Association of Buddhist Studies* 18, no. 1 (1995): 7–45.

——. *A Handbook of Pāli Literature.* Berlin: Walter de Gruyter, 1996.

Holt, John C. *Buddha in the Crown: Avalokiteśvara in the Buddhist Traditions of Sri Lanka.* New York: Oxford University Press, 1991.

——. *The Religious World of Kīrti Srī.* London: Oxford University Press, 1996.

Htin Aung, Maung. *Folk Elements in Burmese Buddhism.* London: Oxford University Press, 1962.

Huntington, Susan L. *The Art of Ancient India: Buddhist, Hindu, Jain.* New York: Weatherhill, 1985.

Inden, Ronald. *Imagining India.* Cambridge: Blackwell, 1990.

——. "Introduction: From Philological to Dialogical Texts." In Ronald Inden, Jonathan Walters, and Daud Ali, *Querying the Medieval: Texts and the History of Practices in South Asia*, 3–28. New York: Oxford University Press, 2000.

Inden, Ronald, Jonathan Walters, and Daud Ali. *Querying the Medieval: Texts and the History of Practices in South Asia.* New York: Oxford University Press, 2000.

Iser, Wolfgang. *The Act of Reading: A Theory of Aesthetic Response.* Baltimore: Johns Hopkins University Press, 1978.

Kapleau, Philip. *Of the Same Root.* Parabola, vol. 8, no. 2. New York: Society for the Study of Myth and Tradition, 1983.

Kapstein, Matthew, ed. *Presence of Light: Divine Radiance and Religious Experience.* Chicago: University of Chicago Press, 2004.

Karunatillake, W. S. "The Religiousness of Buddhists in Sri Lanka Through Belief and Practice." In *Religiousness in Sri Lanka*, ed. John Ross Carter, 1–34. Colombo, Sri Lanka: Marga Institute, 1979.

Kemper, Steven. *The Presence of the Past: Chronicles, Politics, and Culture in Sinhala Life.* Ithaca: Cornell University Press, 1991.

Kinnard, Jacob. "The Polyvalent *Pādas* of Viṣṇu and the Buddha." *History of Religions* 40, no. 1 (2000): 32–57.

Kiribamune, Sirima. "The *Mahāvaṃsa*: A Study of the Ancient Historiography of Sri Lanka." In *Senarat Paranavitana Commemoration Volume*, ed. Leelananda Prematilleke, Karthigesu Indrapala, and J. E. van Lohuizen-de-Leeuw, 125–136. Leiden: Brill, 1978.

Kripal, Jeffrey. *The Serpent's Gift: Gnostic Reflections on the Study of Religion.* Chicago: University of Chicago Press, 2007.

LaCapra, Dominick. *Rethinking Intellectual History: Texts, Contexts, Language.* Ithaca: Cornell University Press, 1983.

Lakoff, George, and Mark Johnson. *Metaphors We Live By.* Chicago: University of Chicago Press, 1980.

Law, Bimala Churn. *A History of Pali Literature.* 2 vols. London: Kegan Paul, Trench, Trübner, 1933.

——. *On the Chronicles of Ceylon.* Calcutta: Royal Asiatic Society of Bengal, 1947.

Le Goff, Jacques. *The Medieval Imagination.* Chicago: University of Chicago Press, 1985.

Le Goff, Jacques, and Pierre Nora. *Constructing the Past: Essays in Historical Methodology.* New York: Cambridge University Press, 1985.

Lévi-Strauss, Claude. *Myth and Meaning.* New York: Schocken Books, 1979.

——. *Totemism.* Trans. Rodney Needham. London: Merlin Press, 1964.

Lincoln, Bruce. *Myth, Cosmos, and Society.* Cambridge, Mass.: Harvard University Press, 1986.

Ling, Trevor. *The Buddha: Buddhist Civilization in India and Ceylon.* New York: Scribner's, 1973.

Little, David. *The Invention of Enmity.* Washington, D.C.: United States Institute of Peace Press, 1993.

Malalasekera, G. P. *Dictionary of Pali Proper Names.* London: Pāli Text Society, 1937.

——. *The Pali Literature of Ceylon.* 1928. Reprint. Kandy, Sri Lanka: Buddhist Publication Society, 1994.

Malalgoda, K. "Millennialism in Relation to Buddhism." *Comparative Studies in Society and History* 12 (1970): 424–441.

Maranda, Pierre. "The Dialectic of Metaphor: An Anthropological Essay on Hermeneutics." In *The Reader in the Text*, ed. Susan R. Suleiman and Inge Crosman, 183–204. Princeton: Princeton University Press, 1980.

——. *Mythology: Selected Readings.* New York: Penguin, 1972.

McCutcheon, Russell T., ed. *The Insider/Outsider Problem in the Study of Religion.* London: Cassell, 1999.

McMahon, David L. *Empty Vision: Ocular Metaphor and Visionary Imagery in Mahāyāna Buddhism.* London: RoutledgeCurzon, 2002.

Mendis, G. C. *The Pāli Chronicles of Sri Lanka.* Colombo, Sri Lanka: Karunaratne & Sons, 1996.

Monier-Williams, Monier. *Sanskrit-English Dictionary.* 1899. Reprint. New Delhi: Munshiram Manoharlal, 1976.

Monius, Anne E. *Imagining a Place for Buddhism: Literary Culture and Religious Community in Tamil-Speaking South India.* New York: Oxford University Press, 2001.

Muller-Ortega, Paul E. "Luminous Consciousness: Light in the Tantric Mysticism of Abhinavagupta." In *Presence of Light: Divine Radiance and Religious Experience*, ed. Matthew Kapstein, 45–80. Chicago: University of Chicago Press, 2004.

Nattier, Jan. *Once Upon a Future Time: Studies in a Buddhist Prophecy of Decline*. Berkeley, Calif.: Asian Humanities Press, 1991.

Nissen, Elizabeth, and R. L. Stirrat. "The Generation of Communal Identities." In *Sri Lanka: History and the Roots of Conflict*, ed. Jonathan Spencer, 19–44. London: Routledge, 1990.

Nora, Pierre. *Realms of Memory: The Construction of the French Past*. New York: Columbia University Press, 1998.

Norman, K. R. *Pāli-Literature, Including the Canonical Literature in Prakrit and Sanskrit of All the Hīnayāna Schools of Buddhism*. Wiesbaden, Germany: Otto Harrassowitz, 1983.

——. "The Role of Pāli in Early Sinhalese Buddhism." In *Buddhism and Ceylon and Studies on Religious Syncretism in Buddhist Countries*, ed. Heinz Bechert, 28–47. Symposium zur Buddhismusforschung no. 1. Göttingen, Germany: Vandenhoeck and Ruprecht, 1978.

Nussbaum, Martha. *Love's Knowledge: Essays on Philosophy and Literature*. New York: Oxford University Press, 1990.

——. *Poetic Justice: The Literary Imagination and Public Life*. Boston: Beacon, 1995.

——. *Upheavals of Thought: The Intelligence of Emotions*. Cambridge: Cambridge University Press, 2001.

Obeyesekere, Gananath. "Buddhism, Nationhood, and Cultural Identity: A Question of Fundamentals." In *Fundamentalisms Comprehended*, ed. Martin E. Marty and R. Scott Appleby, 231–256. Chicago: University of Chicago Press, 1995.

——. "The Buddhist Pantheon in Ceylon and Its Extensions." In *Anthropological Studies in Theravāda Buddhism*, ed. Manning Nash, 1–26. New Haven: Yale University Press, 1966.

——. "Myth, History, and Numerology in the Buddhist Chronicles." In *The Dating of the Historical Buddha*, ed. Heinz Bechert, 152–182. Göttingen, Germany: Vandenhoeck & Ruprecht, 1991.

——. "The Myth of the Human Sacrifice: History, Story, and Debate in a Buddhist Chronicle." In "Identity, Consciousness, and the Past: The South Asian Scene," ed. H. L. Seneviratne, special issue of *Social Analysis* 25 (September 1989): 78–94.

——. "Religious Symbolism and Political Change in Ceylon." In Gananath Obeyesekere, Gananath, Frank Reynolds, and Bardwell L. Smith, *The Two Wheels of Dhamma: Essays on the Theravāda Tradition in India and Ceylon*, ed. Bardwell L. Smith, 58–78. Chambersburg, Pa.: American Academy of Religion, 1972.

——. *The Work of Culture: Symbolic Transformation in Psychoanalysis and Anthropology*. Chicago: University of Chicago Press, 1990.

Obeyesekere, Gananath, Frank Reynolds, and Bardwell L. Smith. *The Two Wheels of Dhamma: Essays on the Theravāda Tradition in India and Ceylon*. Ed. Bardwell L. Smith. Chambersburg, Pa.: American Academy of Religion, 1972.

Obeyesekere, Ranjini. *Jewels of the Doctrine*. Albany: State University of New York Press, 1991.

——. *Sinhala Writing and the New Critics*. Colombo, Sri Lanka: Gunasena, 1974.

O'Flaherty, Wendy Doniger. *Origins of Evil in Hindu Mythology*. Berkeley: University of California Press, 1976.

——. *Other Peoples' Myths*. New York: Macmillan, 1988.
——. *Women Androgynes, and Other Mythical Beasts*. Chicago: University of Chicago Press, 1980.
Olivelle, Patrick. *Pañcatantra: The Book of India's Folk Wisdom*. New York: Oxford University Press, 1997.
Panabokke, Gunaratne. *History of the Buddhist Saṅgha in India and Sri Lanka*. Sri Lanka: Postgraduate Institute of Pāli and Buddhist Studies, 1993.
Panda, Sadhu Charan. *Nāga Cult in Orissa*. Delhi: B.R. Publishing, 1986.
Paranavitana, Senarat. "Mahanama, the Author of the Mahavamsa." *University of Ceylon Review* 20 (1962): 269–286.
Patton, Laurie L. *Myth as Argument: The* Bṛhaddevatā *as Canonical Commentary*. Berlin: Walter de Gruyter, 1996.
Patton, Laurie L., and Wendy Doniger, eds. *Myth and Method*. Charlottesville: University Press of Virginia, 1996.
Perera, Lakshman S. *The Institutions of Ancient Ceylon from Inscriptions*. Vol. 1. Kandy, Sri Lanka: International Centre for Ethnic Studies, 2001.
——. "The Pali Chronicle of Ceylon." In *Historians of India, Pakistan, and Ceylon*, ed. C. H. Philips. London: Oxford University Press, 1961.
Perera, S. G. *A History of Ceylon*. 2 vols. Ed. H. C. Ray. Colombo: Associated Newspapers of Ceylon, 1955–1959.
Pollock, Sheldon. "The Cosmopolitan Vernacular." *Journal of Asian Studies* 57, no. 1 (1998): 6–37.
——. *The Language of the Gods in the World of Men: Sanskrit, Culture, and Power in Premodern India*. Berkeley: University of California Press, 2006.
——. "Literary History, Indian History, World History." *Social Scientist* 23, nos. 10–12 (1995): 112–142.
——. "*Mīmāṃsa* and the Problem of History in Traditional India." *Journal of the Royal Asiatic Society* 109 (1989): 603–610.
——. "The Sanskrit Cosmopolis, 300–1300 C.E.: Transculturation, Vernacularization, and the Question of Ideology." In *Ideology and the Status of Sanskrit: Contributions to the History of the Sanskrit Language*, ed. Jan E. M. Houben, 197–247. Leiden: E. J. Brill, 1996.
Pryzluski, Jean. "La princesse a l'odeur de poisson et la Nāgī dans les traditions de l'Asie Orientale." In *Etudes Asiatiques*, vol. 2, ed.. G. Van Oest, 265–284. Paris: Publications de l'ecole française d'Extrême-Orient, 1925.
Rahula, Walpola. *History of Buddhism in Ceylon: The Anurādhapura Period, 3rd Century BC–10th Century AC*. 2nd ed. Colombo, Sri Lanka: Gunasena, 1956.
Reynolds, Frank E. "The Many Lives of the Buddha: A Study of Sacred Biography and Theravāda Tradition." In *The Biographical Process: Studies in the History and Psychology of Religion*, ed. Frank E. Reynolds and Donald Capps, 37–61. The Hague: Mouton, 1976.
——. "Rebirth Traditions and the Lineages of Gotama: A Study of Theravāda Buddhology." In *Sacred Biography in the Buddhist Traditions of South and Southeast Asia*, ed. Juliane Schober, 19–39. Honolulu: University of Hawai'i Press, 1997.
Reynolds, Frank E., and David Tracy, eds. *Myth and Philosophy*. Albany: State University of New York Press, 1990
Rhys Davids, T. W. *Buddhist India*. New York: Putnam's, 1903.
Rhys Davids, T. W., and William Stede, eds. *Pāli-English Dictionary*. 1921–1925. Reprint. Oxford: Pāli Text Society, 1995.

Ricoeur, Paul. *Freud and Philosophy: An Essay on Interpretation*. New Haven: Yale University Press, 1970.

——. *Oneself as Another*. Trans. Kathleen Blamey. Chicago: University of Chicago Press, 1992.

——. *Time and Narrative*. 3 vols. Trans. Kathleen Blamey and David Pellauer. Chicago: University of Chicago Press, 1984–1988.

Riffaterre, Michael. "Interpretation and Descriptive Poetry: A Reading of Wordworth's 'Yew-Trees.'" *New Literary History* 4 (1973): 229–256.

Rogers, John D. "Historical Images in the British Period." In *Sri Lanka: History and the Roots of Conflict*, ed. Jonathan Spencer, 87–106. London: Routledge, 1990.

Rotman, Andy. "The Erotics of Practice: Objects and Agency in Buddhist *Avadāna* Literature." *Journal of the American Academy of Religion* 71, no. 3 (2003): 555–578.

——. *Thus Have I Seen: Visualizing Faith in Early Indian Buddhism*. New York: Oxford University Press, 2008.

Rousseau, Jean-Jacques. *Discourse on the Sciences and the Arts*. Translated and ed. Donald A. Cress. 1750. Reprint. Indianapolis, Ind.: Hackett, 1987.

Schalk, Peter. "Semantic Transformations of the Dhammadīpa." In *Buddhism, Conflict, and Violence in Modern Sri Lanka*, ed. Mahinda Deegalle, 86–92. New York: Routledge, 2006.

Scheible, Kristin. "'For the Anxious Thrill and Serene Satisfaction of Good People': Rethinking the Pāli *Mahāvaṃsa*." Ph.D. diss., Harvard University, 2006.

——. "Priming the Lamp of *Dhamma*: The Buddha's Miracles in the Pāli *Mahavāṃsa*." *Journal of the International Association of Buddhist Studies* 33, nos. 1–2 (2010–2011): 435–451.

Schopen, Gregory. *Bones, Stones, and Buddhist Monks: Collected Papers on the Archaeology, Epigraphy, and Texts of Monastic Buddhism in India*. Honolulu: University of Hawai'i Press, 1997.

Seneviratne, H. L. "Identity and the Conflation of Past and Present." In *Identity, Consciousness, and the Past: Forging of Caste and Community in India and Sri Lanka*, ed. H. L. Seneviratne, 3–22. Delhi: Oxford University Press, 1997.

——. *Rituals of the Kandyan State*. Cambridge: Cambridge University Press, 1978.

Smith, Bardwell L. "The Ideal Social Order as Portrayed in the Chronicles of Ceylon." In *Religion and Legitimation of Power in Sri Lanka*, ed. Bardwell L. Smith, 48–72. Chambersburg, Pa.: Anima Books, 1978.

——. "Kingship, the *Sangha*, and the Process of Legitimation in Anurādhapura Ceylon: An Interpretive Essay." In *Buddhism in Ceylon and Studies on Religious Syncretism in Buddhist Countries: Report on a Symposium in Göttingen*, ed. Heinz Bechert, 100–126. Göttingen, Germany: Vandenhoeck & Ruprecht, 1978.

——, ed. *Religion and Legitimation of Power in Sri Lanka*. Chambersburg, Pa.: Anima Books, 1978.

——. "Sinhalese Buddhism and the Dilemmas of Reinterpretation." In Gananath Obeyesekere, Frank Reynolds, and Bardwell L. Smith, *The Two Wheels of Dhamma: Essays on the Theravāda Tradition in India and Ceylon*, ed. Bardwell L. Smith, 79–106. Chambersberg, Pa.: American Academy of Religion, 1972.

Smith, Jonathan Z. *Imagining Religion*. Chicago: University of Chicago Press, 1982.

——. *To Take Place*. Chicago: University of Chicago Press, 1987.

Spencer, Jonathan, ed. *Sri Lanka: History and the Roots of Conflict*. London: Routledge, 1990.

Spiro, Melford E. *Buddhism and Society: A Great Tradition and Its Burmese Vicissitudes*. New York: Harper & Row, 1970.

——. *Burmese Supernaturalism*. Philadelphia: Institute for the Study of Human Issues, 1978.
Stock, Brian. "History, Literature, and Medieval Textuality." *Yale French Studies*, no. 70 (1986): 7–17.
——. *The Implications of Literacy*. Princeton: Princeton University Press, 1983.
Strong, John S. *The Buddha: A Short Biography*. Oxford: Oneworld, 2001.
——. *The Experience of Buddhism: Sources and Interpretation*. Belmont, Calif.: Wadsworth, 1995.
——. "Gandhakuṭī: The Perfumed Chamber of the Buddha." *History of Religions* 16, no. 4 (1977): 390–406.
——. *The Legend and Cult of Upagupta*. Princeton: Princeton University Press, 1992.
——. *The Legend of King Aśoka*. Princeton: Princeton University Press, 1983.
——. "Relics." In *The Encyclopedia of Religion*, ed. Mircea Eliade, 12:275–82. New York: Macmillan, 1987. Reprinted with expanded bibliography in *The Encyclopedia of Religion*, 2nd ed., ed. Lindsay Jones, 11:7686–7692. New York: Macmillan, 2005.
——. *The Relics of the Buddha*. Princeton: Princeton University Press, 2004.
Suleiman, Susan R. "Introduction: Varieties of Audience-Oriented Criticism." In *The Reader in the Text*, ed. Susan R. Suleiman and Inge Crosman, 3–45. Princeton: Princeton University Press, 1980.
Swearer, Donald K. *Becoming the Buddha: The Ritual of Image Consecration in Thailand*. Princeton: Princeton University Press, 2004.
——. *Buddhism in Southeast Asia*. Albany: State University of New York Press, 1995.
——. "Hypostasizing the Buddha: Buddha Image Consecration in Northern Thailand." *History of Religions* 34, no. 3 (1995): 263–280.
Tambiah, Stanley Jeyaraja. *Buddhism and the Spirit Cults in North-east Thailand*. Cambridge: Cambridge University Press, 1970.
——. *Buddhism Betrayed? Religion, Politics, and Violence in Sri Lanka*. Chicago: University of Chicago Press, 1992.
——. *The Buddhist Saints of the Forest and the Cult of Amulets*. Cambridge: Cambridge University Press, 1984.
Tirrell, Lynne. "Storytelling and Moral Agency." *Journal of Aesthetics and Art Criticism* 48, no. 2 (1990): 115–26.
Trainor, Kevin. "*Pasanna/Pasāda* in the Pāli *Vaṃsa* Literature." *Vidyodaya Journal of Social Sciences* 3 (1989): 185–190.
——. *Relics, Ritual, and Representation in Buddhism: Rematerializing the Sri Lankan Theravāda Tradition*. Cambridge: Cambridge University Press, 1997.
——. "When Is a Theft Not a Theft? Relic Theft and the Cult of the Buddha's Relics in Sri Lanka." *Numen* 39, no. 1 (1992): 1–26.
Vogel, Jean Philippe. *Indian Serpent-Lore; or, The Nāgas in Hindu Legend and Art*. London: Probsthain, 1926.
Walser, Joseph. "Nāgārjuna and the *Ratnāvalī*: New Ways to Date an Old Philosopher." *Journal of the International Association of Buddhist Studies* 25, nos. 1–2 (2002): 209–262.
Walters, Jonathan. "Appendix: Colonial and National Readings of the Pāli *Vaṃsas*." In Ronald Inden, Jonathan Walters, and Daud Ali, *Querying the Medieval: Texts and the History of Practices in South Asia*, 152–164. New York: Oxford University Press, 2000.
——. "Buddhist History: The Sri Lankan Pāli *Vaṃsas* and Their Commentary." In Ronald Inden, Jonathan Walters, and Daud Ali, *Querying the Medieval: Texts and the History of Practices in South Asia*, 99–164. New York: Oxford University Press, 2000.

——. "Mahāsena at the Mahāvihāra: The Interpretation and Politics of History in Medieval Sri Lanka." In *Invoking the Past: The Uses of History in South Asia*, ed. Daud Ali, 322–366. Oxford: Oxford University Press, 1999.
——. "Stupa, Story, and Empire: Constructions of the Buddha Biography in Early Post-Aśokan India." In *Sacred Biography in the Buddhist Traditions of South and South-east Asia*, ed. Juliane Schober, 160–192. Honolulu: University of Hawai'i Press, 1997.
——. "*Suttas* as History: Four Approaches to the *Sermon on the Noble Quest* (Ariyapariyesanasutta)." *History of Religions* 38, no. 3 (1999): 247–84.
Weber, Max. *The Theory of Social and Economic Organization.* Trans. A. R. Anderson and Talcot Parsons. London: Hodge, 1947.
White, David Gordon. *Myths of the Dog-Man.* Chicago: University of Chicago Press, 1991.
White, Hayden. *The Content of the Form: Narrative Discourse and Historical Representation.* Baltimore: Johns Hopkins University Press, 1987.
——. *Metahistory: The Historical Imagination in Nineteenth-Century Europe.* Baltimore: Johns Hopkins University Press, 1973.
——. *Tropics of Discourse: Essays in Cultural Criticism.* Baltimore: Johns Hopkins University Press, 1978.
Wijayawardhana, G. D. "Literature in Buddhist Religious Life." In *Religiousness in Sri Lanka*, ed. John Ross Carter, 67–77. Colombo, Sri Lanka: Marga Institute, 1979.
Williams, Raymond. *Marxism and Literature.* Oxford: Oxford University Press, 1977.
Winternitz, Maurice. *A History of Indian Literature.* 3 vols. Trans. V. S. Sarma. Delhi: Motilal Banarsidass, 1983.
Zimmer, Heinrich Robert. *Myths and Symbols in Indian Art and Civilization.* New York: Pantheon, 1946.

INDEX

Abhayagiri monastic fraternity, 19, 52, 66, 134, 138, 142; *Dhammaruci* sect, 143; Faxian's account of, 146; Parākramabāhu I and, 148; separation from Mahāvihāra, 139, 141; writing of *Mahāvaṃsa* and, 196n70

adhiṭṭhāna (determined resolution), 50, 52, 103

Adikaram, E. W., 132, 139, 140

Agni (Vedic fire god), 8, 49, 165n36

Ākhyāna poetry, 20, 21, 168n27

Akkhipūja (Veneration by the Eyes) festival, 112, 189n55

alaṃkāra (ornamentation), 27–28

Amitābha (a Mahāyāna Buddha), 8, 165n37, 194n52

Anāgatavaṃsa, 186n25

Ānanda (principle disciple of the Buddha), 99–100, 103, 126, 185n15

Anderson, Benedict, 192n23, 198n107

Aṅgīrasa (epithet of the Buddha), 49

animals, 80–81, 85, 88, 180n33

Anurādhapura, 14, 52, 131, 139, 176n72

Apadāna/Avadāna stories, 73

Asoka (King Aśoka), 2, 51, 96, 161n2, 192n23; appropriated for Theravādin cause, 145; bodhi tree and, 106, 187n34; *Dīpavaṃsa* and, 131; *Mahāvaṃsa* chronology and, 137; Mahinda sent to Laṅkā by, 46; *nāgas* and, 106, 112–13, 114, 181n48

aṭṭhakathā (commentarics), 2, 30, 32, 131, 142, 153

Aṭṭhakathā-Mahāvaṃsa, 169n47, 190n12

Avis, Paul D. L., 10–11

Bartholomeusz, Tessa, 127

Bechert, Heinz, 124

Benveniste, Émile, 37

Berkwitz, Stephen, 7, 129, 168n38, 170n5, 188n48, 197n101; on context of Buddhist histories, 149–150; on creation of the past, 198n110; on medieval Buddhist audience, 151

Bharata, 28

bhikkhus (ordained monks), 34–35, 57, 58, 105; *bhikkunī* (female monks), 106, 107; Mahāvihāra and, 138; as "propagators of a state ideology," 124

Bhūridatta (*nāga*), 73, 74, 75, 85, 179n26; as Buddha-to-be, 79, 94; karma system and, 81–82, 86, 92; *nāginī* wives of, 83; Samuddajā, 75, 178n16, 178n18; transfiguration of, 75–79

Bhūridatta Jātaka, 5, 71, 78, 79, 91, 179n31; animals in, 81; arousal of reader's sympathy for Bhūridatta, 90; introduction to, 72–75; *nāgas*' ontological status in, 86; *nāgas*' soteriological aptitude in, 85; story of *nāga* and *garuḍa*, 84

bhūta devatā (divine beings), 79, 179n30, 183n4
Blackburn, Anne, 8, 41, 161n3, 191n13; definition of textual community, 26–27; on institutional location and interpretation, 18; on literary devices as "ruminative triggers," 40, 49; on simile in *Mahāvaṃsa*, 42–43; on textual community and reading of Buddhist texts, 14–15
bodhisatta [Sanskrit: bodhisattva] (prebuddha), 8, 10, 59, 165n37; animals and, 81; in *nāga* form, 71, 74, 77; path to buddhahood, 91
bodhi tree, 25, 40, 54, 58; arrival to the island of Laṅkā, 95–96, 106; parasol-tree and, 105; relic veneration and, 103, 104; typology of relics and, 186n28
Bodhivaṃsa, 120
Brahmins: Alambāyana, 76, 84, 86; Kassapa, 49; *nāgas* and, 76, 78, 83, 91
Bronner, Yigal, 7
Buddha (Gotama), 3, 25, 150, 161n3, 167n9; animal incarnations of, 81–82; biography of, 51, 52, 59, 137, 171n17; bodhi tree as site of, 54; coming of the *dhamma* and, 58, 60; *dhamma* as gift from, 42, 46; dispensations of, 3, 136; emotions manipulated by, 40, 46; enlightenment of, 21, 24, 48, 50; epithets of, 24, 39, 49; first disciples of, 172n23; as head of the *saṅgha*, 174n47; as "Light Maker," 23–24, 48–49, 56, 57, 168n32; lineage of, 38; *nāga* births of, 68, 74, 85, 92; *nāgas*' relations with, 9, 27, 46, 180n38, 182n2; as one of Three Jewels, 173n40; Pāli language and, 140; presence and proximity of, 6, 17, 32, 39, 71, 103, 119; stylized homage to, 25, 32; Uruvela (Bodh Gāya) and, 53; Veḷuriya jeweled throne of, 57, 96, 104, 105, 107, 174n47, 182n2; visits to Laṅkā and, 151. *See also* Laṅkā, visits of the Buddha to; *parinibbāṇa* (corporeal death), of the Buddha
Buddhadatta, 17
Buddhaghosa, 27, 31, 80, 171n17, 190n12; *Dīpavaṃsa* mentioned by, 130; Mahāvihāra and, 146
Buddha Metteyya (future Buddha), 126
Buddhasīha, 17
Buddhavaṃsa, 17, 182n2
Buddhism, 22, 40; arrival in Laṅkā, 133–34; Buddhist councils, 2, 105, 112, 133, 194n56; Buddhist histories, 7, 8, 68, 129, 131–38, 149–150; Buddhist studies/Buddhology, 6–7, 118; in mainland India, 2; as philosophy and as religion, 137; spirit-deities and, 180n38. *See also* Mahāyāna ("Great Vehicle") Buddhism; Theravāda Buddhism

Campeyya (*nāga*), 73, 74, 75
Cariyāpiṭaka, 73
cetiya (sanctuary, sanctified place), 4, 12, 95, 103, 185n15
Chapple, Christopher, 81
Christianity, 10, 99, 165n34, 184n13
Collingwood, R. G., 121, 191n16
Collins, Steven, 7, 36, 62–63, 164n31, 195n60; definition of *vaṃsa*, 134; on literature in Pāli language, 19; on Mahāvihāra as minority tradition, 141; on *saṃvega* and *pasāda*, 41; on textual production in context of dispute, 139–140; on *vaṃsas* and *purāṇa* literature, 128–29; on the *Vaṃsatthappakāsinī*, 147
Cūlavaṃsa, 19, 120, 148, 149, 176n72, 190–91n13

dāna pāramitā (perfection of generosity), 73
Daṇḍin, 28, 169n41
Dāṭhavaṃsa, 182n1
Dāṭhopatissa II, 120, 190n10
Davids, T. W. Rhys, 20
DeCaroli, Robert, 7, 68, 82, 89, 179n30
Derrida, Jacques, 122
De Silva, K. M., 133, 141
Devānaṃpiyatissa, King, 58, 96, 98, 105, 133, 148, 192n23; army of, 146; as first convert to Buddhism in Laṅkā, 134
devas/*devatā* (gods, deities), 7, 9, 57, 80, 110, 111, 179n30

Dewald, Carolyn, 129
dhamma [Sanskrit: *dharma*] (doctrine), 4, 5, 49, 161n3, 172n23; bodhi tree and, 95; in borderlands, 105; Buddha's enlightenment event and, 58; *dhammadīpa* ("island of *dhamma*"), 63, 176n68; enshrinement of relics and, 97; as gift of the Buddha, 42; introduction to new territory, 40, 79; Laṅkā preordained to receive, 167n9; model reader and, 29; moral community and, 5; *nāgas* and, 45, 54, 60, 86, 91, 163n15; as one of Three Jewels, 173n40; relics and, 116; right and wrong time for introduction of, 51, 52; right practice, 78; transference of, 40, 43, 103, 106, 162n12; unworthiness to inherent, 50–51. *See also* light, *dhamma* as
Dhammacakkappavattana Sutta, 172n23
Dhammakitti, 19, 121
Dhammapādāṭṭhakathā, 34
Dhammapāla, Acariya, 179n31
Dhatarāṭṭha (*nāgarāja*), 75, 83
Dhātusena, King, 1, 143
Dhātuvaṃsa, 185n12, 186n31
Dīghasanda, 146
Dīpaṅkara, 59
Dīpavaṃsa, 2, 6, 28, 38, 95, 111, 166n4; anticipation of the Buddha's visit, 48–58; Buddha's light-making capacity in, 62; on Buddha's visits to Laṅkā, 43, 44, 47; as "Buddhist history," 131–38; as "charter," 123–27; composition of, 19, 58, 130, 151; copying and perpetuation of, 167n16; documentary and worklike functions in, 23; duress and writing of, 142; evolution from oral to written literature and, 20–21, 168n27; grammatical errors in, 19, 20, 169n46, 193n42; as "history," 119, 127–131; lists of kings, 169–170n50; Mahāvihāran textual community and, 14; on *nāga* guardians of relics, 100; as "plea for survival," 39, 139, 145, 151, 170n2; *purāṇas* and, 129, 193n39; reader-interpreters of, 47; shared sources with *Mahāvaṃsa*, 147; textual community and, 118; translations of, 19–20, 167n20
Dīpavaṃsa proem, 4, 13, 31, 33, 36, 98; inscribed audience of, 44; literary effects of, 150; model reader and, 17, 29; narrative of Buddha coming to Laṅkā, 40; reading instructions in, 15, 17; as religious imperative, 24–30
Diwali festival, 9
documentary function/mode, 11, 21–24, 64, 117
double entendre/meaning. See *slesa* [Sanskrit: *śleṣa*] (double meaning)
Duṭṭhagāmaṇī, King, 2, 30, 96, 130, 176n72; anticipated birth of, 126; dates of reign, 134, 148, 196n71; Mahāvihāra and, 134; relics and, 100, 101, 108, 109, 115; role as hero in *Mahāvaṃsa*, 135, 194n57

Eco, Umberto, 4, 17, 52–53, 58; on "empirical reader," 15, 23; on "spectatorly" model reader, 16
Eight Precepts, 104
emotions, 28, 40, 43, 168n38; cultivated in hearts of ideal audience, 74; manipulation of, 4, 40, 46; metaphor and, 38; *nāga* stories and, 87–88; relic veneration and, 7, 78. See also *pasāda* [Sanskrit: *prasāda*]; *saṃvega*

Fausbøll, Viggo, 74
Faxian, 146
Fish, Stanley, 15
Five Precepts, 25, 184n9
Foucault, Michel, 136

gandhabbas (flying musician deities), 82
Gaṇeśa (god), 9, 80
garuḍa (eaglelike creature), 76, 84, 106, 107
Geary, Patrick, 99, 109, 184n13
Geiger, Wilhelm, 20, 24, 131, 147, 163n18, 197n95, 199n6; colorful rhetoric in translation by, 156; *Cūlavaṃsa* and, 120, 148, 176n22, 190–91n13; on *Dīpavaṃsa* proem, 30; on hypothesized urtext of *Dīpavaṃsa*, 169n47; on Mahāsena, 144; on memory verses, 21; on source material of *vaṃsas*, 132; on the *Vaṃsatthappakāsinī*, 146
Gokhale, B. G., 137

Gombrich, Richard, 49, 50, 104, 124, 148
"good people." See *sujana*
Goṭhābhaya, King, 142
Granoff, Phyllis, 182n1
Greenblatt, Stephen, 129
Greenwald, Alice, 98, 125, 183n8
guhyakas (attendants of Kubera), 82
Guruge, Ananda, 113, 164n31, 176n66

Hallisey, Charles, 7, 68, 90, 169n42; on animal characters in moral narratives, 85; on imaginative aspect of empathy, 87, 88; on *lieux de memoire* (memory sites), 185n24; on literary devices as in Theravādin homiletics, 43
Hansen, Anne, 68, 85, 87, 88, 90
Harṣa, King, 10
Heim, Maria, 7, 41, 171n6
Herodotus, 129
Hindu myths, *nāgas* in, 9
history, 2–3, 6, 70, 118, 163n16; chronicles, 128; as creation of Herodotus, 129; *Heilsgeschichte* (mythicized history), 79, 125, 158, 179n29, 192n27; as literary device, 150–52; narrative and, 44–45, 117; nationalist discourse and, 156. See also *vaṃsa*

iddhi (superpowers from meditation), 54, 55, 60–61, 109, 111
Inden, Ronald, 18, 49, 191n16
India, 62, 79, 133
interpretation/interpreters, 15, 49, 121, 133, 140, 152, 198n3; conversion of interpreters, 53; ethical importance of, 153; institutional location and, 18; "interpretive openings," 69; literary devices and, 42, 43; primed interpreter, 39, 49, 51; text shrouded by layers of, 155

Jains/Jain texts, 9, 182n1
Jambudīpa, 51, 171n17
Janamejaya, King, 9
Jātaka tales, 5, 35, 68, 71–72, 73, 126; as acts of social imagination, 88; animals in, 81, 85; snakes and *nāgas* in, 80, 83, 92
Jaṭila sect, 53, 54
Jenkins, Keith, 129
Jetavana grove, 56, 57, 61, 62
Jetavana monastic fraternity, 19, 66, 103, 134; founding of, 141; Parākramabāhu I and, 148; writing of *Mahāvaṃsa* and, 196n70
Johnson, Mark, 11
jyotirliṅgam (Śiva's shaft of light), 9

Kadru (mother to one thousand *nāgas*), 9
Kalingabodhi Jātaka, 95, 103, 106–107
Kāliya (*nāga*), 10
Kapleau, Philip, 81
karma, 7, 81, 92
Kassapa, 49, 53, 54
kāvya (poetic literature), 19, 177n73
Kāvyādarśa (Daṇḍin), 28, 169n41
Kemper, Steven, 198n108
Khuddaka Nikāya, 52, 73
kings, 124, 135, 150
Kṛṣṇa, 10

LaCapra, Dominick, 11, 21–24, 25, 117
Lakoff, George, 11
language, 23, 122, 150
Laṅkā, 14, 29; alternate names for, 56, 59; Buddhist world recentered on, 39, 46–47, 64, 66, 140; development of Buddhism in, 32; *dhamma* transferred to, 40, 97, 103; as island of *dhamma*, 64, 113; *nāgas'* indigenous presence in, 70; preordained to receive the *dhamma* and relics, 50, 158, 167n9; relics of the Buddha in, 36, 46; trade and traffic with mainland India, 133. *See also* Sri Lanka
Laṅkā, visits of the Buddha to, 2, 24, 31, 92, 125, 198n1; anticipation of, in the *Dīpavaṃsa*, 48–58; anticipation of, in the *Mahāvaṃsa*, 58–65; founding of Mahāvihāra and, 134; metaphor of light and, 39, 47; *nāgas* and, 94; relics and, 100
Law, Bimala Churn, 163n16
Lévi-Strauss, Claude, 71, 92
lieux de memoire (memory sites), 185–86n24

light, *dhamma* as, 24, 38, 41, 43, 48, 168n32; in *Mahāvaṃsa*, 59, 62, 156; poetics and, 63; relics and, 102; textual community and, 159
light, religious metaphor of, 8–9, 38, 40, 165nn34–37; as biblical borrowing, 65; Buddhist world recentered on Laṅkā and, 47; compiling of the *Mahāvaṃsa* and, 44; conversion of *nāgas* and, 61; *dīpa* as homonym of "lamp" and "island," 55–56, 63, 64–65, 177n73; image of lamp, 4, 64, 176n72; as ruminative trigger, 40; *sāsana* and, 60
Little, David, 125
Lotus Sūtra (*Saddharmapuṇḍarīkasūtra*), 10

Madhuratthavilāsinī (commentary on the *Buddhavaṃsa*), 17
Mahānāma Thera, 34
Mahāparinibbāṇa-sutta, 108, 115, 187n40
Mahāruhā, 144
Mahāsena, King, 88, 131–32, 143, 151, 191n13; death of, 144; rivals of Mahāvihāra and, 141
Mahāvaṃsa, 28, 79, 95; Asoka cycle (*Mahāvaṃsa* V), 96, 112; authorship of, 6, 11–12, 146; on Buddha's visits to Laṅkā, 43–44, 47, 58–65; as "Buddhist history," 131–38; compilation/composition of, 1, 7, 19, 31, 66, 92, 143; copying and perpetuation of, 155, 167n16; documentary and worklike functions in, 23; Duṭṭhagāmaṇī epic, 2, 96, 97–98, 108, 123, 135; as "history," 6, 119, 127–131; ideal reader-hearer of, 68; as literary work, 118; metaphor in, 38, 40–48, 149; *nāgas*' soteriological aptitude in, 85, 86; as political "charter," 1, 2, 47, 123–27; reader-interpreters of, 47; regular reminders to reader-hearer, 29; relation to history, 2–3; as relic, 159; relic typology in, 103–104; royal narrative in, 151–52; shared sources with *Dīpavaṃsa*, 147; Soṇuttara story, 96, 100–101, 107–12, 114; translations of, 155, 156
Mahāvaṃsa proem, 3–4, 6, 11, 13, 36, 78; distance from "*Mahāvaṃsa* of the ancients," 153; ethical agenda of, 156; inscribed audience of, 44; as instructions, 14–18; literary effects of, 150; narrative about *nāgas* and, 87; repetition of the imperative, 30–36
Mahāvihāra (Mahāvihāran monastic complex), 12, 14, 16, 131; claims to legitimacy and supremacy, 59–60, 64, 66, 156; as community of "good people," 142; *gantha-dhura* (bookish) monks of, 27, 169n40; Gupta-Vākāṭaka imperial formation and, 151, 152; *Jātaka* tales and, 73; legitimization of, 133; lineage of the Buddha and, 38; *Mahāvaṃsa* compiled and preserved by, 70; Mahinda and, 52, 134; as minority tradition, 19, 141; Parākramabāhu I and, 148; *rasa* theory and, 28; relics and, 108; resurgence after persecution, 134; rival schools and, 138, 196n70; tradition transmitted in, 17
Mahāyāna ("Great Vehicle") Buddhism, 8, 69, 141; defense against influences of, 151, 152; Lotus Sūtra, 10; *Prajñāpāramitā* (Perfection of Wisdom) *sūtras*, 181n49, 185n19; *Sukhāvativyūha sutra*, 194n52; Vetullavāda movement, 142
Mahilā, Princess, 144
Mahinda, 2, 30, 46, 51, 58, 130, 131; Devānaṃpiyatissa and, 105; Mahāvihāra and, 52; on relics of the Buddha, 98–99; transference of *dhamma* to Laṅkā and, 106, 133
Malalasekera, G. P., 120, 131–32, 190n10, 190n12; defense of the *Dīpavaṃsa*, 145; on historicity of the *vaṃsas*, 137–38
Maṇiakkhika (*nāgarāja*), 57, 79, 92
manoramaṃ (pleasing to the mind), 28
Maranda, Pierre, 47–48, 50
McMahon, David, 8
meditation, 23, 34, 35, 48, 54
memory verses, 20, 21
Mendis, G. C., 132, 148

metaphor, 4, 5, 19, 42, 140, 149, 189n2; knowledge as light, 8; as restructuring of the world, 11; from Vedic sources, 50
Moggaliputta, 105
Monius, Anne, 8, 117–18
Mucalinda (*nāga*), 83, 180n38
Muluposatha Sutta, 173n40

nāgaloka (subterranean *nāga* world), 75, 76, 78, 81, 113, 178n16, 178n24; Bhūridatta in, 84; bodhi tree graft in, 106; Buddha taken to, 106; Poṭala as capital of, 82; relics of the Buddha preserved in, 100–101, 109, 111, 183n4; relics taken to, 106
Nāgamittā, 144
Nāgārjuna, 69, 70, 181n49, 185n19, 187n41
nāgas (snakelike beings), 3, 24, 31, 119, 137, 149; aboriginal tribes identified with, 163n17; in *Bhūridatta Jātaka*, 73–75; bodhi tree and, 106–7, 187n36; Buddha's lives as *nāga*, 68, 74, 85, 92; Buddha's relations with, 4, 27, 46, 71, 79; in Buddhist texts beyond Pāli sources, 10; in *Dīpavaṃsa*, 53–58; in Indic religious traditions, 9–10, 68, 177n10; legitimating influence to and from, 70; light of the *dhamma* and, 60; metaphor of light and, 38, 44; moral didacticism of, 87–92; *nāgarāja* (*nāga* king), 72, 75, 109–10, 182n2; Nāgārjuna and, 181n49; *nāginī* (female *nāga*), 10, 82, 83; novice monks referred to as, 89, 96, 158, 181n57; ontological status of, 69, 71, 79–85, 86; readers' sense of self and, 67–68; redemptive light and conversion of, 61; as ruminative trigger, 81, 92–93; *saṃvega* and, 39, 41, 67, 69; as symbolic force of chaos, 157, 198n1; textual community and, 159; transformation into Buddhists, 47, 70, 71. *See also* relics, *nāgas* and
nāgas, soteriological aptitude of, 67, 79, 85–87, 93, 113, 157; Bhūridatta and, 94, 179n26; ethical lessons for hearers-readers and, 71; Soṇuttara story and, 100–101, 115
Nāg Panchamī festival, 9
nationalism, Sinhalese Buddhist, 2, 47, 123–24, 153, 156
Nattier, Jan, 136
Nāṭyaśāstra (attrib. Bharata), 28
nekkhamma pāramitā (perfection of renunciation), 74
Nevill, Hugh, 143, 144
nibbāṇa [Sanskrit: *nirvāṇa*] ("extinguishing"), 7, 57, 184n14, 195n60
Nikāya Buddhism, 133
Nussbaum, Martha, 4

Obeyesekere, Ranjini, 28–29, 169n42
Okkāka/Ikṣvāku lineage, 52, 199n6
Oldenberg, Hermann, 131, 132
ophiolatry (snake worship), 9
oral tradition, 20, 21
Orientalists, 135, 155
originality, 2, 13, 154

Padyapadoruvaṃsa, 132
Pāli language/texts, 1, 10, 23, 41, 52, 118; canon of, 139, 195n70; choice of Pāli over Sinhalese, 140–42; continuity valued over originality, 13; homage to the Buddha (*stotra*) in, 32; lack of literary flourish in, 5; "literary" aspect of, 19–21, 167n16; metaphor of light prevalent in, 65, 176n69; model readers of, 16; *nāgas* in, 71, 86, 90, 177n10; proems (opening lines) in, 18, 164n32; translation of Sinhalese commentaries into Pāli, 27
Parākramabāhu I, King, 121, 148, 191n14
pāramitā/pāramī (perfections), 68, 72, 73–74, 91, 92, 177n2
paramparā (teacher-student succession), 97, 129, 130, 133
pāribhogika (relics of use), 6, 57, 97, 103, 107; cuttings/seedlings of bodhi tree, 186n28; *nāgas* and, 104–107; time and, 102
parinibbāṇa (corporeal death), of the Buddha, 51, 94–95, 98; Buddha's absence from community and, 103, 104; *nāgas*' relationship with Buddha

through relics, 67, 71; relics and, 188n44; *saṅgha* and, 132–33; visits to Laṅkā before, 62, 113, 185n16
Pārśvanātha, 9
pasāda [Sanskrit: *prasāda*] (serene satisfaction), 3–4, 6, 28, 34, 88, 126; alternate translations of, 163n18; in *Dīpavaṃsa*, 13, 33–34, 40, 41; explications of, 41, 166n1; of "good people" (*sujana*), 64; in humans and *nāgas*, 39; in *Mahāvaṃsa*, 31, 32, 34–35, 41; *nāgas* and, 67, 69, 96, 115; reader's interpretation of Buddha's acts and, 45; relics of the Buddha and, 7, 102, 105, 112, 170n52; transformation of reader-hearer and, 90, 156
patronage, royal, 14, 39, 60, 104, 142
Perera, S. G., 19
phalaśruti (fruits of hearing/receiving text), 29, 36, 162n12
pilgrimage sites, 61–62, 70
pītipāmojja (joy and gladness), 28, 31, 40
poetry/poetics, 3, 123, 169n42, 171n16, 177n73, 195n63; Ākhyāna poetry, 20, 21, 168n27; compilers of the *vaṃsas* and, 28, 29; *Dīpavaṃsa* and, 52, 130, 139–140; epic poetry, 20, 21; *Mahāvaṃsa* as poetry, 19; originality and, 13; religious community and, 118. See also *Kāvya* (poetic literature)
Prajñāpāramitā (Perfection of Wisdom) *sūtras*, 181n49, 185n19, 187n41
Prinsep, James, 135
purāṇas (legends), 19, 128, 135, 137, 199n6

Rahula, Walpola, 34, 35, 169n40, 169n46; on authorship of *Dīpavaṃsa*, 130–31; on Mahāvihāra, 138; on metaphor of light, 65
Rājataraṅgiṇī (Kashmiri chronicle), 10
rasa theory, 28
relics, 2, 25, 36, 40, 68, 182n1; cultivation of emotions and, 78; disappearance at end of a Buddha era, 102, 186n25; established on Lanka, 3; *Mahāvaṃsa* as relic, 12; miracles performed by, 170n52; offerings (*pūjā*) made to, 168n38, 170n5; tooth relic, 121, 182n1; tripartite classification of, 6; typology of, 103–104; veneration of, 5–6, 69, 104, 162n13, 185n23
relics, *nāgas* and, 6, 68–69, 71, 72, 113–16, 163n15, 181n48; enshrined imagination, 97–99; enshrinement of relics and, 184n14; *nāgas* as guardians, 100; *nāgas* as intermediaries to the Buddha, 96; *nāgas* as relics, 102; *pāribhogika* relics, 104–107; *sarīrika* relics, 107–12; theft of relics, 92, 109, 114; *uddesika* relics, 107, 112–13; value attributed to relics, 99–100; veneration of relics, 94–95, 100–101, 114–15, 159
Ṛg Veda, 49, 165n36
Ricoeur, Paul, 4, 117, 190n8
Riffaterre, Michael, 171n16
Rotman, Andy, 7, 35
Rousseau, Jean-Jacques, 48, 195–96n70

Śaiva texts, 9
Śakyamuni, 194n52
Sākyas (kinsmen of the Buddha), 52
Samantapāsādikā (Buddhaghosa), 131, 196n84
saṃsāra (cycle of birth/life/death), 48, 65, 110, 180n33, 188n49
Samuddā, 144
Samuddajā, 83–84
saṃvega (anxious thrill), 3–4, 6, 28, 67, 88, 126; alternate translations of, 163n18; in *Dīpavaṃsa*, 31, 33, 40; explications of, 41; of "good people" (*sujana*), 64; *Mahāvaṃsa*'s ability to bring about, 31, 32; *nāgas* and, 39, 41, 67, 69, 115; reader's interpretation of Buddha's acts and, 45; relics and, 7, 102, 105, 112; transformation of reader-hearer and, 90, 156
saṅgha (monastic community), 42, 90, 161n3, 173n40; Asoka and, 112; *Jātaka* tales and, 78; kings and, 124; *nāgas* and, 91, 96; relics and, 97, 188n42; "routinization of charisma" and, 132–33
Saṅghamitta, 106–107, 142, 144, 196n83
Sanhā, 144
Śaṅkhapāla (*nāga*), 73, 74

Sanskrit language/texts, 7, 10, 28; as literary language, 5; proems in, 164n32; *purāṇas*, 128; rhetoricians of, 29; *śāstras* (treatises), 29
Sārārthadīpanī, 40, 41, 42, 171n15, 191n13
sarīrika (relics of the body), 6, 97, 100, 102, 103, 107
sāsana (Buddhist teachings and traditions), 2, 31, 40, 161n3, 188n44; arrival to the island of Laṅkā, 98; establishment of, 3; Mahāvihāra as legitimate heir of, 134, 145; Mahinda's role in establishment of, 51; metaphor of light and, 60; *nāgas* and, 5, 54, 94
Schopen, Gregory, 118
Senayake, D. S., 191n20
Seneviratne, H. L., 127, 152–53
Śeṣa (*nāga*), 10
Sīhaḷaṭṭhakathā, 131, 132
sīla pāramitā (perfection of morality), 73, 74, 75, 78
similes, 40, 41–43
Sinhala Thūpavaṃsa, 7, 150, 170n5, 188nn48–49, 197n101
Sinhalese language, 7, 27, 131, 169n42
Sirimeghavaṇṇa, King, 191n13
Śiva (god), 9
Sivalā, 144
Siyabaslakara, 5, 16, 28–29, 167n11, 169n42
Siyam Nikāya, 18
slesa [Sanskrit: *śleṣa*] (double meaning), 4, 7, 65, 162n12
ślokas, 19, 25, 52
Smith, Bardwell, 125, 153, 198n1
snakes, 9, 12, 56; anthill as natural abode of, 76; common snakes (*sappas/sarpas*), 79, 80; as divine beings (*bhūta devatā*), 79. See also *nāgas* (snakelike beings)
Soṇuttara story, 96, 100–101, 107–12, 114
Sri Lanka, 4, 19, 104, 131, 152; civil war in, 124, 198n109; coming of Buddhism to, 22; European colonialization in, 121, 123, 191n20; Faxian's visit to, 146; relics established in, 106; Sinhalese Buddhist nationalism in, 2, 153. *See also* Laṅkā
Stock, Brian, 13, 122, 140
stotra (stylized homage to the Buddha), 25, 32
Strong, John, 7, 184n14
stūpas, 41, 72, 109, 184n14
sujana ("good people"), 13, 35, 36, 71, 123; "island of *dhamma*" and, 64; metaphor in *Mahāvaṃsa* and, 43; *nāga* stories and, 68, 157; reader-hearers among, 90; textual community of, 4, 126
Suleiman, Susan, 44, 46
Sumana (*deva* or *nāga*), 105, 186n31
Sumedha, 59, 175n55
sutta [Sanskrit: *sūtra*] (sermon), 16–17, 36, 54, 68; legitimizing voice of the Buddha and, 194n52; Pāli language and, 140; preservation of, 133
Sutta/Sūtra Piṭaka, 72, 73, 181n56

Tathāgata (epithet of the Buddha), 53, 56, 112, 171n6, 173–74n40
tejas (power, light), 8
textual community, 3, 13, 24, 43, 72, 163n17; anticipated or desired by the *vaṃsas*, 44; creation of, 18; documentary and functions in relation to, 23; of "good people" (*sujana*), 4, 126; interpretation and, 140; *Mahāvaṃsa* as political charter and, 1; metaphor of light and, 39; *nāgas* and, 91, 93, 100, 115; oral and aural practices of, 17; reading of, 15; relic veneration and, 102; role in production of texts, 8; shared, 147; social status of literate interpreters, 26–27; span of time and, 102; stability and continuity in, 167n16; transformative literature and, 118; "world wishes" of, 99; writers and readers in context, 119–123. *See also* Mahāvihāra (Mahāvihāran monastic complex)
theophany, 9
Theravāda Buddhism, 3, 12, 15, 124, 181n56; centrality of *Mahāvaṃsa*, 118; eschatology of, 104; exported to other countries, 148; function of relics, 101; history and, 137; *nāgas* as intermediaries to the Buddha, 96; as non-monolithic institution, 133; path to buddhahood, 91; real and imagined

community of, 1; rethinking of Pāli texts and, 156; tooth relic in history of, 121
Third Buddhist Council, 2, 105, 112
Three Gems/Jewels, 42, 161n3, 173n40
Three Refuges, 25
time, Buddhist conception of, 91, 96, 137, 149, 182n2; *nibbāṇa* (*nirvāṇa*) and, 195n60; relics and, 102; time travel, 107
Tipiṭaka/Tripiṭaka, 27, 72, 131, 139, 169n40, 181n56
Tirrell, Lynn, 87
Trainor, Kevin, 7, 101, 159, 170n52, 185n23
Turnour, George, 120, 135, 155, 199n6

uddesika (image relics), 6, 96, 102, 103, 107, 112–13, 186n28

Vaiṣṇava traditions, 9, 10
vaṃsa (history, chronicle, lineage), 3, 28, 44, 67, 163n16; as "Buddhist histories," 7, 68, 129, 131–38; centrality of relics in, 113; creation of textual community and, 18; history reconstructed through, 148–50; interpreters of, 97; model readers of, 16; present community and, 119; *purāṇa* literature and, 128–29, 193n39; royal patronage and, 14; as "successions" of the Buddha's presence, 103, 186n27; *sujana* ("good people") and, 117; translation of, 172n21; using LaCapra to read, 21–24; "world wishes" in, 152. See also *Dīpavaṃsa*; *Mahāvaṃsa*
Vaṃsatthappakāsinī (commentary on the *Mahāvaṃsa*), 2, 12, 161n5, 190n10; on authorship of *Mahāvaṃsa*, 146; dates of composition, 120; historical context and, 149; Mahāvihāra and, 14, 141, 158; on source text of *Mahāvaṃsa*, 131, 132; textual community of, 65–66
Vāsuki (*nāga*), 9
Vāsuladatta (*nāga*), 109–10, 111, 114, 188n45
Vaṭṭagāmaṇī, King, 139, 196n71
Vedic imagery and ritual, 8, 49, 50, 78, 179n28
Vessantara, 74
Vetullavāda (Sanskrit: *vaitulyavāda*) movement, 141–42
vihāras (monastic complexes), 31, 133, 134, 138
Vijaya, King, 2, 40, 46, 130, 134, 140
vinaya (text of monastic rules), 68, 72, 73; *nāgas* and, 88, 91, 181n56; preservation of, 133
Viṣṇu (god), 10, 182n1
Vohārika Tissa, King, 141, 142

Walser, Joseph, 69, 70
Walters, Jonathan, 3, 7, 50, 63, 143, 170n2; on Buddhist canon, 72–73; on *Dīpavaṃsa* as "plea for survival," 139, 145; on "dispensations" of the Buddha in the *vaṃsas*, 136, 186n27; on goals of *Dīpavaṃsa,* 52; on Mahāsena and *Dīpavaṃsa*, 144; on *Mahāvaṃsa* as Buddhist history, 158; on *purāṇas* and the *vaṃsas*, 193n39, 199n6; on royal narrative in *Mahāvaṃsa*, 151–52; on situated reading of Pāli texts, 122; *sāsana* translated by, 175n59; on the *Vaṃsatthappakāsinī*, 66, 158
White, Hayden, 4, 38–39, 122, 129; on chronicles, 128; on narrative and myth, 44–45; on rhetorical devices in history writing, 117, 189n2
worklike function/mode, 11, 21–24, 25, 26, 64; in history writing, 117; *rasa* theory and, 28
"world wishes," 49, 50, 64, 72, 99, 152, 172n24

yakkhas [Sanskrit: *yaksas*] (class of nonhuman beings), 41, 46, 50, 68, 75, 80, 173n35; Buddha mistaken for a *yakkha*, 179n22; contrast with *nāgas*, 79, 82; expelled by the Buddha, 53, 54, 56, 60–61; inability to embrace the *dhamma*, 55, 86; mythologized past and, 119, 149; as ontological category, 80, 82

Zimmer, Heinrich, 82

SOUTH ASIA ACROSS THE DISCIPLINES

EDITED BY MUZAFFAR ALAM, ROBERT GOLDMAN, AND GAURI VISWANATHAN

DIPESH CHAKRABARTY, SHELDON POLLOCK, AND SANJAY SUBRAHMANYAM, FOUNDING EDITORS

◈◈◈

Extreme Poetry: The South Asian Movement of Simultaneous Narration by Yigal Bronner (Columbia)

The Social Space of Language: Vernacular Culture in British Colonial Punjab by Farina Mir (California)

Unifying Hinduism: Philosophy and Identi ty in Indian Intellectual History by Andrew J. Nicholson (Columbia)

The Powerful Ephemeral: Everyday Healing in an Ambiguously Islamic Place by Carla Bellamy (California)

Secularizing Islamists? Jama'at-e-Islami and Jama'at-ud-Da'wa in Urban Pakistan by Humeira Iqtidar (Chicago)

Islam Translated: Literature, Conversion, and the Arabic Cosmopolis of South and Southeast Asia by Ronit Ricci (Chicago)

Conjugations: Marriage and Form in New Bollywood Cinema by Sangita Gopal (Chicago)

Unfinished Gestures: Devadāsīs, Memory, and Modernity in South India by Davesh Soneji (Chicago)

Document Raj: Writing and Scribes in Early Colonial South India by Bhavani Raman (Chicago)

The Millennial Sovereign: Sacred Kingship and Sainthood in Islam by A. Azfar Moin (Columbia)

Making Sense of Tantric Buddhism: History, Semiology, and Transgression in the Indian Traditions by Christian K. Wedemeyer (Columbia)

The Yogin and the Madman: Reading the Biographical Corpus of Tibet's Great Saint Milarepa by Andrew Quintman (Columbia)

Body of Victim, Body of Warrior: Refugee Families and the Making of Kashmiri Jihadists by Cabeiri deBergh Robinson (California)

Receptacle of the Sacred: Illustrated Manuscripts and the Buddhist Book Cult in South Asia by Jinah Kim (California)

Cut-Pieces: Celluloid Obscenity and Popular Cinema in Bangladesh by Lotte Hoek (Columbia)

From Text to Tradition: The Naisadhīyacarita *and Literary Community in South Asia* by Deven M. Patel (Columbia)

Democracy against Development: Lower Caste Politics and Political Modernity in Postcolonial India by Jeffrey Witsoe (Chicago)

Writing Resistance: The Rhetorical Imagination of Hindi Dalit Literature by Laura R. Brueck (Columbia)

Wombs in Labor: Transnational Commercial Surrogacy in India by Amrita Pande (Columbia)

I Too Have Some Dreams: N. M. Rashed and Modernism in Urdu Poetry by A. Sean Pue (California)

We Were Adivasis: Aspiration in an Indian Scheduled Tribe by Megan Moodie (Chicago)

The Place of Devotion: Siting and Experiencing Divinity in Bengal-Vaishnavism by Sukanya Sarabadhikary (California)

Writing Self, Writing Empire: Chandar Bhan Brahman and the Cultural World of the Early Modern Indo-Persian State by Rajeev Kinra (California)

Culture of Encounters: Sanskrit at the Mughal Court by Audrey Truschke (Columbia)

Reading the Mahāvaṃsa: The Literary Aims of a Theravāda Buddhist History by Kristin Scheible (Columbia)

Negotiating Languages: Urdu, Hindi, and the Definition of Modern South Asia by Walter Hakala (Columbia)